Time and Tide

The Long, Long Life of Landscape

FIONA STAFFORD

JOHN MURRAY

First published in Great Britain in 2024 by John Murray (Publishers)

1

A CIP catalogue record for this title is available from the British Library

Hardback ISBN 9781473686328
ebook ISBN 9781473686335

Typeset in Bembo MT by Hewer Text UK Ltd, Edinburgh
Printed and bound in Great Britain by Clays Ltd, Elcograf S.p.A.

John Murray policy is to use papers that are natural, renewable and recyclable products and
made from wood grown in sustainable forests. The logging and manufacturing processes
are expected to conform to the environmental regulations of the country of origin.

Carmelite House
50 Victoria Embankment
London EC4Y 0DZ

www.johnmurraypress.co.uk

John Murray Press, part of Hodder & Stoughton Limited
An Hachette UK company

Contents

there are so many *inhabited* solitudes
Dorothy Wordsworth

Nae man can tether time or tide
Robert Burns

Prologue: Red Doors, Grey Arches

~

A sudden, scarcely audible swish through the broad hazel leaves beneath a pine tree and a russet flash in the peripheral vision. And there, on a slim branch sticking out straight from the warm trunk is a red fur form catching the afternoon sun. A brown tail bushes around the contours of the bright haunches, brushing down to hide the small head as it freezes under a direct gaze from below. I remain motionless, too. And watch. In a few minutes, the squirrel perks up and looks down. I can see both bright eyes assessing the situation. A gap in the oak canopy beside the pine means that he's spotlit by the September sun – warm, flame red and exposed. A moment later, a soundless hop takes him out of sight, but not out of mind.

I hadn't even hoped for such a treat when setting off. It was just a walk in the woods, beside a winding river on the edge of the Pennines. I have seen red squirrels at Derwent Water, though not for some years, and although Cumbria is one of the counties where a few survive, the odds against spotting them are as high as the pines. The sudden flash was a revelation – a red door opening the moment into other times and places.

I was born in a house with a red front door. A very bright red, as I understand, at least for a few weeks. When my parents arrived at RAF Scampton with two small daughters and a portable mountain of crates, boxes and cases, the Station Married Quarters were still covered in the black and khaki camouflage of wartime defence. All of the houses were the same, their mottled exteriors intended to blend into the dark earth and thick hedges of surrounding fields. Had this been hill country, the doors might almost have passed for the mouths of caves or tunnels. As it was low-lying farmland, they were just black and flat and forbidding. My mother, Gill, who radiated energy wherever she went, saw no good reason to put up with post-war dreariness any longer. She was young and ready for anything – especially for the 1960s. Why blend into the background – least of all when the dominant tone was olive drab?

After breakfast one morning, when my father had gone to work and my sisters to nursery school, Gill opened a tin of vermilion red gloss and spent a satisfying day applying several coats to the dull black door. 'And very cheerful it looked,' she announced proudly, whenever she retold the tale. On his return that evening, my father could not fail on this occasion to notice that something had happened at home, but wisely made no remark. And for a month or more, the entrance to No. 2 Trenchard Square stood resplendent and startling in scarlet. A celebration, a quiet rebellion, an angry protest or perhaps an embarrassment, our glowing door was unlike any other: suddenly it had ceased to match, and stood magnificently out of place.

In due course, the RAF maintenance team set to work, steadily redecorating every window frame and door in the Station, starting with the Officers' Married Quarters. Instead of reinstating the standard black, they introduced a new system. Green, yellow, blue, red – more pastel than primary, but at least each door was becoming part of a sequence of colours. Our dazzling entrance was duly given another fresh coat, to tone it down and make it fit in, but it did not go back to black.

Twentieth-century warfare meant taking cover: among the many long legacies of the First World War is military camouflage. After my grandfather emerged from the trenches uninjured, in body at least, he went to the Westminster School of Art to draw and paint and start again. His daughter Gill, born between the First and Second World Wars, grew up in a house full of colour and a garden bright with flowers and fruit. For her, painting the Scampton front door scarlet meant reinstating normality. As she opened her tin of gloss paint, she was shutting out traumatic childhood memories of the Blitz and the spirit-sapping aftermath of rationing, obedience, austerity. It was not easy to forget. On winter nights in Trenchard Square, shadowy figures loomed by the bedroom windows, troubling sleep. Gill painted the door not just for her own children, but for all the young airmen who were no longer around to see the world returning to colour. A door into the past as well as the future – like so many things that seem out of place, Gill's red door was hinged by time.

I never saw the red front door. Three months after my arrival, the packing crates were out again as Gill rallied to get ready for the new posting. By then the door was Air Force blue, but she had other things on her mind. The red moment was left to fade among the mental embers until a stray breath of air might ignite an unexpected blaze. But we see with the mind as much as the eye. I grew up with the story of the red door, and I've been spotting them ever since – which is why my momentary encounter, many years later, with that elusive red squirrel set me thinking. Though high above, the squirrel's nervousness was only too apparent. He was in no danger at all from me, but still he froze, and stared, and skipped out of sight, propelled by an instinct to avoid humankind. It made me wonder about inherited wariness. This red door was opening to times when nimble little creatures like this were not so rare – and to thoughts of times to come, when they may be rarer still.

A hundred years ago, red squirrels were everywhere. So common were they, in fact, that many people regarded them as pests, threatening young trees or hazelnut crops. Thieving red squirrels were fair game, their rich, russet coats much in demand for fur gloves and collars, the thin leftover flesh for stews and pies. In some areas, 'squoyling' was a favourite Christmas sport, as people got in the festive mood by competing to bring home the biggest sack of squirrel carcases. In the New Forest, skilful squoylers would topple squirrels from the highest boughs, with the strong, lead-weighted sticks known as 'squoyles'. An easier method, more widely used, was to attack their lofty dreys with long poles.

During the famished years of the Second World War, squirrel-tail soup was one of the recommended recipes for eking out ration-ing. At the time, red squirrels could be found running through treetops from Inverness to Land's End – resident in almost every region except Caithness and the Home Counties. Gill saw them in the trees around Windermere when she was evacuated to the Lake District, and then again in Cornwall and the Yorkshire Dales, as constant as familiar birds, when her young life, too, suddenly became a series of strange flits between hotels, guest houses and damp cottages. Today red squirrels are in deep retreat, taking refuge in Scottish forests or pinewoods in the north of England, with a few hardy island survivors fending off extinction in Anglesey and the Isle of Wight. All too soon, the tide turns, and one generation's pest becomes another's precious rarity. When the grey squirrels introduced as novelties to grand Victorian gardens went forth and multiplied, their small red relations were driven from their old homes. As they settled in, the newcomers doomed red squirrels to decades of dwindling until eventually they became the rarities.

Unlike red squirrels, Gill's scarlet door was only temporarily out of place. Its rapid return to 'regulation blue' was a reminder of norms and uniformity, of neatness and rightness and order. Everything from the white stones around the Officers' Mess to the airmen's shining buttons and boots had to fall into line, to uphold eternal standards. And yet, such 'norms' were relative newcomers. Only a few decades earlier, there had been no officers, no Mess, no Trenchard Square at Scampton. In those days, the old Ermine Street, always known as the 'Ramper', still ran as straight as when the Roman army laid it down on their way from Lindum (Lincoln) to Eboracum (York). Until the first flimsy biplanes landed beside it in the middle of the First World War, the site had been open country-side; by the mid-1930s, regulars at the bar in the Midge Inn were taken aback by the news that their pub was to be replaced by a runway. What could be more out of place in a Lincolnshire field? Their grandparents would have been astonished by the very idea of flying. All would have been baffled to learn that one day Scampton's village pub would be called the Dambusters Inn. For centuries, the only changes had taken the form of seasonal ploughing, sowing and harvesting, as the rich, brown soil sprouted spring green, which gradually warmed into pale gold before being ploughed again. Occasionally, the perennial cycle was unexpectedly disrupted – but never for very long.

One bright morning in 1795, labourers tasked with extracting stones from a field beside the Ramper unearthed a few shards of terracotta. The local Rector, Cayley Illingworth, was so intrigued that he told them to carry on digging, deeper and deeper, excite-ment mounting as they turned up more and more red fragments. After several hours of heavy spadework, they reached a hard, flat, level surface several feet down. The broken terracotta turned out to be a trail of buried clues, leading to a hidden, underground world. In a matter of days, the mud was removed to reveal a grand mosaic of rich red, yellow, black and white tiles, laid out in intri-cate geometries.

Roman remains were much in the news at the time, because of similar revelations in Bath. Belief in the therapeutic benefits of 'taking the waters' had boosted the city's appeal to wealthy invalids and fashionable society. As Bath boomed, so did the local construc-tion industry. But the soaring demand for elegant houses and hotels often entailed rather more digging than the architects anticipated. Work on the new Pump Room in the city centre was halted by the discovery of a buried pavement, and then, on further investiga-tion, steps, stones, Latin inscriptions, and dozens of damaged sculptures. The unsuspecting citizens of Bath had evidently been going about their business for centuries, unaware of the classical temple lying beneath their feet.

Now the tiny village of Scampton turned out to have Roman baths of its own – or at least a large villa, a bath house and a natural spring. The colourful mosaic was just the start of an extensive excavation. And yet, once uncovered, the glossy floors began to fade rapidly, their grandeur not helped by curious visitors, who liked to take home a tessera or two. Even a temporary building couldn't quite preserve their lustre. The underground wonderland was fast becoming less wonderful. In rural Lincolnshire, interest in wheat also outweighed even the keenest antiquarian curiosity, and so there were compelling reasons to avoid unearthing anything more. After the excavation, what remained of the villa was reburied and quickly disappeared under the plough. Firmly in place since the first century, the Roman residence was splendidly, but inconveniently, out of place when it resurfaced in a working farm some 1,750 years later.

Apart from this brief moment of fame, Scampton remained a relatively self-effacing village. Between the Romans and the RAF came Saxon settlement and a medieval abbey, but neither left many traces to intrigue later generations. Willingham Franklin Rawnsley, commissioned to describe the *Highways and Byways of Lincolnshire* in 1914, was much more impressed by the broad, open views from the Ermine Street as it ran northwards along the Lincoln Edge than by the villages scattered below. He listed Scampton along with Burton, Carlton, Aisthorpe, Brattleby, Cammeringham, Ingham, Fillingham, Glentworth, Harpswell, Hemswell, Willoughton, Blyborough and Grayingham, perhaps to demonstrate that he knew what he was about when declaring that 'nothing of importance' could detain the traveller between Lincoln and Kirton-in-Lindsey. Neither did the clear eye of Frederick Griggs, whose light pencil sketches provided the book's atmospheric illustrations, alight on a suitable subject anywhere along the limestone ridge running north from Lincoln.

When he finally reached Barton-upon-Humber after nearly forty miles, he made up for it by making two sketches, inspired by both the Saxon church and the small boats moored in the haven at low tide.

Had Rawnsley paused to turn off the highway and explore the byways around Scampton, he might have discovered a weathered monument standing alone on the edge of a copse beside the village. If you take the narrow lane running westward from the High Street, which doesn't seem to go anywhere in particular, and stop to look across the wide field towards the church, you might just spot it. Not in the summer, when the hedge beside the lane is dense with green leaves, but during the weeks when the days are shortest, often greyest, and yet the clouds sometimes break to allow the clearest light. It is not easy to see. Through the thick, criss-cross tangle of spiked twigs, crumpled leaves, ivy fronds and scarlet rose hips, the form of a pale arch is just visible against a clump of bare trees. When the sky changes, it is less distinct. In mist or heavy rain, it disappears. Grey and ghostly on a dull day, in bright winter light the stone shape stands out, solid and solitary. Pale gold on a bank of grass, an old arch frames the darker woodland beyond. You could only reach it by continuing along the hedge to the private road at the next bend, ignoring all the signs forbidding access, and then tramping across the muddy field. I prefer to avoid upsetting the farmer and so look through the hedge, wondering what's there, what might be on the far side of the distant ruin.

The grand old arch on the edge of the dark wood reminds me for a moment of George Dobson, the Edinburgh coachman who found himself one night driving his horses through an unfamiliar gateway, realising only too late that he was on his way to hell. But in the morning light, there is nothing too ominous about this strange remnant of vanished splendour. Defiant in solitary grandeur, it seems to disdain the straggle of unremarkable farm buildings to the left of the wood and even the church tower, away to the right. Grey-gold rather than red, it signals a striking difference from everything round about, standing as an entrance to some-where that cannot quite be seen.

Though forbidding in its monumental being, the arch seems to beckon to ages past, mocking the present with an air of eternity. Indistinct shapes on the massive frontage and what might be a plaque above the keystone may once have guided visitors on the proper way to approach. The worn stones have long since ceased to tell their tales. Still, in the empty space beneath, the outlines of earlier existence begin to form. Stand here long enough at dusk and the shadows of horsemen, coaches, carriage dogs might well start flitting in and out.

By the time of Cayley Illingworth's excavations at the site of the Roman villa in the 1790s, the old Jacobean hall at Scampton had been reduced to rubble, the great, grey, top-heavy gateway, with its solid supports and slim Doric pillars, all that remained. It might have come into its own as a fashionable folly, had a smart, new Georgian mansion arisen nearby. Instead, it seemed odd and out of place, prompting the rector to brief meditations on the vicissitudes of time and the transience of worldly power.

Whatever the fate of Scampton Hall, the arch itself was built to last. The monumental gateway was commissioned by Sir George Bolle, after he was ennobled by James I and VI for obeying the will of heaven rather than kowtowing to the king. As Lord Mayor of London, Bolle had attempted to maintain order in the bustling city by forbidding all Sunday travel, even when the royal entourage was on the road. Though initially incensed, the king quickly came to admire Bolle as a man of upright character and religious principle. A baronetcy was conferred accordingly. Such an honour deserved a country house to match – and an entrance which would remind all comers of the owner's elevation.

Sir George's heirs carried on riding through the triumphal arch until 1714, when the last Sir John died without issue, leaving the estate to his sister Sarah in Shrewsbury. Since Sarah had no interest in moving to Lincolnshire, the great house was left to crumble: as rain pounded down on the unrepaired roof, and frost fractured the window frames and walls, the grey stones were quietly diverted to humbler building projects. With no great house to generate traffic, the drive fell into disuse, while grass and saplings shot up and the moss steadily spread. Generations of local farmers carried on ploughing the land around but left the old stone arch alone. Designed to command attention, Sir George's gateway survived its original owner and all his descendants, to stand alone amid the weeds.

The entrances that catch my eye are often less noticeable than the red door I never saw – more like the grey arch that only occasionally comes into focus. A solitary encounter can open the way into invisible worlds, past and present, to places far away, or near at hand, but hiding in plain sight. A grey arch, a red squirrel, wonderful in itself, is also the start of a story, beginning in the middle of things and ending – who knows when or where?

The rarity of red squirrels, and other phenomena, natural and man-made, results from circumstances. What may seem settled for ever can all too easily come to look as out of place as a freshly painted scarlet door or a solitary grey arch from nowhere to nowhere – but how does this happen? Rarity depends on *place* as well as *time*. Among the quieter domestic excitements of late December is the sight of the cotoneaster in our back garden beginning to tremble and then shake quite vigorously. Within a few hours, the heavy clusters of blood-coloured berries have gone. What might seem baffling – and not a little disappointing – as an afternoon discovery is intensely diverting when witnessed as part of an urgent natural process. If you happen to be looking out when the vibrations start, it quickly becomes clear that the thick, shining evergreen leaves are full of birds: quite sizeable birds, resembling puffed-out thrushes with strongly speckled breasts and flushed with red beneath the wings. Once a year, if we're lucky, redwings land and feast and fly away, leaving the branches both lighter and darker than before. Sometimes it's just a single bird, bright and out of place in the dying days of the old year.

Flocks of fieldfares, lapwings and wild geese are regular high-lights of my local winter calendar, but redwings are rare, unpredictable visitors. Their very occasional arrival in a garden shrub makes me wonder about their chances of survival. Are they destined to alight on the Red List of Conservation Concern or even to disappear for ever from our shores? Was there a time when they were commonplace and so may be again one day? Some birds have an inherent strangeness or wonder-inducing quality – I don't believe you could ever get used to peregrine falcons, even if you were lucky enough to see them every day. With other birds it is harder to tell whether their power to arrest attention arises from natural character or from rarity – so I like to find out how they were regarded by earlier generations, or by people in other regions.

Redwings merit a short chapter in Walter Swaysland's four-volume book of *Familiar Wild Birds*, which gives me a sense of how things stood in the Edwardian era. There's the redwing, painted in full colour on the page, perched on an ivy-covered gate in deep snow. Redwings never ventured into gardens, apparently, and though known as 'Norway Nightingales', no one in Britain ever heard them singing. An air of mystery seems to have hung about them then, too. This is evidently one of the not-so-familiar wild birds in Swaysland's book.

Flying back another century, Thomas Bewick, the brilliant engraver and observer of the natural world, knew redwings as winter visitors, appearing just a few days before the fieldfares and immediately joining forces with them. They must have arrived a little earlier in eighteenth-century Northumbria than they do in our modern and more southerly garden, judging from his note about the unlucky bird picked up on 7 November 1785 after it smashed into the old lighthouse at Tynemouth. What strikes me as out of place may have been more familiar in the past, then – or even rarer. The RSPB website tells me that, though fewer in number than they once were, thousands of redwings still land and feed in British fields and orchards each year. So perhaps they are just not very taken with our garden.

My sense of what's out of place may not exactly match yours – as a recent trip to the Malverns brought home. I was out walking with a group of tree lovers, and so when I spotted a gargantuan clump of mistletoe suspended from a flimsy branch of acacia, I stopped to look. A light-hearted comment about how pleased Getafix would be was stalled by a few puzzled expressions. My new friends were quick to tell me that 'Hereford is the county of mistletoe' and so this clump was hardly a curiosity – though they were surprised by my surprise. Mistletoe is relatively rare in the woods and hedges where I usually walk, but common as a cloud elsewhere. The little exchange also made me realise that although familiarity can deepen our understanding of nearby places, it can deflect us too. It's all too easy to cease to notice the red doors nearest home, so I like to see how visiting friends react to the birds, buildings and fields I see every day. Would anyone else be surprised by a redwing?

Or a Red Arrow? Some years after we left the house with the red door, the skies of North Lincolnshire began to acquire multi-coloured streaks, as Scampton became the base for the RAF display team. The Red Arrows' spectacular aerobatics attracted crowds everywhere – except at Scampton, where people saw (and heard) them every day. An air of imminent danger needed bringing down to earth. As the youngest of the Armed Forces, the RAF has always been adept at both inventing and invoking tradition. When the station at Scampton was built in the 1930s, the Headquarters and the Married Quarters were designed in a neo-Georgian style, as if to keep in step with the well-proportioned farmhouses nearby. By the time my mother painted her red door, a strange new bend had been introduced to the ancient Ermine Street, out of line with Roman principles – an innovation triggered by the need to accom-modate a longer runway for massive Cold War Vulcan bombers. The new station badge featured a symbolic longbow, to reflect the old Roman road in the vertical bowstring, the re-routed Ramper in the braced bow, and the long, straight runway in the arrow. Nuclear defences, it seemed to say, were really not so different from the days of Agincourt. No wonder then, that when the Vulcans flew away, the Red Arrows settled in so easily.

This book is a personal response to the surprise of landscape and the gradual revelation of what's hidden from immediate view. It wanders and wonders over things out of place and in, be it redwing, red squirrel or Red Arrow, pausing to look for clues about how they came to be there, their chances of survival and revival. What seems out of place now may one day settle in – or vanish altogether. Seemingly empty places often turn out to be the fullest. Red doors stand out in green spaces but are often even more arresting amid blue and grey, as the tides of time ebb and flow. On the south coast near Rye, a bright red door in a black, wooden fisherman's hut is striking enough to feature in tourist guides as an icon of local heritage. But the 'doors' in this book come in all shapes and sizes, colours and kinds, natural, man-made, metaphorical. My zigzag journey through sea-, land- and skyscapes stops and starts at the unexpected, at the red doors in the grey wings that can open a way into unfamiliar times and places. The world is full of stories, with characters only just off stage. At the edge of a wood at dawn or dusk, a grey arch can slowly emerge from the shadows.

I like to be stopped in my tracks, to be led unpredictably through places thick with experience, with forgotten hopes and hidden lives, among generations vanished or unborn, yet still somehow present. Some of my red doors have an inherent strangeness – a natural out-of-placeness, while others are accidentally odd, isolated by surrounding transformations, or designed to be ahead of their times. Think of a kingfisher flashing from a low-lying branch above a river in a city centre, shooting away over floating cans and chip trays. Gone almost before you realise it's there. Or the shiver provoked by a dark figure with outstretched oblong wings, caught in the mirror as you speed along the A1 at Birtley. Or the duller intake of breath when visiting old friends and finding a familiar street utterly changed. A high-rise hotel, a sports centre, a new road layout can seem out of place if you're returning to old haunts, though your friends, used to seeing them every day, may already have forgotten how it once was.

Red doors are red lights: signals to stop. Once you stop, you can begin to feel what is there, to turn aside and follow an unplanned, unpredictable track. Places are lit up by what is out of the ordinary, by what's counter, original, spare and strange. But they can be darkened too. The last fat old oak beside a new rail construction depot contracts the heart by looking out of place.

From red squirrels and redwings to red kites and red springs, from waves resonating in grey sea caves to the sudden cries of migrating geese, from medieval red-brick castles to modern steel suspension bridges, from a blazing chimney in a green shaded valley to a church half submerged in water or wildflowers, there are many portals to the past, to the future, and to the elsewhere. Even an unfamiliar word or a curious place name can act as cracks in the present, opening into worlds only just out of sight. It is always worth pausing to see what might be there, before it hops away soundlessly into the shadows of the forest, or washes out to sea.

Drained

~

If you search a map, you will still find 'Whittlesey Mere'. The words are printed plainly on a road atlas, not far off the A1, a few miles north of Alconbury. But there is no pale blue shape beside the name. On Google Earth, Whittlesey Mere is pinpointed with a bright red balloon (rather than a door). It floats above a large, green space defined by a long, undeviating track and what looks like a ditch running perpendicular to it, cutting straight through another rectangular field. This agricultural geometry is like a vast Mondrian earth canvas – though he never painted in such sludgy greens and browns. The defining feature of this place has vanished from sight, so Whittlesey Mere survives in name only – a signal through time from what was once a national land-mark. But how do you find something that has been lost for many years – even something as big as Whittlesey Mere?

When the intrepid seventeenth-century writer, Celia Fiennes, set off on her horse across England in the 1690s, she rode across unknown stretches of country without any real sense of what she might see, or how long her day might turn out to be – and left an invaluable record of what caught her eye. I've never ridden side-saddle in a long skirt, so the ladylike conventions of three hundred years ago make her seem more heroic than ever. She's a good ghost to glimpse on a strange road or coastal track: a woman who noticed things but didn't pay too much attention to whether she was being noticed or not. She jotted down what she saw and heard and often got things a little bit wrong. When she set off for York, her journey took her through the old county of Huntingdonshire, where she was struck by a great, shimmering expanse 'like some Sea'. The ground around was wet and marshy and furrowed with narrow channels running towards the vast sheet of water. The flat, boggy land offered little to break the winds rushing in from the east or north, blasting travellers on horseback, making their hands and faces sting. She listened to stories of storms sweeping out of nowhere, racing across the open water to rip into sailing boats before they knew it – just as if they were out at sea. And she caught the name 'Whitlesome Mer'.

Whitlesome, Whittlesea, Whittlesey: names as slippery as the place they attempt to fix. Here the wide skies shift very rapidly from clear blue to soft white mackerel scales to smooth slate, leaden grey and dark charcoal. In flat country like this, the sky is dominant but rarely still. Unpredictable clouds suit the land below, which has changed more slowly but no less dramatically. For the great lake that surprised Celia Fiennes is no longer there. Who took the *sea* out of Whittlesea?

On foot, things are not quite so clear-cut as on the screen – no scarlet balloon to pinpoint the spot. The area still called 'Whittlesey Mere' stretches out across fields dotted with wind turbines, isolated farms, old mills bereft of sails, and tall, slim, brick chimneys. Narrow lanes called Gosling's Drove or Two Pole Drove echo with lost activity. Far away on the horizon, the spire of Whittlesey Church marks the old market town which still greets approaching traffic with a flower-filled boat called 'The Spirit of Whittlesey'. But the spirit of Whittlesey can be felt more powerfully in the flat land once covered by the waters of the great lake.

Dark, straight dykes cutting between the fields ooze with the lifeblood of this low-lying district. Even in August, the air breathes through hidden lungs, heavy with unknown vapour and drifts of white seed. Tall maize masses on either side of deep, duckweed-green cuts. Bindweed wraps the quill-headed sedges and the edges of corn and kale. The white flowers open innocently, as thin strings strangle the nearest sunflowers. Bog reeds and bulrushes burst up, along, above, beside and into the sunken channels. Peat and beet. A kestrel hovers over long, collapsing grass and yellowing nettles. To the right are the low, pale humps of scattered sheep, far to the left the mophead silhouettes of distant willows. Nearby lines of alder and poplar offer perches to the noisy jackdaws. Telegraph poles stand in wait for flocks of smaller birds to turn the high wires into an aerial score. Everywhere, the land is in limbo, holding its secrets, biding its time.

A delivery driver, weaving slowly between deep pocks and potholes, watches over the side of the van door to see if his wheels can keep within the jagged edge of tarmac. 'Wouldn't want to try this every day,' he calls out.

I smile and nod, while trying to find a less crumbling spot to stand as he crawls past. As I watch him making his unsteady way onwards, I think about the people who do come and go every day and what it might be like to live in a house where the ground falls away. But there is no one around to ask – and if there were, it would be an ill-judged opening gambit. The narrow track ahead buckles into cracks and crevices, as gravity turns the surface into rough gravel and rocks. The old mere is getting its own back. Below the precarious track, a red-billed moorhen nips beneath big blades of flag iris, her small black chicks quick to follow.

Whittlesey or Whittlesea? The spelling that now marks the mere's absence is deeply rooted in the old place. The 'ey' suffix has its source in Old English and means 'island'. You see it in the nearby fenland villages of Thorney, Yaxley and Ramsey St Mary's. It's easy to see why someone's 'ey' became a 'sea', as memories of the Saxons were submerged in the settling generations that came and went and stayed in this amphibious region. But 'Whittlesea Mere' is still overflowingly maritime, because 'mere' itself originally meant 'sea'. 'Mere' springs from the same fountain as the French *mer*. But perhaps something more vital and magical was going on when Whittlesea Mere acquired its name. The verb 'to mere' once meant 'to purify or refine' and gathered its gleams from an old Sanskrit ray of light (*marīci*) and an Ancient Greek 'sparkle' (μαρμαίρειν). The Vikings brought their own shining words, *merla* and *mura*, as well as their swords. But 'Whittlesey Mere' was well enough known to merit a mention in the *Anglo-Saxon Chronicle*, in an entry that long pre-dated the arrival of the Vikings. In 656 it was already distinguished from all the other mere 'meres' in the surrounding area by the name of 'Whittlesey'. For many centuries the biggest mere glistened among deep, peaty brown expanses, washed by waves of new people. Now its old name seems oddly out of place in the flat, dissected fields southeast of Peterborough.

Whittlesea was once one of England's great lakes. When John Clare first saw the Thames flowing through Westminster, he was disappointed to find that the river he had heard so much about was hardly a stream compared with Whittlesea Mere. But just how big was the Mere? The sea seen by Celia Fiennes was some '3 mile broad and 6 mile long', but she was probably relying on what she had been told on the journey north, or what she read on her return. These were the dimensions recorded in William Camden's grand survey of Britain, with its final-word-on-the-matter kind of title – *Britannia*. No traveller cantering along a lake as big as the sea would really have any reason to quibble, especially as a 'mile' was rather more elastic in those days.

If you pore over the map of Cambridgeshire designed by Robert Morden for the new edition of Camden's *Britannia* in 1695, you can see 'Wittlesey Meer' on the western county boundary. I have an old hand-coloured print, showing a dark blue shape rather like a flintlock pistol. Underneath is the scale of the map, with three different lengths of mile 'Great, Middle, Small' – so measuring a mere depended on which gauge you used. There were other cartographers who put Whittlesea Mere at a fraction of this size. In his research into the fluctuating history of the lake, Paul Middleton discovered a late eighteenth-century map of the area where it occupies only two miles in length and a mile and a half in width. A later recording made it five miles long. The greatness of this natural phenomenon seems to have depended on the eye of the beholder – until you realise that its boundaries were in fact remarkably fluid.

Even in its heyday, Whittlesea Mere wasn't always in place. In the baking summer of 1826 it vanished altogether, evaporating in the heat to leave a mass of squirming fish. In less exceptional years, the fish in the Mere were so abundant that they were routinely caught, kept fresh in barrels of water and loaded onto horse-drawn wagons bound for Billingsgate. The Fens were rich in fish, the villages full of fishermen, the rivers and lakes lined by anglers. Distant kitchens cooked tench, trout, perch, pike and eels hauled from the brown waters of Huntingdonshire, Cambridgeshire and south Lincolnshire – none more famous than Whittlesea Mere. And yet the defining feature came and went, shrank and grew, froze and melted and flooded. The untidal mere was a natural shapeshifter, swelling and receding with the seasons. Fenland archaeologist Francis Pryor suggests that the great lake might have covered 3,000 acres in winter, but only 2,000 during the summer months. What you saw of Whittlesea depended on when you went to see it.

The poet John Clare tramped a few miles cross country from Helpston to study the flora of Whittlesea, spending happy days with his friend Joseph Henderson discussing the rare ferns, cranberries and dwarf willows that grew in the boggy land around the Mere. So rare were many of the flowering waterweeds that they had yet to be honoured with 'christenings from modern botany'. Plants peculiar to the area often had local names but remained as yet unclassified in the Latinate categories of the Linnaean system. Throughout the summer, the bog plants flickered with rare moths and butterflies. A sharp-eyed observer might spot the smudge and feather of a gypsy moth or the flush of a rosy marsh moth among the leaves of bog myrtles. Marsh carpet moths, blotched as the layers of an old, peeling stump, were harder to see than silver-barred moths with their two light chevrons. In July, large copper butterflies opened brilliant orange wings, outlined in black with just a dusting of white. Swallowtails, translucent in lemon and black, looked as if tiny angels had taken flight from a stained-glass window to alight on the thistle-heads at Whittlesea.

The reed-wooded Mere was alive with waterbirds, too – wild geese, mallard, wigeon, teal. Bitterns, beaks raised, brown pin-striped breasts hidden in the rushes, boomed across the broad fenlands. Clare understood why shy, ground-nesting birds roosted in the boggy ground, where human beings ventured at their peril and eggs had a chance of hatching. The 'huge flag-forrest' and 'stagnant floods' offered safe refuge to the snipe, the 'lover of swamps'.

Masses of waterbirds meant that fowlers flocked here, too, float-ing stealthily on flat punts, imitating their prey as they hid among the reeds. A more efficient (if less sporting) method was to create a duck decoy and drive the unsuspecting birds through narrowing channels into capacious nets. Like the eels and fish, wildfowl from Whittlesea furnished tables near and far. Dishes of duck or goose were a staple of cramped cottages and Cambridge colleges alike. The generous Mere sustained rich and poor, young and old, and those amorphous bodies in between. From reed beds to home-steads: across the Midlands, thatchers laid thick, waterproof roofs, builders packed muddy walls, and weavers wove rush matting for the floors with Whittlesea reeds.

The great Mere was a natural leisure centre, too. Students often rode over from Cambridge to see the races: sailing in the summer, skating through the winter. When Lord Orford and his friends embarked on a summer holiday in the Fens in 1774 in a somewhat eccentric armada, they spent whole days racing and fishing at Whittlesea Mere. The shallow water, the reeds and weeds, the

submerged nets and sudden squalls made progress excitingly unpredictable for those on board and those cheering – or jeering – from
the shore. Since his lordship's fleet with all those tall masts had
already demolished four bridges, not everyone was delighted to see
the sails spread as the races got under way.

If regattas were mainly a fair-weather pleasure, winter brought
skating and 'bandy games' – an early version of ice hockey. The
best skates for speeding ahead were known as 'Whittlesea Runners'.
Blades two feet long, curled up at the front as in an Avercamp
painting, took experienced skaters flying across the ice. Everyone
had a pair. Through the shorter days of the year, the hard mere was
scored with mysterious patterns. When the Fens froze and breath
was visible in white clouds, the shouts of a crowd watching an
impromptu race rang out for miles. There were organised races,
too, like the midwinter contest at Whittlesea in 1841, when sixteen
local skaters competed for a £10 prize and had the satisfaction (or
embarrassment) of seeing their performances reported in the
Cambridge Chronicle. To cross the Mere at top speed, you had to
swing your arms and your whole body with rhythmic vigour.
Master skaters became local heroes, like the Smarts of Welney and
the Watkinsons of Ramsey. 'Fish' Smart held the speed-skating
record from 1881 to 1912, though he was unable to compete at
Whittlesea Mere as his grandparents had done, because by the time
he was born, the great ice rink had gone.

Where did it go? The Mere drained away into a grid of ditches,
cut in straight lines, deep, dark, neat. One across, five across, two,
three, four down. Everything so cleverly devised that the solution
seemed complete, though there were no clues to the black squares.
It took the determination of Victorian engineers to tackle such a
vast stretch of water. Once the aptly named William Wells, MP for
Peterborough, decided on drainage, the days of Whittlesea Mere
were numbered. At the Great Exhibition of 1851, among the elms,
the ear trumpets and Axminster carpets, the telegraph machines
and the Trophy Telescope, the leopard skins, pistols and printing

presses, the weather forecasters, false noses, folding pianos, Jacquard looms, jewels, majolica jugs and Maori baskets, Wells spotted a prize-winning pump invented by John Appold. The remarkable invention promised to shift water at the phenomenal rate of 16,000 gallons a minute. This was just the thing for rapid lake removal – and within two years Whittlesea Mere had been turned into farm-land. So rapid was the disappearance that it took time for the transformation to sink in – *Black's Guide to England and Wales* was still telling travellers a decade later that the Mere 'produced excellent fish, and is much frequented by pleasure-parties'.

And yet by the time the Appold Pump got to work, Whittlesea Mere was already something of a relic. Even before Celia Fiennes rode across the Fens, ambitious drainage projects were well under way. The diarist and tree-lover John Evelyn, visiting Newmarket in 1670, gazed in amazement at areas of newly drained land, 'so exuberant and rich' that the banks of the freshly cut channels were sprouting plants as high as a man on horseback. In place of swarm-ing gnats and infested swamps, Evelyn saw wind- and watermills, pumps and engines sucking water from the sodden land and discharging it into carefully designed dykes.

Since the Middle Ages, when the area filled with abbeys, efforts had been made to direct excess water into cuts and leams. St Guthlac's quiet island retreat at Crowland steadily became more accessible as causeways and embankments were laid down across the wide, wet, empty plain. A few hundred yards from the Abbey, Trinity Bridge stands at the centre of modern Crowland as a reminder of a progressive medieval approach to the local streams. Low stone steps, worn down by centuries of pedestrians, rise from three directions into steep cobbled paths converging at a central slab. The triangular bridge of small Gothic arches once spanned a point where the River Welland divided, allowing the monks and the townsfolk dry crossings over the confluence. The threeway bridge made sense to those who built it and to those who added sculptured figures to the solid stone walls. But now that the streams are no longer there, the bridge crosses from pavement to pavement to pavement over a pavement. The grey arches are out of place at the road junction in modern Crowland: from the smooth slab at the top you look down on roads, cars and shops. After school, children race up and down the cobbled slopes under the stone stare of King Æthelbald. And the old bridge still offers a dry haven, as there's just enough room to avoid heavy rain by taking cover underneath.

After the Reformation ambitious landowners became preoccupied with the rumoured riches beneath the soggy wasteland and murky marshes. Ben Jonson was quick to see the comic possibilities: in *The Devil is an Ass* characters called Merecraft and Engine con the greedy, gullible Fabian Fitzdottrel into thinking that he might capitalise on the enormous potential of the Fens and become 'Duke of the Drowned-land'. The satire was only just exaggerated, as the Earl of Bedford and a band of Gentlemen Adventurers began commissioning Dutch engineers to redirect fenland meres and streams into freshly dug channels. The projectors left their names with their dykes and drains – Sir Philibert Vernatti is immortalised in Vernatt's Cut, the Earl of Bedford in the New Bedford River, which ran rather less sinuously than the old one.

The new king, Charles I, took drainage seriously: within months of his accession, he commissioned the famous Dutch projector Cornelius Vermuyden to get to work in the Isle of Axholme. Soon he was gripped by a vision of untold wealth flowing from a great drainage project in the Fens. Although plans were rapidly overtaken by national events, Vermuyden survived better than his royal master, continuing to design dykes and pumping stations for the Earl of Bedford after the Civil War. Local opposition to drainage projects was often intense, as people saw their common land being not just transformed, but repossessed. The gleaming prospect of reclaiming land and creating wealth – as the Dutch had done so successfully – acted as an unstoppable engine of change, and so the voices of fenland fishermen were steadily drowned out by the galumph of pumps and swish of sluice gates.

The arguments for wholesale dehydration were strong. What serious objection could there be to schemes designed to reduce disease and increase produce? The rich, peaty fenland soils were the very definition of fertility; the flat terrain, once drained of its bogginess, made cultivation straightforward. Daniel Defoe, never a fan of the Fens, 'for 'tis a horrid air for a stranger to breathe in', was far more inspired by ambitious drainage projects than by insects, birds and bog weeds. His idea of a good place was some-where useful, healthy – and lucrative. Far better to drain the land and plant it with hemp and high-yielding crops than to let it lie fruitless, stinking with fish and fog. As channels straight as Roman roads were cut between the old winding rivers, and surges of water came under control through sluices and pumping stations, the landscape began to change. Gone were the vast marshes of medi-eval Britain, and in their place came the Bedford Levels and the modern Fens.

As the largest of the meres, Whittlesea was the last to disappear. The fish and frogs were the first to go, but almost as soon as the water dried up and the mosses dried out, the large copper butter-flies ceased to stretch their orange wings. Soon the snipe and the bitterns flew away. As the years passed, more and more local butter-flies, flowers and waterbirds went with them. The Whittlesea satin moth has vanished in all but name. Gone is the cotton grass, bog rosemary, marsh hellebore, grass of Parnassus, great sundew and bog asphodel. Plants once abundant at Whittlesea are now as rare there as their botanical names. The mallards and moorhens stalked by the wildfowlers were the ancestors of the birds I watched glid-ing along the dykes. But the rhythmic grate of the corncrakes fell silent years ago.

It is hard to imagine the psychological impact of such a drastic change in the landscape; to think of a lake five times bigger than Grasmere draining away and taking with it not just the distinctive wildflowers and wildlife, but an entire way of life and being. We can glean some sense of it from the more recent experience of

Peter Carter, the last eel fisherman in the Fens. He finally gave up his work in 2016 after a catastrophic decline in the eel populations. He knew he had been on borrowed time ever since he started fishing in the seventies, as most of the eel men had already found other trades as the Fens turned steadily into arable farmland. Still, the sense of his heritage was with him daily. The Carter family have been fishing for eels in East Anglia since at least the fifteenth century, their unrecorded ancestors for far longer. 'I feel I have let all the eel men of the past down,' he admitted on his last fishing trip. 'Three thousand years of Fen life has finally gone.'

His great-great-great-grandparents, like the fenland fishermen and sedge-cutters at Whittlesea, never welcomed the inexorable desiccation of their homeland. Living so close to the land and water, they were among the first to see how rapidly the surface of the ground started to sink once the wet peat disintegrated into dark dust. It was William Wells himself who had an iron pole driven deep into the damp soil at Holme Fen to monitor the lie of the land. Between 1848, when it was first fixed in place, and 1860, when the Mere had been gone seven years, the level of the ground descended by nearly five feet. It has now sunk to a further eight feet below the pre-drainage level – so far down in fact that people now travel here to see Britain's lowest lying point. What was lauded as a triumph by progressive Victorian engineers soon became witness to the unpredictable character of Whittlesea and an unsettling truth: a personal vision of a better future can, when realised, turn out to have unexpected side effects.

William Wells could not have guessed that draining Whittlesea Mere would inadvertently fuel environmental disaster. He was entirely unaware that the exposed peat had been imprisoning carbon in underwater cells for centuries, or that quick-dry drainage would set free tons and tons of greenhouse gases. Like all fen-pumpers before him, he thought he was improving the local countryside by making it more productive. But long before the dangers of carbon dawned on the modern world, the disappearance of the old wetlands began to worry a few naturalists, as well as those whose livelihoods depended on fishing, fowling and reed harvesting. When the National Trust was founded in 1895, the very first Nature Reserve to be offered protection was Wicken Fen, some twenty miles southeast of Whittlesea Mere. It was a gift from Charles Rothschild, whose enthusiasm for insects was helpfully enabled by a career in banking. He also bought a parcel of fenland at Ramsey St Mary's, inspired by a vision, very different from Wells's, of a land rich in butterflies, fleas, moths and dragonflies. Woodwalton Fen, lying just south of the old site of Whittlesea Mere, was saved for the insects – and so sustained some of the rare fen flowers admired by John Clare.

Rothschild's dream of conservation helped to attract interest in the Fens as a unique habitat, though almost a century passed before Darlows Farm on the north of Woodwalton Fen became foundational to the Great Fen Project: a concerted attempt to reclaim reclaimed land. William Wells's iron measuring post still stands upright in its original spot, but it is surrounded by sinuous silver birches and curling bracken in what is now the Holme Fen Nature Reserve. The wood is quiet and oddly pale. It looks as if the dark brown ground has sucked the colour from the slim white trunks, though in fact they are richly fed by the peat at their feet. Through the ghostly trees, you may catch the odd glimpse of a swan, head held high, neck paler than the birches. In a small lake hidden inside the wood, cygnets paddle their way through grey water, camouflaged in shiny, dappled feathers. Greylag geese, mallards, moorhens and great crested grebes glide between the weeds and trees. If they seem a pale reflection of the old spreading Mere, these wooded lakes are the first signs of its recovering strength. As the Great Fen has begun to return, so have the bitterns and the butterflies. One day the waters may well return with a vengeance, though whether through the carefully controlled recreation of wetlands, or a rather less welcome inundation, remains to be seen. Whittlesea Mere is biding its time.

The Great Fen Project is the mirror image of the ideal that drew seventeenth-century projectors here. The recreation of a vast flooded area of wetlands and waterbirds, a re-peating of ground slowly composed over centuries through the natural processes of rotting moss and sodden leaves, is a strange damp vision of redemptive decay. It makes me think of Rupert Brooke's imagined fish-eye lens on an aquatic paradise:

> And in that Heaven of all their wish,
> There shall be no more land, say fish.

But not everyone sees eye to eye with the fish. Farmers have been working the land at Whittlesey for 150 years, priding themselves on their produce. During the Second World War, the Fens offered a life support system for the British people. While bombers roared overhead, armies of land girls moved in to help the local farmers with the vital labour of ploughing, drilling, harvesting crops. In peacetime, too, potato and sprout pickers worked in the stone-cold winter fields with blue fingers and raw cheeks to keep the shops stocked. Hard work in a hard place.

From Norfolk across to Huntingdon, from Cambridge to Lincoln, the Fens have gone on providing lettuces, carrots, parsnips, cabbages, potatoes, sprouts, sweetcorn, sugar beet, kale, sunflower seeds and oilseed rape. Even new understanding of the urgent need to protect peatlands does not mean that local farmers are necessarily delighted by the prospect of seeing their family fields flooded. Like Peter Carter, they have their own sense of family traditions and duties, their own views of the land and local wildlife. John Ayres, who farmed land near Ramsey for many years until it was sold for the Great Fen Project, saw the development as 'a disaster'. As far as he was concerned, the return of 'wildlife' in the shape of foxes, badgers or buzzards posed a severe threat to many of the other local birds and small animals. He is sympathetic to ground-nesters, just as John Clare was, but sees the return of marshy wetlands as just another danger zone rather than a safe haven.

How many years does it take to make a place? Those who are born, raised and employed in the same area grow up with a strong sense of what their home is like and should be like. They have their own sense of what is and is not in place, based on years of first-hand, if largely unconscious daily experience. No matter how different it might have been a century or two before they were born – they know their home better than anyone. Their ancestors protested about the drainage projects that threatened their way of life, but this does nothing to dampen the fears that the Great Fen Project may be an omen of wholesale flooding. The modern conservationist-projectors maintain that its scope is modest, its potential to curb other local flooding immense; still, a wholesale transformation to the character of a place can be deeply unsettling. And yet, if the last century or so has witnessed a steady slide towards environmental disaster, the gradual restoration of land to an earlier condition, to a time before living memory, might be a step towards a very much better home. A lot depends on perspective and the point from which a view is taken. A sense of place dawns, deepens, dips, drops away and redevelops over decades, centuries, millennia. Is there an optimal point for arresting time, for defining the quint-essential character of a place? In the fluid Fens, it is difficult to find firm ground.

Drowned

~

John Clare made poems to show his feelings about the casual destruction of old trees and bushes, about ploughing up heathland, enclosing the commons, wrecking homes and turning the local wildlife into 'outcast refugees of mother earth'. Though the language of modern ecology would be alien to him, his understanding of the vital connections between different species and their habitat was well ahead of his time. A felled tree, a diverted stream, a dried-out well: each was a deeply felt personal and shared loss. Unbridled demand for grain and industrial components provoked alarm, sympathy and indignation: the poem known as 'The Lament of Swordy Well' takes the voice of 'a piece of land', denuded not just of trees and bushes, sand, grit and stone, but also of bees, rabbits, mice and beetles. One man's building material was another species' home.

Clare was sometimes able to find relief from his distresses in quiet, familiar places. On the shady banks of the Gwash, as it wound through the riverside trees and long grass not far from Helpston, Clare could escape himself and give thanks:

> when old willows lean
> Thus their broad shadow—runs the river bye
> With tree & bush repleat a wilderd scene

& mossd & Ivyd sparkling on my eye—
O thus wild musing am I doubly blest
My woes unheeding—& my heart at rest

What might he have felt and written, had he lived to see his favourite river dammed and swollen out of all recognition to create
England's largest reservoir?

Only a few miles northwest of the lost and last great mere at
Whittlesey is Rutland Water. The lake formerly known as
Empingham Reservoir was created in the 1970s by flooding the
Gwash Valley just outside Oakham. Since then, the reservoir has
been rebranded with the more natural-sounding name of Rutland
Water. Rutland had lost its independent identity shortly before
the reservoir submerged much of its acreage, during the grand re-
structuring which also abolished Cumberland, Herefordshire,
Westmorland and Worcestershire. But the tiny county returned in
triumph in 1997, with Rutland Water at its heart. The new lake,
covering over 3,000 acres, is large enough for birds and boats, fishing and swimming, wildlife and watersports – many of the leisure
activities once pursued at Whittlesea Mere.

There are differences, of course. Bicycles had yet to be invented
when Whittlesea was drained, but the low-lying slopes around
Rutland Water offer safe and easy cycle tracks. The sailing dinghies
and small motorboats have fibreglass hulls, while the fishing is all
for sport. When the reservoir opened for visitors, the new butterflies brought in to delight children on family days out were bright
blue, big-winged, tropical insects in warm glass houses. Wild
insects are now abundant once more, though they are not quite so
showy and need a bit more effort to find. What might surprise
William Wells the most, however, is the transformation of St
Matthew's Church, Normanton.

The parish church has had a long and unusual life, beginning
in the thirteenth century, but experiencing a major eighteenth-
century makeover that left the nave encased in neoclassical columns

and balustrades. A new tower, open to the winds, added an air of elegant antiquity. And there it stood for many years in proud isolation, after the nearby cottages were demolished to clear the views across Sir Gilbert Heathcote's parkland. Plans for the new reservoir in the 1970s meant that St Matthew's was finally destined for the same fate as the cottages, until a public campaign was launched to save it from the imminent inundation. As a compromise, the lower half of the nave was filled with rubble, leaving the upper storey, with its cream colonnades and baroque tower, to rise above the waves. The church now stands on a small, rocky peninsula, casting reflections in the placid lake below. From the broad grassy bank sloping down to the water, it looks like a romantic island chapel, or – depending on your point of view – a stranded paddle steamer. From the pebbly path on the causeway, you can stand right beside the arched stone windows and see the waves and the clouds and the distant trees shining and distorted in the squares of glass.

The old houses at Normanton were long gone when the Gwash Valley was flooded. The nearby villages of Middle and Nether Hambleton were marked for clearance as the work went on. On the larger peninsula in the middle of Rutland Water, the cluster of houses on the hill is now known simply as Hambleton, since the more happily placed Upper Hambleton no longer needs to be distinguished from its ancient, drowned neighbours. There's only one road to the village, running east from Oakham. Water laps along the fields and trees on either side as the lane runs up to what feels almost like an island community: quiet, cut off, but under no immediate threat from the waves. The village has kept its old pub and church, and just beyond, a drive winds through tall dark trees to the many-gabled, multi-chimneyed and half-timbered Hambleton Hall.

When the teenage, mildly tubercular Noël Coward arrived here for a therapeutic visit in 1915, he was struck by the unfamiliar atmosphere of a country house, though felt he could become accustomed to the life of the landed. His mother, battling with 'poverty-stricken gentility', had had to pawn her last diamond ring to pay for his train fare to Rutland. Hambleton Hall was relatively new when Noël Coward came to stay – the date, 1881, is clearly visible above the grey arch over the front door. It had been built for hunting parties, in keeping with the tastes of the surrounding gentry, but once Mrs Evangeline Astley Cooper moved in, the new French motto carved into the stone porch, 'Fay ce que voudras' (or 'Do as you please'), signalled a distinct change of mood. Evangeline, less typical of her class than Coward assumed, was an enthusiastic artist who liked to surround herself with creative spirits. Among her many house guests was Charles Scott Moncrieff, who politely drank tea or cocktails while working on his translation of Proust. He dedicated the first volume to his hostess. The stately evergreens circling the front lawn must have been slimmer then. It is easy to imagine Evangeline drifting among the cedars, a young Noël Coward arranged on one of the low, spreading, chaise longue-like boughs.

It was here that Coward learned to dress for dinner and descend the grand, polished staircase without slipping in his new patent leather shoes. He liked the orderliness of the domestic arrangements, the easy style of his hostess. He was struck, too, by the way Upper Hambleton rose above 'chequered fields, polite and green and neatly hedged'. This was well-run rural England. The county of Rutland, 'compact and tidy', seemed to sleep through the summer 'gently and a little stuffily', though it woke up for the winter hunting season. And what might Coward have thought if he returned today to gaze from the windows of Hambleton Hall? 'Very wet, Rutland.'

In place and out of place. The waters running through the British Isles have often struck certain influential people as being in the wrong place. And yet, while the engineers commissioned to drain or drown valleys are applauded for their extraordinary technical achievements, there are often less enthusiastic reactions to the irreversible transformations, too. As great bodies of water well up or flow away, so do the tears.

In the High Peak between Manchester and Sheffield, the drowned village of Derwent lies hidden beneath the Ladybower Reservoir. In an exceptionally hot summer, its ruins rise from a hidden, watery cave for a few days, before the waves close over again. The strange dark shadows in the shallows are no lurking sea monster waiting to wreak havoc on the land, but they are troubling enough in their own way. The waterlogged stones that appear and disappear are a sporadic reminder of what went underwater. Occasionally remnants of a vanished world are uncovered from drying mud. In 1989, when the reservoir receded in the heat, a cricket scoreboard from Derwent Hall emerged to spark memories of lazy afternoons and cricket teas. A few years later in the drought of 1995, the 'alphabet stone' which once helped local children learning to read, became visible among the ruins of the village school. In the hot summer of 2018, what survived of Derwent Hall resurfaced through exceptionally low water, while the even hotter summer of 2022 exposed the latch of an old gate. As summers become drier and drier, the form of the drowned village becomes easier to trace, though fewer and fewer are left to flesh out the well-washed bones of their childhood home.

Old photographs hold something of those who once lived and worked in the Derbyshire valley. Solemn children strictly grouped for a school photograph, a stagecoach and four sleek horses stopping outside the Ashopton Inn, Scouts in their best uniform assembled for a rare royal visit, smiling faces in an open-topped bus setting off on a trip to Scarborough. The faces in shades of fading grey gleam for a moment on the surface of the reservoir or gaze out from the shadows in the wooded slopes along the shore.

As the waters rose to erase homes, Ladybower left deep marks. Years after they left school, girls who were evacuated to Derwent Hall in 1940 remembered the nuns who tried to make things seem normal in spite of the sirens. All the time, work on the great dam across the green valley carried on, with a black flag raised whenever one of the men was killed. Hilary Mantel grew up in nearby

Glossop, fascinated from childhood by the drowned village that came and went in the waters. The past had strange ways of re-emerging in the present. The poet James Kirkup was gripped by the idea of an underwater world, where fish swam through trees 'too full of tears for weeping', where coffins were 'launched like death-ships' over yews 'now green for ever'. Although the graves at Derwent were opened before the valley was flooded and the human remains moved to Bamford, his haunting poem about 'The Submerged Village' conveys the shock of finding peace disrupted and permanence proving illusory.

The last service at Derwent Church took place on 17 March 1943. In his address, the Bishop of Derby expressed the mood of a generation battered by years of bombardment: 'We build churches with the idea that they will endure for ever, but we know in our hearts that our buildings will not endure, for we have seen so much destruction during the war that we no longer have the illusion of permanence of the work of human hands.' When the waters finally closed over the old fellside community, the outcome of the war was still unknown. Walter Rouse, who had been the vicar of Derwent Church for forty-seven years, died in 1945, two years after the demolition of his parish. The spire of his church stood amid the waves a little longer, before being blown up in 1947.

The Ladybower Reservoir secured essential supplies of water to the growing populations of nearby Sheffield, Derby and Nottingham. As Liverpool was just as thirsty, plans to dam the River Tryweryn and create the Llyn Celyn Reservoir were announced in the decade after Ladybower opened. But what was vital to the health of expanding cities sucked the life from smaller, rural communities. For the tiny Snowdonia village of Capel Celyn, the news that it was suddenly in the wrong place fell like a dead weight. The handful of families who lived there took their protest to Liverpool, but too much was marching against them, and so, after a nine-year and increasingly desperate fight, they abandoned their homes to the invulnerable tide. The words *Cofiwch Dryweryn*

('Remember Tryweryn') painted in large letters on the wall of a ruined cottage beside Cardigan Bay expressed the reaction of those who felt helpless in the face of unstoppable forces. Graffiti, the instant art that asserts its angry out-of-placeness, can prove more permanent than anticipated. Meic Stephens's spontaneous protest was rapidly turned into correct Welsh – *Cofiwch Dryweryn* – and has since been repainted on a dragon-red wall. Words splashed out in fury have taken on a life of their own, lifting the story of Capel Celyn from the bottom of the man-made lake.

Deadly in excess, deadly in absence. We need water in the right places. The difficulty is finding a place for everyone in grand irrigation plans. In 1994 Norman Hoyle and Kenneth Sankey published a booklet to celebrate the centenary of a new supply of fresh water to Manchester. Their story centres on the grand Victorian fountain in Albert Square but is more concerned with the radiating lines of pumps and pipes, dams and aqueducts, which brought the miraculous gift of clean water to overcrowded, disease-ridden homes. As Manchester grew exponentially over the course of the nineteenth century, the new textile mills and factories drew in workers from far and near. So rapid was the city's industrial expansion that the quickly built terraces were immediately over-full, but under-supported. Elizabeth Gaskell's Manchester novels offer glimpses of families living in cellars, nursing sick children, coughing cotton fluff from infected lungs and navigating the raw sewage in the narrow streets. Fresh water saved thousands of lives. But where did the clear jet spurting up from the new fountain in Albert Square come from?

The water was piped over fells, under roads, across rivers, down valleys and into Manchester from Thirlmere in the Lake District. Work started in 1890, and within four years, the ambitious, life-changing project was complete. The grand dolphin-adorned fountain that now stands in the Square was erected in 1897 for Queen Victoria's Diamond Jubilee, but the real emblem of hope and health was the more modest construction that enabled the first flow of fresh water in 1894. The centenary booklet, *Thirlmere Water*, was sold in support of WaterAid, a charity committed to helping communities in the Global South secure safe water, and with it, better sanitation, hygiene and life expectancy. The story of the Jubilee Fountain seemed only too apt: retelling Manchester's success story could help in addressing the plight of contemporary communities deprived of vital supplies of clean water.

While lives were immeasurably changed for the better in late Victorian Manchester, the effects on those at the northern end of the pipes were more equivocal. We learn from the celebratory booklet that 'a number of farms and associated livelihoods disappeared with the flooding of the valley but . . . the waterwork created a new and larger local economy'. This win-win story is rather different in tone from Ian Tyler's book on *Thirlmere Mines and the Drowning of the Valley* or Margaret Armstrong's account of Basil Lawson, the Victorian curate of Wythburn. As soon as the focus is on the old communities and characters who lived and worked in the valley flooded to form the reservoir, the powerful Water Company tends to be cast as the enemy rather than friend of 'the people'.

As at Ladybower, the Thirlmere dam cost the lives of construction workers, the livelihoods of local shepherds, farmers, miners and teachers. At Wythburn a hamlet known (bafflingly) as 'The City' went under, along with several farms, the school, the Cherry Tree Inn, and the parsonage. All that survived of Armboth Hall was the old summerhouse, which still stands empty among the trees, except for the squirrels and wrens. The ancient Celtic or Wath Bridge which spanned the kissing point of the east and western shores vanished as the familiar figure-of-eight lake swelled around the middle. The small islands of Box Holme and the Scarf Stones disappeared with the distinctive character of the old lake.

Delight in Manchester meant despair in Thirlmere. A photograph of Reginald Bewley, taken around 1900, shows the elderly shepherd standing straight-backed, stick in one hand, well-grown lamb under the other arm, staring over the place he had known all his life. His home, Quayfold, survived the initial inundation, but when the reservoir expanded in the First World War it was demolished.

Many visitors to the area drive swiftly past Thirlmere on the A591 between Keswick and Ambleside, barely aware of the shape of the lake they're passing. The road passes beneath the lower slopes of Helvellyn, whose massive bulk and height, though hidden from view, makes its presence felt. If you have more time, it is worth taking the narrow, winding road along the west side of Thirlmere and scrambling down through the tall beeches and pines to the water's edge. The contours of the fells haven't changed much since Reginald Bewley was a boy; the wooded form of Great How is still there, with the high, bare beak of Raven Crag beyond. But there are no cottages along the shore, no cattle drinking in the shallow water, no causeway crossing from side to side.

Last time I was there was late summer and the water was low. The rough expanse of grey rocks, dry stones and slate kept the still waves at a distance. A bleaching sheep skull lay beside a pair of pale, slightly contorted branches that must have been stranded when the water level sank. Hard to think that they were ever alive and covered with green leaves. A strange sense of absence wasn't helped by the dullness of the day. Under the heavy cloud, the flat sheet and jagged edge of the water seemed utterly drained of life. Not a single boat or solitary angler to be seen. Armboth Hall, which once stood nearby, was famous for its ghostly lights, ringing bells and a black dog haunting the lake below. A murdered bride would occasionally rise from the water, too, and attend a nocturnal feast in the Hall. No black dog on that September day, just a faintly melancholy feeling of vacancy. The only sound came from the stream of cars on the far side of the reservoir.

Victorian Thirlmere never lacked determined defenders. Octavia Hill, a child of Wisbech in the Fens, was an ardent campaigner for better living conditions in the slums and the conservation of areas of outstanding natural beauty. Her vocal opposition to the plans for Thirlmere attracted support from influential figures with passionate, personal attachments to the Lake District. But neither John Ruskin nor Matthew Arnold could halt the plans of the Manchester Water Company. Hill's friend and co-founder of the National Trust, Canon Hardwicke Rawnsley, joined the vigorous fight to save the beautiful, historic valley beneath Helvellyn. But to no avail. The Lake District was famous for its natural beauty and cherished on both sides of the Atlantic as the home of poetry. It was also known for the pure, abundant rainfall that swept in from the ocean to sustain the green fells and valleys – and hence the Manchester scheme.

Among the casualties of the new reservoir was a rock, well known as a natural drinking fountain by travellers on the old road from Keswick to Ambleside and fell-walkers on their way up or down Helvellyn:

> An upright mural block of stone,
> Moist with pure water trickling down,
> A slender spring; but kind to man

It was a good friend to William Wordsworth, who wrote these lines after a trek up the mountain.

For most of the nineteenth century, the tall rock with its ready supply of fresh water was embellished with a line of carved letters: DW, JW, WW, MH, SH, STC. Far from being graffiti cut in anger, these were the initials of friends, siblings and lovers: Dorothy, John and William Wordsworth, Mary and Sara Hutchinson, and Samuel Taylor Coleridge. The 'Rock of Names', halfway between Coleridge's home in Keswick and the Wordsworths' cottage in Grasmere, marked days of intense happiness and creative conversation. The initials made the local landmark a monument to mutually sustaining love, or so they hoped:

. . . fail not thou, loved Rock! to keep
Thy charge when we are laid asleep.

When William Knight was editing Wordsworth's work a few decades after his death, he became acutely conscious of the changes taking place in the poet's landscape. He knew that the Rock of Names would soon disappear under the new reservoir, but drew some comfort from a recent application to move the rock 'as uninjured as possible' higher up the hill to stand beside the new road. Instead the Rock was blown up by the team working on the water supply to Manchester. Canon Rawnsley rescued what survived the blast, including a few fragments of stone with carved initials. He reassembled them as well as he could and had them set into a memorial cairn above the new road. The cairn was to be a lasting monument to the monument that had turned out to be less lasting than Wordsworth hoped.

Rawnsley's attempt at permanence proved no more enduring than Wordsworth's. Although the cairn stood above Thirlmere for almost a century, a new generation of Wordsworthian admirers, led by the poet's great-great-grand-nephew Jonathan Wordsworth and Robert Woof, Director of the Wordsworth Trust, decided to restore the Rock of Names. The cairn was removed from the hillside and smashed to pieces so that the precious initials could be reset in a new stone and placed in the garden of Dove Cottage. The Rock's significance now resides not in its original location under Helvellyn, but in a dozen letters. Wordsworth's symbol of enduring love and permanent in-placeness has proved unexpectedly mobile.

The power of letters and objects to stand for human attachments often emerges most strongly when their physical settings are under threat or changed utterly. Familiar landscapes may be drained or drowned, dried or dammed, their features exposed, distorted or swollen, yet still the old places speak to later generations through storied fragments and chance survivals: through ordinary things

made marvellous by the loss of home. And yet there is still something to be said for standing at the edge of Thirlmere and staring
into the broad waters to trace the ancient lineaments of the lake
and catch the echoes of old voices.

A Crossing with Red Pillars

~

E ven when the Solway's pulse is slow, at low tide on the most placid day of the year, everything flows. This is the sea that never sleeps. On rare days when the wind forgets to get up, leaving the wetlands wrapped in white, the coast underneath is still as restless as ever. Dark stones along the shore, settled into thick mud and drenched sand, look as if they belong there, but soon they are on the move, too. The stones beyond are smaller, scattered among the sea-brack and the thin, glistening lines of water, ridged banks and pools. Tufts of reeds turn into islands now, then back to muddy reed mounds again. Everything lies quiet, while the water comes and goes. It is hard to say whether the tide is flowing in or out, ebbing, flowing, or on the turn, as the river makes its way into the sea, the sea into the river, stirring in slow-motion backwards and forwards as if a full circle would be too much. The birds understand things better here, cutting across just above the surface, taking quick steps across the flats, sweeping down like scattering speech marks. The only sounds are from the sky. Sharp shouts, cries, rhythmic mewings, duller moans: many voices talking at once. Somewhere, a warbler is singing.

All along the north Cumbrian coast are signs warning of treacherous marshes, quicksands, inundations too sudden to escape. The bus stops on these small, well-made roads display photographs of local buses ploughing through floods. Impossible to avoid the sense of danger all around. There are ways to cross the firth when the tide is out, but only if you know when and where – and only if you're quick. There are so many tales of people who got it wrong – the pair of wildfowlers who drowned in pursuit of geese, the passengers who mistakenly disembarked on a sandbank in the middle of a storm, the Scottish and English soldiers caught by the Solway Bore during a desperate and, as it turned out, ill-judged retreat across the sands. The course of the river, the character of the bank, are constantly in flux. Where there are now fields and farms, once there was seawater. The currents move and move again, making the old 'waths' harder to find. The Solway is named by its crossing places – the waths that meant so much to those living on either side or passing through. 'Sol' may derive from the geese (*súla*) that have always flocked here, but probably comes from the Norse word for a pillar – *súl* – referring to the Lochmaben stone, a prehistoric megalith on the coast near Gretna Green. If it were once part of a larger stone circle, the pillars, grey and austere, may have symbolised gratitude for a safer crossing place – without taking anything for granted. The waths have moved with the tides.

Those who know their way – or think they know – can easily be caught off guard by the speed of the tide. As the Irish Sea sweeps in to do combat with the combined force of several rivers in full charge, the Solway churns into terrifying action. The roar of the Solway Bore has sent shivers down spines on either side of the estuary – and, worst of all, in the middle. In Scott's Border novel *Redgauntlet*, the wheels of a cart carrying Darsie Latimer across the Firth at night are caught in quicksand. As the captive of unknown enemies Darsie is doubly stuck: 'I soon not only heard the roar of this dreadful torrent, but saw, by the fitful moonlight, the foamy crests of the devouring waves, as they advanced with the speed and fury of a pack of hungry wolves.' The Solway tides are always highest when the moon is full. Storytellers have an easy time when their tales are set around this unpredictable estuary – all they need to do is listen to the local accounts of lost lives and near misses.

Charles Dickens and Wilkie Collins spent a couple of nights eating shrimps and drinking brandy at the Ship Inn in Allonby, where the great mouth of the Solway opens wide to meet the Irish Sea. Collins was laid up with a badly sprained ankle after they got lost in a storm on the top of Carrock Fell and came slithering down in the dark. Dickens, increasingly frustrated by the enforced interruption, was irritated by the rain, the noise of wailing children, and the dismal guest houses, which matched the beach: 'all more or less cracked and damaged as its shells were, and all empty – as its shells were.' Collins, who spent more time staring out to sea, listening to the wind and the seabirds, would take the hero of his mystery story, *The Woman in White*, to a remote part of northern Cumbria soon afterwards. Memories of the Solway seem to have surfaced again a year later in the Shivering Sand of *The Moonstone*, where the sea leaves 'the waves behind it on the bank, and rolls its waters in smoothly with a heave, and covers the sand in silence'.

On the banks of the great estuary, there are obvious danger spots where only the foolhardy or desperate might think of venturing into the restless tide. At the mouth of the Nith, the river races towards the sea while the estuary waters are advancing upstream, lapping up the reeds like an inadequate breakfast. There is no need for a sign here telling the unwary to keep away from the agitated waves. But across the Firth at Cardurnock, the green grass stretches out invitingly, smooth as a carpet leading down to the sea. Here the dangers are hidden. The merse is all awash with secret, serpentine channels and sunken lakes below cliffs of sand, where a child might look in and never be seen again.

On each shore, seaward lanes turn suddenly from tractor-tyred mud into moss-beds, hiding sand holes and ways into some subterranean world of salt and samphire and sea-filled caverns. In the wetlands, nothing stays in place. The air tastes of the sea, the mists merge sea and sky, the seashore is an ambiguous space of mossy islands, marsh and meandering streams. As the estuary rises and subsides, submerged sandbanks and scars heave flat, deceptive backs into sight from time to time. The fluid margins of sea and land are nowhere more distinctive or less clear-cut than in the Solway Firth, at the westerly edge of the old debatable lands.

What's surprising about this endlessly moving seascape is that anyone ever tried to fix things in place. But something about the open estuary has always provoked straight lines. From the square-cut Roman fortifications to the rusting sewage pipes still visible in some spots at low tide, the slippery, sinuous Solway has been dug and drilled and dredged and determined. Walls and wharfs, railways and radar masts, canals and caravan sites have come and gone, stamping their rectilinear characters on surfaces where nothing really sticks for long. A recurrent revelation is that what was here has gone again, with most of the remnants washed away. Still successions of powerful men surveyed the scene and felt impelled to stamp their mark on the shifting surface. The Emperor Hadrian decreed that Bowness signalled the end of the great Wall, but the sea paid no attention and ran on around the Cumbrian coast. Soon they needed forts further west.

Where the Romans drew a straight line to divide Britannia north from south, their nineteenth-century heirs commanded the perpendicular. A railway right across the Solway Firth was a Victorian vision of money-making modernity. The Lakeland fells were famous not just for pure water and natural beauty, but for being rich in all manner of minerals – coal, lead, iron ore, tungsten, copper, arsenic, graphite, plumbago. The rail project would connect the mines and quarries of the northern Lakes to the factories and ironworks on the Clyde – just as Thirlmere's water would soon be flowing south to Manchester. Even Hadrian might have been impressed by James Brunlees's viaduct, with its marching iron columns cross-braced to bear parallel rails and heavy freight at a steady eighty feet above the seething waters: flat and straight and efficient as the best Roman road.

The railway opened in 1869 and for the best part of fifty years, steam engines rattled across north and south, south and north, pulling the heavy loads of minerals, goods and passengers. An exceptionally hard winter in 1880–1 brought heavy blocks of ice coursing down the estuary. When they smashed against the cast-iron trestles, big sections of the viaduct crashed down into the waves. But it took more than icebergs to deter Victorian business-men once they had made a start. Fading photographs of grey days on the Solway show steam funnelling from the chimneys of deter-mined steam trains, in thick puffs barely distinguishable from the low, louring clouds. A black viaduct cuts right across the scene, marking a machine line of intricate stitching between the river and the sky. What was once an image of modernity now looks like a still from a very early movie. You almost expect an ambush or a stick of dynamite beneath the track.

The unlikelihood of the Solway Railway Viaduct was obvious from the start. Even Brunlees had his doubts about the commis-sion. For a generation who had witnessed the spectacular opening of the Clifton Suspension Bridge, however, a low-level viaduct across the Solway Firth seemed to require nothing more than grit and perseverance. As it turned out, that was the problem. The shifting sands and the ceaseless tides kept up the relentless war of attrition until 1921, when the viaduct was finally declared unsafe for rolling stock. Schoolboys in the 1920s and 1930s, including my father, still faced the winds daily, treating the long iron road as a footbridge to take them from Bowness-on-Solway across to school in Annan. I can see why he grew up with no fear of heights – or indeed much else.

The seemingly empty shores on either side make the historical facts harder to believe than the historical fictions of the area. Unless you know something of the grand Victorian plan, you would be very unlikely to guess that the Solway Firth was once crossed by elevated steam trains. The viaduct has vanished and the waters flow on, impervious to human attempts at control. And yet the old line can still be traced from a striking red door into the past.

On the Cumbrian side, it is more overgrown than at Annan. You can make your way through the trees from the little coast road and scramble up the lower slopes of the steep stone embankment onto the ridge. The unnatural structure juts out into the waves, like an oddly well-organised long barrow, covered in a scrub of brambles and shrubland – something between a bier and a pier. At low tide the sand below cleaves into dark ravines, snaking about the causeway as if intent on bringing down the whole show. When you finally reach the furthest point, high above the lines of wet mud, marbled sand and heaving waves, you can see far into Scotland, England and out to sea. More startling are the six vast columns left behind by the demolition crew. They stand in line, linked by what's left of the iron braces – crumbling saltire crosses, dark against a pale blue sky. The iron pillars have rusted into a dull red, as if to match the huge sandstone blocks at the base. A few feet away, the broken stumps of another row of pillars juts up from the pile of disorderly boulders. Nothing else remains of the long straight metal railroad that once ran for more than a mile across the sea.

On a clear day, the colours of this rusting, ruined Parthenon are as rich as any emperor might desire – ruby and garnet, tourmaline and gold, glinting as the light shifts. The weather-beaten pillars are brighter now than when they were rammed into the causeway – until the sun goes behind a sudden cloud. Far below, the sand gleams opalescent. Opalescence and obsolescence – ruins and radiance – accidental intensity born of opposition. The old borderland of the Solway is deeply resistant to hard edges and defined lines.

It is easier to see the dismantled track from the Scottish bank, just a short walk from the red sandstone town of Annan. From what is now a raised path straight out to the water's edge, you can see the Firth, shimmering in each direction, with a few fishing nets hanging out to dry on the marshy banks below. Cumbria is more than a stone's throw in these winds, but near enough to see the small houses in Bowness staring back. There's room for everyone here, but hardly a person in sight. Once it was full of boats and fishermen, nets and creels and life. Where has the busy port gone? A solitary dog walker nods and puts up his collar against the wind.

The open mouths of the Solway, the rivers and streams north and south, mock any ideal of solid ground. Earth, sand, rock, reeds, salt and fresh water meet and mingle. The sea constantly reclaims its own, contemptuous of opposition. When Robert Burns came to Annan Waterfoot, tasked with imposing excise duties on goods arriving by boat, he understood at once the scale of the place. Troubled by finding himself alone at 'this wild place of the world', he kept up his spirits with rum. The strangeness of the Solway put him in mind of ghosts, witches and bogles. The local water spirits, known as kelpies, were 'haunting the ford, or ferry, in the starless night, mixing a laughing yell with the howling of the storm and the roaring of the flood' as they watched the 'perils and miseries of man, on the foundering horse, or in the tumbling boat!' The chilling atmosphere on the coast made him think of 'the world beyond the grave' and the precariousness of his own life. Perhaps the massing clouds and shrieking seabirds caught in the wind over the great expanse of water were a cold, fleeting premonition of his early death.

Four years later and four miles from Annan at the small village of Brow, Burns spent his last painful weeks, drinking the red-tinged waters at Brow Well and wading into the Solway each day on disastrous medical advice. He died in Dumfries at the height of summer and was buried in the corner of St Michael's graveyard. William and Dorothy Wordsworth were among the earliest literary pilgrims to call on his widow Jean and the surviving children, and to weep over his unmarked grave. From the road along the coast, they looked across the broad estuary to the clear silhouettes of Skiddaw and Scafell. The familiar outlines of the Lake District mountains brought home the nearness and eternal distance of Robert Burns: 'Neighbours we were, and loving friends we might have been.' Had the railway been built a few decades earlier, they could have rattled across to Annan and caught the West Coast train to Dumfries.

Almost twenty years after Burns's death, a gleaming white mausoleum with neoclassical columns was erected in the kirkyard at Dumfries to celebrate Scotia's chosen son. A new boat named in his honour was launched in the Solway, just as the grand mausoleum was nearing completion. Half a century later, as work started on the viaduct, the *Robert Burns*, laden with passengers bound for a new life in America, set off down the estuary passing Brow on the starboard side. I'd rather think of those on board singing Burns's songs than shedding tears as they sailed 'on the seas and far away'.

Throughout its long, fluctuating history, the Solway coast has been a site of adventures, invasions, defences and retreats. If the landscape now seems a sanctuary from the heavy urbanisation of the twenty-first century, its seemingly vacant spaces are brimming with turbulent, only half-hidden experience.

You don't have to dig to find Roman remains – they are there along the seashore and in the contours of the fields. It's just a matter of thinking to look. The sea washes away the past, but still the flotsam and jetsam of generations is lying around. The church at Bowness is built from stones repurposed from Hadrian's Wall. Just down the road at Hesket House, the keystone in the lintel carries a Latin inscription: *matribus suis milites*. Two thousand years ago, Roman soldiers carved a prayer to the mother goddesses, hoping for protection in this most remote extremity of empire. Perhaps they were just young men, a very long way from home, missing their mothers. Letters can survive through centuries, though the means to their meaning may be washed away.

Across the water on the Scottish shore at Ruthwell, a stone cross not quite so old, though old enough, carries an Anglo-Saxon legacy. The narrow, angular letter forms of the runes running around the cross's tall Christian sculptures can still be decoded as quotations from *The Dream of the Rood*. The Old English poem offers the words of Christ's cross, or 'rood', forced into a terrible role by Roman soldiers following their own gods. The lines are carved in stone and stood for centuries in the graveyard at Ruthwell, until smashed by Presbyterian soldiers enraged by what struck them as a monument of superstition. The pieces were rescued, reassembled and rehoused in the nineteenth century, ready for any railway passengers with antiquarian interests. The village takes its name from its ancient monument, though over the centuries, 'rood' melted into 'ruth'.

Place names quietly record unquiet times. Dumfries means 'a woodland stronghold', while across the Solway Moss, Drumburgh derives from 'a fortification on the ridge'. The fortification is still there, a red pele tower built in the Middle Ages with stones once cut for Hadrian's Wall. People in these parts lived their lives fully armed. Further down the coast at Skinburness, once one of Britain's busiest ports, the name recalls 'the promontory of the demon-haunted stronghold'. But I wonder whether it was haunted by more demons than anywhere else along this ravaged coast. Newton Arlosh carries its own story of destruction and renewal in a name that means 'a new farmstead at the burnt place'. 'Arlosh' is rooted in the old Celtic language that flourished here before the Romans or Saxons or Vikings arrived and still reminds us of how settlers would often build on ancient sites. Whether the Celtic community had already been routed by Roman troops, whether the Dark Age settlers were dispossessed in turn by Scandinavian invaders, is more than a short name can disclose. Where the coastline is perpetually shifting, there is little expectation that anything man-made will prove permanent. A sense of uneasy anticipation is incorporated in the architecture – the church tower at Newton

Arlosh has a fortified turret on one side of the parapet, the church at Burgh-by-Sands resembles a pele tower. The waves of new people inundating these flat lands did not always leave clearly de-cipherable marks – they are *felt*, rather, as deep, endless, inexorable movement, a human counterpart to the restless tides. The anchor, a biblical symbol of hope, has special resonance here – no wonder the pub at Port Carlisle was called the Hope and Anchor.

Long before the Victorian viaduct, the ultra-efficient Roman legions arriving at the end of Hadrian's Wall marched right across the Solway to secure strategic spots such as Caerlaverock. There they found an Iron Age hill fort ready to provide firm foundations for their own encampment. Centuries later, the Lords of Nithsdale built closer to the shore – perhaps the Solway had slipped a little further south by then. The same site became Sir John de Maxwell's solid Norman castle, but soon after it was finished, the new Lord of Caerlaverock decided it did not quite measure up to his sense of Maxwellian magnitude – or perhaps the Solway seemed dangerously close for comfort. Sir Herbert ordered a new castle a few hundred yards further inland, with the grandest towers and battlements. It was no match for Edward I, whose legendary ambition to hammer Scotland found an immediate target at Caerlaverock. When the Maxwells rallied to pledge allegiance to Robert the Bruce, whose lands ran through neighbouring Annandale, the Bruce returned the compliment by having their castle demolished because of its proximity to English Crown territory.

Subsequent generations of Maxwells grew gradually more secure and, as the Border was settled, an even grander castle rose above the mighty Solway. With the crowning of James as King of Scotland and England, it seemed safe enough to adorn the great inner walls with decorative grey stone arches and a fine, sculptured façade. But at last Caerlaverock fell to the Covenanters. The castle now stands, in ruined splendour, with gaping windows where the ghosts of the Maxwells look down on tourists wandering as free as sheep in their once-great hall. In the woods nearby, the site of the older castle is carefully marked out. Beyond the clearing, the waters of the Solway move on and on.

In the centuries following Caerlaverock's last stand, new visions of power and prosperity inspired new development projects. By 1820, a consortium of enterprising Carlisle businessmen employed teams of impoverished Irishmen to dig a canal all the way from their city to the tiny coastal settlement of Fisher's Cross. When the canal opened three years later, one elderly resident refused to believe that he had seen ships sailing into town. I can sympathise with his surprise, having been caught off guard near Lochgilphead one morning by the sight of a yacht speeding across a field: it was in fact taking a short cut across the Kintyre peninsula and moving swiftly along the Crinan Canal. The new basin in Carlisle had room for eleven splendid, flag-flying schooners below the castle. Apart from the *Menai* and the *Crown*, the ships assembled for the opening ceremony in 1823 sound more like a party than a fleet: the *Robert Burns*, the *Miss Douglas*, the *John*, the *Nancy*, the *Sarah*, the *Rosina*, the *Mary*, the *Henry Brougham* and the *Irishman*.

Despite the celebrations, despite the new shipping companies that instantly sprang up, despite Fisher's Cross being rebranded as Port Carlisle, the new canal became redundant within thirty years. By then, the railway ran all the way to the harbour at Silloth ten miles down the coast, west of Port Carlisle. What was not filled in to make room for rail tracks now lies in the woods, full of duck-weed, alongside a remnant of Hadrian's Wall.

The old quay at Port Carlisle is just visible: the huge blocks of stone form a surprisingly grand ha-ha for the cottage gardens. An old sandstone capstan protrudes through the grass and looks a more likely resting place for a garden gnome than a tall ship bound for America. Though the lock and the dock are silted beyond recognition, solid shapes of earlier days can be traced beneath the slopes and the sudden precipices of grass and sand. On the road above, a straight two-storeyed terrace of perfectly proportioned late Georgian houses stands like a street detached from some invisible town. The doors are portals to the past. Old names fashioned in the cast-iron fanlights hark back to a time of shared expectation: Sea View, Harbour View, Navigation House. Solway House, with its Ionic portico and perfectly proportioned windows, has seen busier days. The sun set on Port Carlisle when the rising generation saw a brighter future forming in the mirror of the broad Solway. Railways were criss-crossing the world, like the iron girders of the new Solway viaduct.

This is a place where people have come and gone by sea, road, rail and air, sometimes by choice, sometimes by necessity, sometimes fleetingly, sometimes staying rather longer than they'd planned. Those who stayed have always made the best of whatever was left. Why venerate or execrate old stones, if you could use them to build a byre? And if the railway track has been taken up, then sleepers can be repurposed to create steps or flood defences. Walls and ditches have turned into waterways and dykes, railways into roads, mariners' cottages into Indian head-massage parlours. It's a practical attitude to challenging, changing circumstances. Pick up the pieces and just get on with it. Rebuild walls, reuse old materials.

There are countless unpretentious monuments to those who worked with what they found. The churchyards hold their own private histories of young men drowned on fishing trips, girls lost to thin ice, workmen killed by falling cranes, smugglers caught on reckless voyages, older men and women who died peacefully in their beds. Those who moved with the tides have generally fared the best. Solway fishermen have always known how to wade into the dangerous waters to catch the passing salmon. Their permeable hand-held haaf-nets have survived far longer than the heavy, unbending constructions that have been built and unbuilt and rebuilt over long centuries. In this fluid, in-between world of shifting light, everything goes with the flow.

Overhead, pink-footed geese fly in loose S-shapes. A heron lifts from a hidden salt-lake at no great speed. The barnacle and the bean geese feel safe enough in the Solway, unaware that from the shore they are viewed as rare survivors. And the red-legged oyster-catchers, untroubled by being a little more commonplace, carry on their urgent business, finding crustaceans on the mudflats.

Haaf-Nets and Half-Netting

~

I wanted to find out more about haaf-netting. It is something I've always known about – or half known about. My father used to tell us about how he and his brothers, his father and their friends would stride into the Solway when the tide was right, forming a line across the estuary. 'You have to hold on tight and keep your eyes peeled.' They would all stand for hours chest deep in salt water, stepping from foot to foot to stop the sand dragging them down as the water rose. The tides were swift, the currents were strong: you needed your wits about you. It was the same voice for a rugby scrum or reefing a sail in a Force 8 gale – all fine if you knew what you were doing, but not something for the faint-hearted or easily fazed. He spoke in a clear, matter-of-fact way, as if one day we might find ourselves trying to catch salmon in a tidal estuary when the advice would come in handy. But the bright light in his eye and the dramatic dips and falls in the story showed that the thought of haaf-netting sent him off through the years and miles to experience more raw and adrenalin-filled than the comfortable life he now led.

'Haaf-net' is another red door, opening to different times, but always leading to the Solway Firth. The Vikings who arrived a thousand years ago knew how to make nets strong and buoyant enough to survive the double flooding and ebbing, strong enough to catch the estuary's wealth, to bring in the great silver fish. They also liked to give things names. Their sagas are full of names for the places they encountered, the leaders who found them, the weapons, tools, animals, fish and plants they took and traded. The local languages of the North of England are coloured by Scandinavian threads. Words once foreign to the people who lived there are now intrinsic to local identity, in village names ending in '-howe' or '-by' or '-thorpe'. From How in Cumbria to Howden in the East Riding, from Appleby in Westmorland to Somersby in Lincolnshire, from Thorpe in North Yorkshire to Gunthorpe in Nottinghamshire: for the past millennium people have lived by the names chosen by Scandinavian invaders. The Northern fells run with becks rather than streams, while Yorkshire and Lincolnshire farmers build *stacks*, run up *stees*, call their young livestock *gimmers* and *gilts* and, if a sheep turns over on its back, rescue it from being *far-weltered* or *rig-welted*. 'Haaf-net' shares the Scandinavian ancestry of the North country, deriving from *haf*, an Old Norse word for a sea channel.

The spelling given in the *Oxford English Dictionary* is 'halve-net', as used by Allan Cunningham, who seems to have been the first person to commit Solway fishing nets to print. Cunningham, who trained as a stonemason but achieved more success as a poet and storyteller, was born in the Dumfriesshire village of Dalswinton, fifteen miles north of the coast. As a young man, he helped to bear Robert Burns's coffin to the graveyard in Dumfries and, as a slightly older one, supplied collectors with old – or seemingly old – songs and stories from Nithsdale and Galloway. His 'traditional tales' appeared regularly in the *London Magazine* in the 1820s, giving people far away a taste of the Solway's sharp, salty air. 'The Ghost with the Golden Casket' includes a cameo of two young fishermen singing a mournful duet as they dry their 'halve-nets' one evening on the shore beneath the ruined castle of Caerlaverock. Haaf-nets have since been fished from the cool web of official words to recover their older, Scandinavian form. It is easy to see why

Cunningham referred to them as 'halve-nets'. At some sixteen feet across, the broad rectangular nets are twice as wide as they are high. They are strung along a broad crossbeam and attached horizontally to a tall, central staff with shorter poles at either end, like a very wide, flat fork. You could be forgiven for thinking that the bottom section had been lost or removed, leaving only half a net to cover the frame.

Cunningham's tale brings home the precariousness of ordinary life. Had he left out the fishermen (who do not add much to the plot), a long line linking modern lives to their Viking ancestors would have been left to float in the uncertain tides of oral tradition. A place name, an incidental detail in print, an old photograph: these are the accidental means to earlier moments, to those habitual experiences that so easily slip away.

Victorian paintings can offer glimpses of what's been lost. William Ferguson's picture of *Haaf-Net Fishing near the Solway*, painted around 1885, shows nets spread like a pair of thin square wings in the morning light. The pale mesh shimmers with flecks of white paint, a gossamer film transfiguring the trees and meadow and sky beyond. A tall fisherman, bearing the net and its wooden cross on his shoulder, pauses to chat to a red-haired woman in a head scarf, who carries a wicker basket while staring out to sea. On the sand below, another figure, wrapped in oilskins, holds his haaf-net firmly in front and walks towards the shore, where a third fisherman is stepping into the river, his net invisible as it meets the sky-white water. On the shore, cross propped against a pole, a haaf-net, gathered like a wedding veil, is hanging out to dry. The net blurs the outlines of three of the small gaggle of white geese that are making their way to the water. It's a scene of utter stillness, all action and anticipation suspended for an instant. Old pictures hold the past in place, while demonstrating its distance.

The coast remains little changed from when William Ferguson painted the scene. He must have been looking down to the estuary near Glencaple on the bank of the Nith. The fishermen may well be descendants of those observed by Allan Cunningham a little further down the river at Caerlaverock. They are long since gone and though their special method of fishing survives, it is now hanging by a thread.

There was a time when haaf-netting was protected by royal decree. In 1612, the right to fish with haaf-nets in the Solway was secured by a charter signed by James I and VI, VI and I (or just VI, or just I, depending on which side of the border you are standing and how much difference that makes to you). Some Solway fishermen still preferred other methods, hammering fixed nets into the sand or galloping along the shore with spears poised above the flowing shallows. Unsurprisingly, this was the type of fishing featured by Walter Scott in *Redgauntlet*. As the hapless Darsie Latimer gazes over the wet estuary sands for the first time, he is astonished to witness a salmon hunt: 'they chased the fish at full gallop, and struck them with their barbed spears, as you see hunters spearing boars in the old tapestry. The salmon, to be sure, take the thing more quietly than the boars; but they are so swift in their own element, that to pursue and strike them is the task of a good horseman, with a quick eye, a determined hand, and full command both of his horse and weapon.' Scott, who had evidently watched people spearing salmon in the Solway on one of his many visits to the coast, was eager to convey not just the intense excitement of the hunt, but also the camaraderie and the extraordinary skill of those involved. As Darsie listens to the shouts, the bursts of laughter and applause, there is a strong sense of admiration and exclusion. This is an intensely fulfilling experience for those who know how – for those who are part of the band.

Outside the pages of Scott's adventure story, where galloping horses and hunting with spears offered a more thrilling spectacle than a row of men standing motionless in the sea for hours, haaf-netting continued as it always had done. Families on either side of the Solway were kept well nourished by their fat fish, which at certain times of the year became so plentiful that workmen were known to request a limit of three times a week on salmon suppers. Before industrial fish farms turned salmon into everyday fare, the hours spent patiently waiting in cold water were well repaid. During the 1950s, a decent living could still be made by catching salmon and sea trout with haaf-nets: there were some seventy full-time haaf-netters in Annan alone. Since then, a way of life that characterised the place for a thousand years has steadily disappeared. Lines linking father, son and grandson across the tides of time can very quickly be swept away.

The decline in haaf-netting was directly tied to the severe decline in wild fish stocks. For centuries, huge shoals of wild salmon and sea trout have been fulfilling a remarkable marine life cycle, from their spawning grounds in the local rivers of Cumbria, Dumfriesshire and Eskdale, into the Solway estuary and then away on their great journey across the Atlantic towards Greenland and the Arctic Ocean. A year or two later, fattened on what they find in the far north, they make their way back past Iceland and onwards to their original home waters. How salmon navigate thousands of miles of seawater is as baffling as the annual migrations of wild geese. These are mysterious silver creatures of the deeps and shallows, slipping easily between fresh and salt water, yet with homing instincts as strong as any bird. With such extraordinary natural survival skills, it is sobering to witness their struggle with the challenges of the twenty-first century.

Even when their long, long voyage is nearly over, salmon have always had to hazard the haaf-netters in the Solway and the anglers further upriver to reach their native breeding grounds at last. In recent years there have been many other threats. Marine pollution, plastic infestation, parasites, viral disease are all grave enemies of the travelling salmon: dangers intensified by global warming and climate change. As if this were not enough, many of the stony, spawning streams in Scotland and the North of

England have been disrupted, making breeding more difficult even when the great fish have finally arrived home. No wonder their numbers have declined. How much of the damage was the fault of the fishermen remains contested, but as licences to catch salmon in the Solway were steadily restricted as part of the urgent conservation effort, haaf-netting ceased to be a way of life. Under legislation designed to protect the local ecology and enable the restoration of salmon and sea trout, any fish caught in the estuary must now be released or inspected by scientists. The ancient practice of haaf-netting is now a sport rather than a way of making a living. Whether the wild fish populations will ever recover remains to be seen.

Between May and September, a few determined fishermen still regularly wade out into the waters of the Solway with their licences and haaf-nets. Many come from old fishing families, including Barry Turner and John Warwick, who feel a strong commitment to family and local tradition. Or George Willacy, who is very proud of his biggest catch – a mammoth 34-pounder. But he's prouder still of his fishing forebears. Since his father and his grand-father both died during fishing expeditions, each trip into the Solway is a kind of family tribute.

Deep in the flowing water, face to face with the seabirds and seals, geese and porpoises, the haaf-netters are participating in the full life of the estuary. George Chalmers, who fished different stretches of the Solway for many decades, remembers an unsettling moment when a large, dark shape appeared in the sea not far enough away from where he was standing. It looked at first like a submarine but turned out to be a whale. Unlike some forms of angling, haaf-netting, with its line of linked fishermen, fosters a special camaraderie. The men may be competing for the biggest fish but are more concerned with looking out for each other in the dangerous waters. Memories of those who went over the edge and failed to resurface in time generally last the longest.

A sense of being the last of their line has made the Annan haaf-netters eloquent advocates of their ancient skill. Their website abounds in portraits of the key players, photos of the wide sands and tides, shots of men struggling into waterproofs, wading into the sea, carrying their haaf-nets, catching the great fish, standing together in cheerful solidarity. There are videos, too, on the history of haaf-netting, or about how to make a haaf-net or a crossbeam and then tie them together. Most affecting of all is the film called 'The Last Tide'.

When I walked along the north bank of the Solway near Annan, looking across to my father's old home at Bowness, I tried to spot the Altar Stone, a boulder lying in mid-channel, marking the boundary of the Annan fishing grounds. The Annan haaf-netters are keen to point out that when the tide runs north of the Altar Stone, both sides belong to them. Information boards beside the white fishing shed above the water reiterate the point, with a fine photograph of the stone. Against the wall, a solitary wooden haaf-net was resting.

I took out an old family photograph to study the line of figures standing behind an open haaf-net. Most have moustaches, one or two have beards, all are staring directly at the camera. Their bodies are blurred into ghostliness by the billowing nets, but above the broad, horizontal pole their heads are oddly distinguished by different hats. Flat and not so flat caps, bowlers, top hats, broad-rimmed fishermen's hats, deerstalkers and something that looks almost like a fez. The photograph was taken by T. Kirkpatrick of Lenton Street, Carlisle, and on the back fifteen names are listed in fading ink and a clear hand: Billy Elliott, Laurence Cowan, Joe Wood, John Holmes, Robert Holmes, Billy Fell, Pat Lawson, Johnny Bateman, Jack Linton, Geordie Hodgson, B. Holmes Ogle, Geordie Holmes, Jack Stafford, Bob Percival, Johnny Wood. In fainter pencil are a few of their nicknames – Tibby, Lorky, Whistler, Old Gunner. These must be the Bowness haaf-netters, who were probably less keen to preserve the traditions eddying around the Altar Stone.

Solway fishermen holding their haaf-nets. Early
twentieth century photograph.

The gulls were flying across the Bowness Wath, untroubled by
old rights and national borders. I could make out a few low roofs
and chimneys on the other side and the silhouette of the remaining
pillars of the derelict railway viaduct. The shore was ringing with
the piping sound of oystercatchers and the curlews, stooping at the
edge of the reeds to spear shellfish with their thin, curved bills. As
I couldn't see what was under the surface of the sand or the water,
the entire estuary seemed to belong to the birds.

In the Annan Museum in Bank Street, there are surprisingly few
displays relating to the local fishing practices; only one or two
pictures and, resting on top of a glass display case, a capacious
wicker creel opening like a clamshell. It was specially made for
carrying the salmon caught in haaf-nets and stake nets. Apart from
this, there is little on show to suggest that haaf-netting was regarded
as a defining activity of the town. Annan has other claims to fame

and when I last visited, the museum was devoting its ground floor to Solway smuggling.

To try your hand at a haaf-net seems to be a badge of honour nevertheless for writers on the Solway. In *The Marches*, Rory Stewart describes wading into the estuary to stand waist deep in water under the careful guidance of Mark Messenger. I wonder if there's a height restriction, as for the more dangerous rides at theme parks. What might be quite all right for the long-legged could quickly prove fatal for the more vertically challenged. A six-footer's waist-high tides would be sweeping over my head in minutes. And yet Ann Lingard reveals in *The Fresh and the Salt* that she too has been out into the waves with Mark Messenger. Not only did she live to tell the tale, but to write vividly about standing in the water with a fast tide forcing the haaf-net against her, soaked by rain and spray, still warm in her waterproofs and waders and exhilarated by being 'in the Solway' rather than observing from the margins. Once haaf-netting came to mean leisure rather than livelihood, the exclusively male pursuit was open for women to experience. I still have a strong feeling that if I were to try, things might not go quite so swimmingly. When I spotted that sea-stained haaf-net drying on the shore, I felt no impulse to carry it into the waves. But I was pleased to see it there and know that others still did, if only because haaf-nets and -netters have always been part of the Solway.

Haaf-nets seem half net, half wing, and utterly at home in this amphibious region, where the land becomes sand and the flat banks of seagrass are punctured by saltwater pits; where the sea swirls through channels and sandbars, leaving scars in its wake; and everywhere the seabirds coast along swift currents of air and water, before dropping or surfacing again. This fluid land of the in-between, half Scottish, half English, half ebb, half flow, half seen, half hidden by clouds and mist and changing winds, is the perfect habitat for the Viking haaf-net. The fishermen balance them on their backs ready for moving across the water like great dragonflies or tiger moths with light, boxy wings. But this is cold, hard work. A tough way to earn a living, exposed to bitter winds and driving rain, to deadly currents and quicksand. How many haaf-netters have taken a wrong step and been swept away by the tide? Yet still the pull of the wind and water is strong – the raw struggle between man and the elements. There's a Viking longing deep inside many of those who now spend their days in warm rooms in front of screens. Mental haaf-netting is hardly a match for feeling the freezing water surge against your legs and chest, the cold biting into hands and face. Like so much of what we learn, it is knowledge mediated and filtered by layers of other people's tales, records, photographs, technology. But second-hand experience can still take you by surprise.

In a desultory search for haaf-nets, I stumbled across a short black-and-white film from the BBC archive, first broadcast on 3 March 1965. The piece opens with a young, clean-cut, evidently rather chilly Julian Pettifer on the Cumbrian bank of the estuary at Bowness-on-Solway. He stands out in his smart leather gloves, long dark overcoat, neat white collar and narrow tie, against the flat, hazy, grey levels of the Solway. 'It's a griew day, and the breist is a wee bit clarty underfoot,' he begins, speaking slowly in hushed tones, beautifully articulated, to give viewers a chance to follow what he is saying. But in case this proves too difficult, he immediately translates 'from Cumbrian English into Standard English', explaining to anyone who has struggled to work it out that 'it's a raw, cold day, and the bank's a little bit muddy underfoot'. What he really seems to be saying is that here is a man from the BBC in anthropological mode, about to shine a light on the natives of the region just as he might in central Africa or deep in the Amazon rainforest. 'This is my Scotland pocket and my English pocket, as they say up here,' he explains, slapping the respective pockets and gesturing across the estuary to where Scotland lies on his right. It's also a place where fishing is not exclusive to 'the privileged few', he tells us. This is something everyone can do, 'as long as he can walk as far as the water'. Though what followed made me wonder.

The camera shifts to two men walking across the ridged sand, with broad white tridents, hung with nets, balanced across their shoulders. The man wearing a rather jaunty beret, who is smoking a pipe as he walks along, is identified as the Vicar of Bowness, the Rev. Maurice Allen. He's followed by his sexton, Mr Bob Rome, and then the pub landlord, Mr David Tunstall, though there are fewer men out than normal because of the cold (or perhaps because of the camera crew). The footage of the trio lined up in the deep waves, rhythmically smacking their bare hands against their arms, brings home how cold it is – and perhaps their awareness of how the outside world might enjoy the spectacle of an ancient ritual. The haaf-nets are plunged, prongs first, into the waves, but, as the long wait for fish begins, the film cuts to the merse, where a figure in a felt hat is sitting close to the shore, fully absorbed in making a net. With the tall interviewer perching on the rough grass, he carries on with his netting, hunched against the wind looking rather like a wombat, or, to my surprise, remarkably like my father. As the clipped BBC voice politely asks Mr Stafford whether haaf-netting has changed since he started fishing over forty years ago, the realisation breaks over me. This is my grandfather, John Topping Stafford, in the brimmed hat and tweed suit I remember so well from early childhood.

Mr Stafford, in his soft Solway voice, explains that although the fishing practice hasn't changed at all, not many people are still making nets. The one he's making now, which hangs neatly before him on a low frame as his skilled hands work away, will take a good two days, 'but not an eight-hour day'. 'What, a twelve-hour day?' asks Julian Pettifer, warming to his subject, despite the raw morning. 'Yes, a good twelve.' They talk about fishing and how hard it is – how some haaf-netters go weeks without catching a single fish: 'Not one salmon . . . Not one.' Mr Stafford makes the point with dramatic pauses and a twinkle in his eye, while his hands carry on working. It turns out that it is Grandad who talks of his Scotland pocket and his England pocket – their identities presumably depending on whether he is facing inland or out to sea. As the salmon sweep in from the Atlantic, the haaf-netter stands on a sandbar in the Solway, staring westwards and waiting for his net to tug and tighten with a thrashing fish.

When asked whether he had ever been carried away by the current, Grandad looked quizzically from under his brim. 'Oh yes, more than once.' Like my father, he was always good at hooking a listener, even if the salmon sometimes evaded his skilfully crafted nets. By now, they were getting on well, Pettifer grinning and animated, my grandfather allowing a pause in his netting and smiling broadly. 'I once went over the deep and over to the other side.'

'Over to *Scotland*?' Julian Pettifer, rising to the excitement of the tale, uttered the words as if speaking of the moon.

Grandad nodded, smiled, and decided not to mention that his wife was Scottish or that Scotland was only a mile or so from Bowness, if you went by the most direct route. But it must have felt a very long mile of unexpected drifting in the strong, swift tide.

'And what happened, exactly?'

He had been fishing on a hem, a ledge along the deep, where currents cross and fish sometimes congregate, when a great pile of rubbish swept passed, filling his Scotland pocket and breaking the right-hand pole of his haaf-net.

'Well, I went down and, to tell you the truth, I was frightened, make no mistake about that,' he chuckles, 'but when I came up and could see I wasn't going to drown, I thought the best thing I could do was to see if I could paddle over to the other side. So I gathered up my net, kept hold of the beam, and tried to keep my head, as far as possible. The flood tide was coming up at the same time –' he pauses again, and gazes towards the estuary – 'but eventually I got over to the other side.' Luckily there were a couple of men on the Scottish shore who pulled him from the water and onto the sand. 'Well, they tipped me up and ran the water out and pulled my boots off. And that was all there was to it.'

And that was all there was to the short film. But the shock it delivered and the emotional depth charge detonated have lasted much longer than the modest seven minutes of grainy, grey footage.

The monochrome film opened a window on the past, a national, international and deeply personal past. Haaf-netting belongs to the Solway, but links the estuary to the North Atlantic, and to the people who came and went by sea centuries ago. The nets and their names knit the Solway to the Isle of Man and Ireland, Norway, Denmark and Iceland, a broad, barely visible web of ancient threads. Astonishingly well-travelled salmon and sea trout once linked the haaf-netters to fishmongers, chefs and diners across England, Scotland, Wales and Europe. They have been caught, in turn, in a mesh of legislation and conservation, specially made to sustain the fish. My grandfather's net was strung from local strands, tying the tiny village of Bowness to the other side of the Solway, to the other side of the Atlantic, to the other side of time.

My screen had turned unexpectedly into a virtual haaf-net. If I had a second screen, as many people do, the resemblance would be even more striking. But the single rectangular shape shows me what can still be caught – and let go again. In the virtual world, we perpetually catch sight of half-lives, of things half netted or slipping away. The internet offers glimpses of an elusive past, fleeting chances to see what's beneath the surface and imagine what else might be there. In the half-life of the world wide web the marvellous resurfaces before going down into the dark once more. If the BBC remove the clip of film, Grandad will go down again, with his haaf-net and his hat.

Wild Geese and Tame

~

Y ou hear them first – a faint rhythmic cry, amplified by many voices, not quite in time, rippling through the clear sky. Impossible to ignore as the sound gets louder, the pitch varying like the approach of an airborne crowd on the way to some unknown, marvellous event – excited, urgent, each voice shouting to be heard above the din. By the time they sweep into sight, the air is loud with exuberant calling, calling, calling, across the currents, careless notes dropping to the ground as they go. Strong, slow dips of those great wings cover the distance in no time, necks stretched out, smooth bills open, closed, open in the sheer affirm-ation of being. *Here we are, here we are*, the wings beat, the cries repeat. Count the geese as they print the sky in even, invisible patterns, leaving only their calls on the air. Ten, twelve, sixteen, eighteen, twenty-six, thirty, forty, more.

Sometimes, it's a more intimate party. Two pairs moving asymmetrically as a fin, voices slicing through the cold, damp air. They say that geese mate for life, making the sight of a single goose the sign of private catastrophe. A single, crying bird circling in the pale, milk-pink sky, may be mourning a lost part-ner. But the lone gander I watched one winter afternoon showed no obvious hint of distress or alarm, as he sailed above the bare trees. He looked more like a scout on reconnaissance, sharing his observations in short, echoing reports. The rest of the flock were not far away.

However often you hear or see wild geese in flight, it is always startling. In a world of their own as they move overhead, at home in the air, in place and out of place everywhere. Wild geese seem to know their place. Whether they fall into line companionably or compete for prime position at the head of the flock or take turns at different stages of the journey is hard to tell as the aerial flotilla sails past. Craig Sharp, a veterinary and sport scientist as well as an old friend, understood the movement of birds. He once explained to me that wild geese have a leader to guide the flock on its way from place to place, from wetlands to drowned fields, from estuaries to lakes. The geese follow their leader in relaxed formations, spreading across the sky in wavering chevrons, until there's an emergency. Then another goose will leave the trailing lines, stepping up swiftly through the current to spearhead the skein to safety. The idea of having an executive manager for routine guidance and a crisis chief to rise to the fore when occasion demands confirmed my instinctive sense that wild geese know what they are about. Their well-measured lives are proclaimed in each matched beat across the cloudless horizon, in their regular arrivals and departures.

I'm always impressed by their annual appearance just after the corn harvest. Even though it happens every year, it still makes me stop. They sweep from the sky, landing surprisingly quietly in stubble fields to feed on what's left among apparently empty husks. Though surely ravenous after such a journey, they amble around, pecking, preening, inspecting the ground and generally making themselves at home. Unperturbed by surface differences, wild geese mix and muck in together. Mottled old-snowy-breasted greylags mingle easily with their more decisively marked barnacle companions. Canada geese, dark-necked, with dirty white bellies and heads held high, stand out from the gabbling crowd in human eyes, but none of the other geese takes much notice. Bent on their collective task of tucking in, they're more likely to startle at a dog or a rambler. Hundreds of geese land, feed and take off, swirling in great chattering waves before alighting again in a neighbouring field to carry on where they left off. They're fattening themselves on rough stubble and thistle seeds after their great flight from the far north through thousands of miles of unforgiving winds.

One of Aesop's brief but brutal fables reflects the feeding habits of geese. Wild geese land in a field, where some tame geese who have escaped from a nearby farm are busy gobbling up the corn. All the geese then feast together amicably until they are rudely interrupted – by a fox in some versions, by the angry farmer and his men in others. While the wild geese immediately fly off to safety, the tame geese, less agile and more used to being fed than foraging, fall prey to the unexpected intruders. The inevitable moral lays blame on the tame geese for being richer and fatter, in other words for being greedy, lazy, over-privileged and unable to remain content with what they have. This strikes me as rather unfair, since the failure of the tame geese to take flight fast enough is entirely due to their domestication. All too often, 'goose' is a byword for foolishness, a big, comfortably built bird domesticated by humankind and then held in contempt for its obedience. If taken at face value, the old fable is just as unsatisfactory – would a farmer choose to slaughter his own flock and leave the wild birds to fly free? Men have been hunting geese for as long as they have had effective weapons, apparently gaining more satisfaction from bagging a wild goose than disposing of a tame one.

And yet the old fable does reveal an important truth: while human observers make clear divisions between the domestic and wild, between those kept firmly in place and those free to fly away, the birds themselves show no interest in the distinction. And why would they? White farm geese and wild greylags are very closely related – it is just that their evolution has been utterly changed by human rather than natural selection. Geese have been kept by humans almost as long as they have been hunted. From China to

Egypt, they had their place in the ancient world, inspiring artists as well as supplying cooks. Their distinctive silhouettes can be seen standing or stooping for corn in skeletal hieroglyphs on Egyptian tombs. There is more realistic depiction on a tomb painting from Thebes, now in the British Museum, of a great flock being fed, rounded up and counted, before being stacked into baskets for slaughtering and plucking. Strange to see four-thousand-year-old geese looking out with just the same increasingly agitated expressions as you might see in a gaggle today.

The ancients knew that geese belong to three elements – water, air and earth. For the kind of writer who shifts from tone to tone, topic to topic, with as little fuss as these great birds make on their way through the elements, a goose quill was a gift from the heavens. I'm not sure what the keyboard equivalent could possibly be. The mystery of geese is not dependent solely on their capacity to appear in the sky as if from nowhere. Nor on their ability to descend into water so smoothly that it's hard to think they were ever airborne. Their breathtaking take-off or landing gathers force from the unlikeliness of their plump, low-slung, flat-footed forms, which are only fully apparent on the ground. Geese are full of hidden secrets. It is when they move between elements that their unearthliness breaks out.

The fat, white birds dawdling across a muddy farmyard do have a very grounded, no-nonsense character. I remember being amazed by the size of a goose egg, a present some years ago from kind-hearted neighbours whose small flock kept them oversupplied once the family had grown up and left home. A single egg was enough for a family-sized omelette, though I could never quite bring myself to break the gargantuan gift. Why did it seem so different from a hen's egg? The huge, smooth, white shell felt heavy and somehow momentous, as if I were holding the world in my hands, or an opaque, oddly swollen, crystal ball. The idea of cracking it open was unthinkable. When John asked how the goose egg had been, I said (truthfully) that it was wonderful.

For John, the well-meaning benefactor, farm geese had clearly defined roles – they were kept for producing eggs and goslings, flesh and feathers, and for keeping unwanted visitors at bay. An angry goose, neck pulled up and puffed out, is not to be messed with – and unhappy the man who attempts to cross a pair protecting their young. The honk-volume turns up when geese are riled, to announce the arrival of unwanted visitors – whether four-legged, two-legged, two-wheeled or four. If the intruders stand their ground, the anserine guard advances with wings outspread, to launch a barrage of spit and hisses.

Though often despised by cyclists and delivery drivers, geese are just demonstrating their legendary heroic character. In Ancient Rome, geese sacred to the goddess Juno were kept with great care at her temple. Any mild resentment about these plump birds among the less well-fed citizens quickly turned to reverence after the geese saved Rome from invasion. The enemy moved at night, so silently that even the dogs slept on oblivious. The sacred geese, on the other hand, set off such an angry hullaballoo that the garrison woke up in time to see off the marauding Gauls. From that day on, Juno's geese were known as the fearless defenders of the Capitol.

Whether it was Juno's protective character that made geese a congenial species in the first place is not part of the story. But it is easy to see why the goddess of birth and motherhood might have chosen the goose. Though a different kind of protection from the incandescent puffing of a goose standing its ground, the confident, matronly form of a well-nourished goose offers all the reassurance of an experienced nursery nurse. The perennial figure of Mother Goose is comfortable and capable, protective and proud. After all, domesticated geese are at their best when leading a fleet of soft-plumed, dirty-blonde goslings across a pond. John Clare loved watching spring goslings waddling across the grass or swimming 'with wild delight', while their hissing guardians sent the village children scampering. Wild geese are good parents, too: in their well-organised society, new mothers are helped by the more experienced birds. In 2018 a 'nanny' goose was spotted sailing across a Canadian lake with fifty-one goslings in her care.

Whenever these birds move into another element, everything changes. As soon as they launch into water, geese lose their land-lubberly gait. From stout to stately in a simple, smooth step, they glide across dark, limpid pools, elegant and bold as waterlilies. Even the best-fed goose will shed the heavy weight of awkward-ness once afloat. They gravitate naturally to regions where land and water meet and mingle – to broad river mouths, estuaries and lakes. Vast skeins circle around the Solway, the Moray Firth, the Cornish coast, the Scottish islands and the Wash.

The amphibious region of the Fens was always renowned for huge flocks of geese. Above the dark waterlands, small knolls would turn from fresh green to brilliant white as the geese began to feast. The old village of Goosetoft in South Lincolnshire was called after the grassy tuft of higher ground popular with local geese. Not that this was necessarily an enviable distinction, judging by John Taylor's view:

> The people there have neither Horse or Cowe,
> Nor Sheepe, nor Oxe, or Asse, nor Pig, or Sowe:
> Nor Creame, Curds, Whig, Whay, Buttermilke or Cheese,
> Nor any other living thing but Geese.

Fat, well-feathered farm geese were utterly at home in fenland villages, and yet they were still subjected to frequent removals. Their down might be harvested for pillows and cosy, lightweight quilts several times in a single year. Great gaggles were regularly driven many miles along long narrow lanes or droves – like Gosling's Drove near Whittlesey. Since their webbed feet were unfit for iron shoes, they were sometimes walked through sticky tar and sawdust before setting off to give their soles a better chance on the long walk to market. At the old Michaelmas Hiring Fairs, hundreds of geese and labourers assembled with little sense of where they might be by the end of the day. Roast goose was a traditional dish for Michaelmas, so it was as well that the birds were unaware of the possibilities. Crowds still flock to Nottingham in early October for the Goose Fair, but now it is humans getting together for rides on the ghost trains, dodgems, waltzers and wall of death, though 'Goosey', the large fibreglass 'Goose Fair Goose', alights on a nearby roundabout for the duration.

There is something oddly human about a goose on foot, stepping along left, right, left, right. A large flock is not so much regimental in its movements, though, more of a companionable crowd, jostling together, veering in and out. But why geese put up with the long march to market is a mystery. Unless their wings are clipped, it seems to be another example of misplaced trust in their keepers. Even the most enlightened poultry farmers have ulterior motives for their kindly care. The Botteril family have been rearing very healthy free-range geese in the Leicestershire village of Croxton Kerrial since the 1940s, accruing plenty of experience in training enormous flocks for the daily walk from farm to field. The trick is to instil habits of obedience as soon as the goslings have fledged and are old enough to walk out. The smart, glossy gaggle, in matching white, steps briskly and noisily down the village street each day, until the morning of their final walk. I can't help wondering whether one day a pair or two might celebrate the festive season by breaking open those magnificent wings and wheeling away.

The obedient amble of farm geese brings home their distance from their greylag relations. A rich diet designed to fatten growing birds puts the ancient element of air further and further beyond them. For it is in the air that geese really come into their own, alchemised from solid earthiness to float and fly above the pond, the lake, the water-meadow, off into the translucent fields of cloud and sky. And while wild geese are never as firmly grounded as their domestic counterparts, their transformation from low-slung, well-rounded, short-legged creatures waddling across an autumn field into graceful, aerial agents of the heavens is still one of the world's natural miracles.

In flight, calling geese are free from the faintly ludicrous timbre of the farmyard honk. Amplified, echoing from the low clouds, the sound is strange and otherworldly. The cry of geese, rising and falling with the wings and winds, brings in the air of elsewhere. Among rocky island outcrops, across windswept sands, all around the coves of Britain and Ireland float empty shells of old maritime traditions, telling of how migrating seabirds carry the souls of the dead. Terns, petrels, gannets and gulls have all been cast as aerial ferrymen, but the wailing of geese and their strong, certain flight from the familiar affirms their right to the final journey. Nan Shepherd, acutely sensitive to the life of the Scottish mountains, was powerfully affected by the sound of migrating geese. Though so familiar around the coast and caught often over many years, their call remained harsh, alien, haunting, their sudden appearance in autumn a glimpse of 'primeval forces'.

The spectacle of the vast flock embarking on their arduous journey into the unknown can also stir a host of corresponding feelings in those lucky enough to witness their departure – awe, excitement, restlessness, anxiety, pity, perhaps even guilt over a startled yen to fly far away from the familiar. The oblivious flock flies high above earthbound observers, crossing a point of confluence charged with imminent parting and promise. The geese are on their way – away from England, Ireland, Scotland or Wales – to nesting grounds and new life. Wild geese choose the coldest places for nesting, beating across thousands of miles of wind and sea to the Arctic shores of Iceland, Greenland, Spitsbergen; in place on either side of the ocean, their presence everywhere intensified by thoughts of imminent absence.

Bernard O'Donoghue, a friend and colleague, remembers the yearly departure of wild geese over the River Lee during his childhood in the West of Ireland. Time was marked by the overlapping cycles of hedging, drilling, lambing, shearing, haymaking, harvesting, ploughing, and of ebbing light, cooling nights, falling leaves, migrating birds, budding, blooming, ripening, returning. The movement of geese brought together the natural and agricultural, as well as marking the differences. The farmer's boy who grew up to be a poet was attuned to the uneasiness of the field geese, too, as their wild, migrating relatives flew away overhead. In his beautifully balanced poem 'Geese Conversations', memories of the wild flight are mixed with the unquiet sounds erupting among the heavier, farm-fed birds, which he recalls growing restless,

> preparing to call out
> to the Canada geese flying overhead
> to regions of thick ribbëd ice, far away.

This snapshot of an earlier time includes two flocks, physically close and yet painfully distant. When wild geese embark on a scarcely conceivable journey across the North Atlantic, leaving the field geese behind on the well-managed levels, they seem almost as far removed from each other as a chihuahua from its primitive ancestor, the wolf. It's a moment of startled recognition – of kinship and difference. And yet, the spectacular, natural movement agitates the grounded flock, as if stirring memories of their greylag ancestry. The winter-clear memory has remained with a poet whose own life has for many years involved regular flights between Ireland and England. Thoughts of geese, wild and tame, brim with sympathies divided and shared, with possibilities and a dim sense of perennial sorrow.

'Geese Conversations' was called into being not only by personal memories of geese, but also of a friend who had been similarly affected by their annual movements. It is dedicated to Ian Niall, or John McNeillie, the writer, naturalist and countryman. The distinctive sound of geese in flight called Niall back to his youth in Galloway and to more distant ancestors in a far-northern country where 'the cry of the migrating goose' was 'seared into their souls'. The 'talk of geese' meant winter in a hard world far removed from the insulated existence of modernity. Mesmerised by the mysterious flocks passing overhead, he too had been struck by the way 'every goose on the farm pasture hears their crying and stops grazing the turf to call in reply'.

Though accurately observed and unsentimental, something of the old fable of wild and tame geese echoes in Niall's attitude to the farm birds, who 'would take to the air if they could, but alas . . . are no more equipped to join the flight than a portly stockbroker is equipped to hunt the mountain for his food'. Plump, well-fed geese, unfit for flight, unfit to fend for themselves, cut oddly poignant figures as their distant relatives sail through the sky above. When Niall himself left for the regions of thick ribbed ice, O'Donoghue was left to remember their conversations and lament.

The comings and goings of wild geese, habitual and remarkable, are witnessed each year by kindred spirits in different places. As converging lines of airborne geese mirror the vanishing point of the grounded, their dual perspectives reflect past and future: bringing back lost years, heralding those to come in what is still a supreme assertion of presence in the present. Keenly felt congenialities and gulfs between the winter visitors and those who stay put crystallise in each beating wing, in each haunting cry. The high lines of geese, poised, diminishing, dissolve in the distance. The heavy flock below is left to gaze and graze. But geese have an earthly, aquatic, and aerial reality resistant to the human impulse that would make emblems of them all. Geese may have lent us a language of parallel behaviour, but they retain their special secrets, their freedom to fly away.

The calls of wild geese are elusive, ever given to slipping away from the known world. Theirs are international, border-crossing voices, familiar to those on either side of oceans yet baffling to both. Geese migrations, inevitable as the lengthening day to those who see them every year, never lose their miraculous qualities.

Insistently local as they wing their way above riverbeds and estuaries, wild geese are global, too, passing overhead, alighting easily wherever they may be, retaining, always, a powerful sense of elsewhere.

Wild geese come and go, careless of their effects on those below. Memories often start up suddenly from the mental wetlands, in response to things that have vanished from sight. A chance remark, a strain of music, a few lines in a newspaper, a sudden cry caught on a clear winter day and the past is rising unbidden. Even the most grounded can be caught off guard.

Perhaps the geese flying over County Cork each year were heading for the same frozen grounds as those heard long ago in Galloway? The geese seen by Ian Niall may have been the very same skeins that flew over my father, when he was a boy on the other side of the Solway. Perhaps they followed the course of a low-flying phalanx heard by Nan Shepherd one October day, as it swerved through a gale in Glen Callater. They may have flown from further south, sweeping over the wet fens from the Wash. Geese cover the miles of air, land and sea with easy grace. And who can say where they may be going or what havoc the innocent geese might cause as they sweep overhead with their loud, lazy calls? Their cry is an aural vapour trail, lingering long after they have flown away.

Otters and Cockles

~

There are no fences on the road around the bay, only a natural perimeter fringe of soft green. The machair, bursting with wildflowers, circles the lagoon like the bright pattern around a dinner plate, colours changing with the seasons. In spring, the new grass gleams with flecks of white and pale gold, as primroses and daisies put out fresh petals in defiance of spring gales. By the summer, the primroses are gone, but the gold deepens into corn marigold and buttercup yellow, offset by red clover and poppies. The Cockle Strand, also known as Tràigh Mhòr (which just means 'big beach' in Gaelic), forms a bright crescent running from Ardmhòr towards Eoligarry in the northern tip of Barra. On the vast expanse of shallow water and wet sand, scattered crab claws, longline razorshells, spiralling winkles and round, ribbed cockleshells wash up daily to form long, low, straggling heaps. The seashells, smashed and ground by the pounding waves and washed ashore, balance the acidic soil and help to feed the flowers of the machair. I'm always on the lookout for otters in the Hebrides, always resigned to not spotting them. The open shore of Tràigh Mhòr looks a bit too smooth and exposed for an otter sighting, though the chances of seeing geese, ducks, divers, gulls, even gannets on this long, empty road beside the sea seem good enough.

But there, beside the narrow, winding road, is a pillarbox-red sign warning walkers to watch out instead for an orange windsock and flashing lights. Though it seems a world away from Heathrow, the small building visible across the beach is the island's chief – and only – airport. From here, regular flights carry passengers to Glasgow, where they can change planes and travel on to Europe, America and across the world. Unlike Glasgow International, the scheduled flights from Barra take off from the beach, with arrivals and departures dictated by the tides. And yet, however well attuned to the natural rhythms of the island this tiny airport may be, it still seems magnificently out of place on the old Cockle Strand.

The red sign seems out of place, too, because there's very little danger to unsuspecting hikers (except perhaps for the hard of hearing). When a plane is coming in to land, the drone of the Twin Otter engines carries far across the open sea. You can spot the imminent arrivals, as a dark dot in the pale cloud above the eastern horizon enlarges rapidly. Among gulls and terns and fleeting petrels, sporadic small planes swoop suddenly from the sky, skimming the bay to splash down in the shallows before swishing to a halt on the gleaming sand. The wide stretch of white beach inclines so slowly into the turquoise sea that there is more than enough room for a small runway. In fact there are three, triangulating the wet sand with tracks and lines to guide approaching aircraft. Occasionally, things go wrong and the little planes, dropping too heavily, get stuck in the soft mud. But new pilots quickly get the hang of landing in shallow water.

In recent years, airline staff and frequent flyers have found the airport facilities a little limited, so plans were approved for a major makeover, which began in September 2022. I am glad to have been there before the promised improvements and to have seen the tiny café selling coffee and sandwiches and colour-enhanced photographs of Barra's untouched wilderness, just next to the Check-In hatch. There was no need for screens ordering passengers to 'Go to Gate', because there is only one gate – the back door onto the beach. The single approaching plane was easy enough to spot from the terminal window. Baggage Reclaim was located just outside – a suitcase-sized shelf on rollers under a blue bus shelter.

When the Twin Otters are growling in the sky, the local seabirds flop lazily out of the way. They are used to sharing their airstreams. Planes have been taking off regularly from Tràigh Mhòr since 1936, when small airstrips began to erupt across the world in the most unlikely spots. In the early days of aviation, any strip of land big and flat enough for light aircraft could be turned into a temporary runway – in the Isles of Scilly, the little planes touched down on the golf course at St Mary's. During the 1930s, flying became a fashionable – and exciting – alternative to long trips by sea, rail and road – it is the only activity appealing enough to lure Aunt Ada Doom out of self-isolation in Stella Gibbons's comic masterpiece. Aunt Ada takes off for Paris, but had *Cold Comfort Farm* been published five years later, she might have headed for the Hebrides. Once Barra Airport opened, more and more visitors began dropping down on the Cockle Strand.

Barra has been on the Scottish tourist trail ever since, with its USP of landing on the beach. The small flocks of summer island-hoppers are still far less populous, though, than the seasonal skeins of wild geese and mergansers, eider ducks, whimbrels, and golden plovers. A few miles down the coast at Castle Bay, CalMac ferries swallow and disgorge the larger crowds. Getting to Glasgow by sea means a voyage to Oban of nearly five hours and then a long drive or train ride. As the Twin Otters fly overhead in a matter of seventy minutes, it is easy to see why the airport has kept its place, however surprising to those arriving for the first time. The tourists are generally infrequent, fair-weather visitors, but all year round the planes provide quick flights for Barra businesses and a life-saving service to islanders in urgent medical need. The life of a critically ill patient was saved by one of the earliest flights from the new airport and, in the years since, hundreds of people have been flown to hospitals in Glasgow, Inverness or Stornoway. Unlikely as it

seems, the airport has made its mark on the shifting sands of Tràigh
Mhòr.

As the small planes drop down towards the sand, they pass into
a world unlike any other. Lives lived long ago haunt the paths and
landing places, unhindered by dates and years. As the small planes
manoeuvre for take-off from the beach, they prepare to pass into
another element, flying higher than the geese and gulls, carrying
passengers away. What's gone and what's to come are only just
beyond the horizon. In the hours between flights, when the tide is
in and the wind rips the surface of the bay, or when the water is
low and the cockle pickers are quietly raking the sand, you get a
sense of Tràigh Mhòr in the centuries before the first plane arrived.
It is not so very different now. While the waves wash in and out,
the thin, broken ring of land holds its history as well as its present.
The Cockle Strand has always seen perpetual arrivals and departures from sea, land and air. Planes arrived late in a very long line.

Of all the bright, white beaches in Barra, Tràigh Mhòr is the
longest and widest. No wonder St Barr was drawn to this vast,
shimmering halo of sand. If, as legend rather than the written
record has it, his Irish name was Findbarr and he came all the way
from Cork in a leather-covered coracle, this gently sloping bank
must have seemed a heavenly destiny. However strong his trust in
God, the open prospect of Tràigh Mhòr was a much more promising landing spot than a hard jagged creek – safer for the hull of his
small boat and allowing a little distance to gauge the mood of any
reception party before disembarking. There was no guarantee that
people living here would be pleased to see a stranger arriving from
the sea. As it turned out, the islanders renamed their home in his
honour. Whether or not he made the legendary personal visit,
over many centuries the *idea* of St Barr became foundational to
Barra's sense of itself.

Just to the north of the strand where he supposedly landed is the
spring that bubbled up when St Barr struck the ground with his staff.
It is close to the churchyard of Cille Bharra, where low stone walls

stand open to the sky among gravestones, grass and wildflowers. Set into a broken wall of the ruined church, a grey arch, inside another grey arch, which might once have been the top of the door, lies half buried in the ground. A peaceful place to spend eternity.

There has been a church in this spot since the eighth century, though the original was rebuilt in the twelfth. Just as the work was getting under way, the sacred statue of St Barr vanished, miraculously reappearing some way away from the building site. As this happened on a daily basis, the plans were revised and the new church (which now seems extremely old) was built on the spot where St Barr's statue kept reappearing. Thoughts of St Barr continued to revolve around the great circular bay near his church. Each year, on 27 September, St Barr was celebrated with ceremonial horse riding on the wide sands, then three times around the chapel at Cille Bharra, in keeping with the movement of the sun and an age-old understanding of time's eternal cycle. The Twin Otters circling over the Cockle Strand may seem a very modern intrusion into this ancient site, but are oddly in accord with the sky and shore, and the generations who followed natural patterns in their worship. The annual horse riding went on for centuries after St Barr's departure from the island. In 1840, the Rev. Alexander Nicolson, sent as a Minister of the Church of Scotland, was surprised to find the 'superstitious ceremony' still in full sway.

St Barr's spring sustained generations of islanders with fresh water and cockle spawn. When the seventeenth-century antiquarian Martin Martin sailed over from Skye to examine the customs of neighbouring islands, he remained sceptical about their old tales, dismissing much of what he was told as 'the most ridiculous fancy', but he was very interested in what people ate and how they fished and farmed. Unsurprisingly, his request to see the holy statue was refused. St Barr's flock, adhering defiantly to the old Catholic faith, preferred their own ways and were not very receptive to patronising visitors. Martin was not too disappointed – he was much more interested in whether or not cockle larvae were really to be found in the holy well.

Barra has always been famous for cockles. The very earliest account, written in 1549, dwells on the 'grate Cokills' of 'Trayrmore', exclaiming that there 'is na fairer and more profitable sands for cokills in all the world'. The sea molluscs from the Cockle Strand were big, blue and abundant. When other food was scarce, as in the hungry years of the 1790s, the whole island depended on Tràigh Mhòr. Every morning from May to August, the great beach filled with people, praising St Barr and harvesting basket after basket of cockles. As the tides swept yesterday's tracks away, the islanders waited to load their horses with the water's bounty.

Still at low tide, the rake-scrapes of the cockle pickers criss-cross the narrow sandbars, left to dry as the waters retreat. The tides inscribe their own special patterns in the sodden, golden parchment, intricate as a medieval manuscript. Only the gulls and the plovers and the geese can read this ancient Celtic text. Even the triangular tracks of the plane tyres are purified by the waves and rain into alchemical symbols of water and air.

The arrival of an airport at Tràigh Mhòr was a catalyst for a new wave of curious, though not necessarily any more welcome, visitors. The poet Louis MacNeice and artist Nancy Sharp, working very closely together on a book about the Hebrides, were among the first to try the new air service. When they landed one morning on the Cockle Strand in 1936, right outside Compton Mackenzie's front door, they were rapidly sent on their way by his housekeeper Chrissie MacSween. She could not say when Mr Mackenzie would get up, but 'when he did get up he would be busy with his mail'.

Compton Mackenzie, lying in Barra 'like a barrel of gunpowder', was the island's main attraction for the young poet, as for many of the writers who landed there in the late thirties. Mackenzie was not a Barraman born and bred, but chose to live there because, as he later told the world, 'Barra is an extraordinarily happy place'. After meeting Barra's great storyteller, the postmaster John Macpherson (universally known as the Coddy) at a council meeting in Inverness, Mackenzie had travelled to the island and fallen under its spell. Unlike Martin Martin, Mackenzie was deeply sympathetic to the old ways, to the Catholic tradition, to the unique atmosphere of Barra. Instead of arriving, observing and leaving swiftly, Mackenzie had a bungalow built at Tràigh Mhòr, looking out over the bay towards Orosay, Fuday and Eriskay. As things turned out, the plans went a little awry, so the new house had only one window facing out to sea. But once given a gold frame, the view from the window became a perpetually changing seascape on the wall of the library. The tide flowed in and out over a thousand years of cockleshells, 'sometimes sky-blue, sometimes dove-grey, sometimes a pale green, the colour of a cowslip spathe'. It reminded Mackenzie of the Mediterranean.

He did not move to Barra to get away from it all. Like his friend and regular house guest Hugh MacDiarmid, he felt no further from 'the centre of things' in the Scottish islands than in London, New York or Tokyo. Barra was its own place and there he could see more clearly. Actively concerned with Scottish Nationalism and international politics, with fishing rights, crofting legislation and the future of Gaelic, while still working away on his book about Pericles, Mackenzie enjoyed both the immediacy of the neighbourhood and the perspective brought by an island outlook on the world. Every Sunday evening, he welcomed Barra friends to Suidheachan to down gin and whisky and share books, billiards and stories. Chrissie often kept the gramophone going until three in the morning. During the week, he could stay at home and write – or take flight. Flying, which Mackenzie found 'most exhilarating', meant he could be away from Barra whenever he wanted. With only a very short walk from his house to the airport, he could be in South Uist in a matter of minutes.

The arrival of the airport gave writers like Mackenzie and MacDiarmid an unprecedented view of the world. 'It is only now, with the use of the aeroplane,' wrote MacDiarmid, 'that the Scottish islands . . . can be seen effectively, at one and the same time in their individual completeness and in all their connections with each other.' Suddenly maps had become three-dimensional, geological formations, vivified. It is difficult now to grasp the sheer astonishment of writers in the 1930s experiencing their first flights – though a Twin Otter from Barra Airport probably offers the nearest thing. The completeness and connection of small islands had always been understood by those who lived by the sea, but the arrival of an airport allowed them to take on an eagle's perspective.

As Mackenzie listened to the Coddy's bottomless well of tales, he was struck by the way old Barra families talked matter-of-factly about things invisible to outsiders. The gold that suddenly materialised for the Jacobite cause when Bonnie Prince Charlie landed in Eriskay was still a regular talking point. The conversation shifted between European politics and basking sharks, Greek oratory and Highland cattle, shipwrecks, sea monsters, Mary's beans, births and marriages. Mackenzie evidently talked a lot, judging from the mischievous cameo left by Louis MacNeice after he was finally invited to Suidheachan: 'Mr Mackenzie told me of his earlier years. He could read at twenty months, learnt Latin at four, Greek at eight, and at eleven was translating Shakespeare into Greek iambics.' Mackenzie, for his part, was less than impressed by MacNeice's 'cocksure air' and guessed that his visitor had taken offence over the general lack of interest in his poetry.

Food for thought was as abundant as the cockles. Inspiration for Mackenzie's most famous novel just floated in on the tide one winter day during the Second World War. On 5 February 1941, the heavily laden SS *Politician*, on the dangerous voyage from Liverpool to New York, was struck by a powerful storm in the Sound of Eriskay. As the winds roared and the waves reared, the ship began to founder and the captain commanded the crew to abandon her. The lifeboats were launched into the biting cold of the turbulent sea. What made the wreck so memorable was not the miraculous survival of the crew, but their cargo. In the hold of the *Politician* were cases and cases of whisky, some 28,000 in all, together with thousands of pounds in banknotes. If you happen to be having a drink in the pub in Eriskay, which is named after the *Politician*, look out for the row of salvaged whisky bottles in the bar. What happened to all the others remains a mystery. Once the great storm subsided, the police conducted a thorough search for the missing cargo, but although a few bold men of Barra were arrested, most of the bottles and the banknotes were never found. The Coddy was full of tales of the '*Polly*' and the peculiar frustration of returning to a rabbit hole where a bottle or two had been popped for safekeeping only to find it empty.

It did not take Mackenzie long to rake together what he needed for *Whisky Galore*. Friends and neighbours appeared in thin disguise, while Barra became 'Great Todday'. The airport came into its own when Ealing Studios decided to film the novel in Barra. While the cast and crew flew in and out, the director did not have much trouble finding extras: the Coddy and Mackenzie both made fleeting appearances in the film. The flotilla of dark bottles washing towards Great Todday's white sands under bright Hebridean light worked perfectly in black and white. Since then, the old film has developed an otherworldly quality, as the long-departed whisky-drinkers sing on into endless night.

Past and present co-exist amicably in Barra. The ghost of St Barr's first church can still be glimpsed among the ruins of Cille Bharra chapel. When Compton Mackenzie died in Edinburgh in 1972, his body was flown back to Barra, landing in a November gale so severe that at first the plane missed the airport. When the pilot managed to bring it down safely, Mackenzie was piped to his final resting place by his old friend Calum Johnson, who was so overcome that he collapsed and died. In the small churchyard at Cille Bharra, Mackenzie, the Coddy and their friends lie quietly among the old grey stones and Celtic crosses.

The clarity of the air and light, the sharp taste of the salt water, the cries of seabirds on the gusting winds and the wide, level lines of sea and sand and grass open the mind to other worlds and ways of thinking. Among the brilliant circle who came to Suidheachan was the Gaelic collector and campaigner for island life, John Lorne Campbell. As he immersed himself in real, spoken Gaelic, the language of the islanders, Campbell was also struck by the atmosphere of the place and 'an ever-present sense of the reality and existence of the other world of spiritual and psychic experience'. His friend, Hugh MacDiarmid, though resistant to any idea of 'the presence of spirits', still tried to convey a feeling of the uncanny in his poem, 'Island Funeral', grappling to find words for an 'indefinable something . . . which you feel in the air, / And are conscious of by some instinct'. MacDiarmid recognised that arriving at Tràigh Mhòr meant 'passing into a spiritual climate of its own to be found nowhere else'.

The sense of another world, not quite legible, not quite tangible, crosses in and out of consciousness at the Cockle Strand. Just behind the terminal a steep bank of sand rises from the level bay like a miniature mountain range, with tufts of marram grass and gorse hinting of something beyond. It is easy enough to make your way up through the dunes to discover, within metres of the airport, a very different side of the island. This is Tràigh Eais, where the full force of the Atlantic smashes against black boulders, whisking tattered brown seaweed in brilliant white surges, hurling ashore lumps of blanched driftwood, scattered tangles of old blue rope, odd flip-flops, bits of bright bone, green bottles and plastic bags. Lifting and landing, in and out of place: ancient and modern alike are whirled and hurled, smashed and drowned and washed up again on the western shore by the airport.

The neck of narrow dunes connects Eoligarry to the larger body of Barra. The few steps through the sharp grass and soft sinking sand from the airport to the Atlantic coast bring home the precariousness of island life. This is a meeting place of elemental forces, where air, water and earth collide, where the lines of land and sea are never settled, where past meets present and no one knows what the future will bring. Barra's geography hangs by a thread. From above, it's only too clear: the gannets and the Twin Otters can see that the sea may wash across one day, cutting the island in two.

If the smooth, open countenance of Tràigh Mhòr smiles over limpid aquamarine, Tràigh Eais has a tougher aspect altogether, frowning down the perpetual battering of the breakers on the west, where the hills are jagged, the dark rocks sheer, and the beach harder than the January winds. Its austere features are picked clean by the blast of salt and storms. In keeping with these contrasts, the sand-mountain passes are watched over by double-dressed butterflies. The fragile guards of this Janus-faced isthmus flash wings of brilliant summer sea-blue, edged with glistening white. When they land on a stickle of gorse, the blue folds away to reveal tawny underwings speckled with flame and dark dots – a tiny, portable map of the small isles. In Barra folk-lore, butterflies are sent from heaven to alight in the machair like angels.

If the elemental clashes of primordial rock and endless break-ers give Tràigh Eais an eternal quality, Tràigh Mhòr moves with the tides and the times. After Compton Mackenzie gave up Suidheachan, it became a factory for pounding seashells into grit, until eventually his great-nephew, the actor Alan Howard, and his wife Sally Beauman restored it to former glory as a five-bedroom seaside villa, reviving the family tradition of writing and inviting congenial friends to fly over to the Cockle Strand. When Alan turned seventy, his friend Julian Barnes wrote him a short story about the Twin Otters bringing travellers back to Tràigh Mhòr. For Sally Beauman, who had lived mostly in the south of England, Barra was a revelation – her 'favourite place on Earth'. Like the original owner of her Hebridean house, she found the 'spectacularly beautiful' light and seawater equal to the Greek islands, spending hours looking across the bay, loving the way 'the islands in between assume new shapes' and where the 'weather is completely sea-borne', blowing in with the winds and altering fast. Suidheachan was once again the perfect home for a storyteller.

The Coddy was always prepared to look backwards and forwards. He lived on the island's oral heritage but was just as committed to the well-being of the living and quick to take a job with the new airline. He bought Barra's first car, too. When the Coddy retired, his son Angus took over management of the airport before handing it on to his sister, Katherine. She ran it efficiently for another thirty years and, equipped with a walkie-talkie and local expertise, became just as well-known as her father. Far from being out of place, the airport has made its mark on the island's long history, passing through the Macpherson family as surely as the old tales.

At Barra Airport, a sense of other times, other worlds is power-fully present. Boarding a small plane there is reminiscent of the closing scene of *Casablanca*: as the propellers whirr and the sand begins to fly, the force of the island becomes intense. Once on board, the plane gives a shudder as it charges across the beach and away from the terminal. For a few fearful moments, it seems that the pilot, seized by some desperate, suicidal urge, is heading into the sea, taking everyone on board down with him. But then the plane pauses for a breath, turns around in the shallow water and rushes back across the beach, lifting from the sand and wheeling over the thin road, the scarlet sign, the pale dunes, the ring of low, green hills and grey rocks around the cobalt sea. All too soon, Barra shrinks and disappears.

However hard you try to keep an eye on the island, it vanishes into the haze and the distance, lost in the vast Atlantic. Though a few passengers are visibly excited about being on their way, I felt a sharp pang of severance and thought how much sharper it must be for those who live here. As we swept away towards the south, the clear prospect of a hundred tiny isles and lochs below was blurred by the smirr of silent rain. Louis MacNeice and Nancy Sharp left Barra by ferry from Castlebay, but still MacNeice caught the peculiar feeling of leaving the island, 'Restless as a gull and haunted / By a hankering after Atlantis'. Barra was not his Atlantis, but he could feel the power of elsewhere.

Other Edens

~

A sense of being restless as a gull is no stranger now than when Louis MacNeice watched Castlebay harbour shrinking into the distance over the white and brown wash of the ferry. His wistful words may resonate rather differently in an era when gulls are as likely to be spotted over a corporation dump in the heart of England as along the coast, but birds take time to moult their old plumage. In the 1930s, seagulls still belonged to the sea and to poets expressing their yearnings for elsewhere. MacNeice's friend Wystan Auden conveyed a deep sense of longing in his evocation of 'the salt smell, / Shadow of gulls on the road to the sea'. While the physical distances flown by gulls may change, the feelings they evoked in the 1930s remain. Atlantis is somewhere lost inside most of us, a dream, a memory, a promise. The vision of an unspoilt island can spur us into setting off for open spaces, rocky fastnesses, bare beaches swept by the winds and scoured by ocean waves. To Ardnamurchan, to Barra, to Beara, to Connemara, to Cork, to Cornwall, to Galway, to Galloway, to Piel, to Pembroke. The difficulty of getting there just adds to the appeal. And yet, the ultimate goal for the cooped-up and wilderness-hungry is attained by few, as Andrew McNeillie admitted in a wry poem, 'On Not Sailing to St Kilda'. Those who do get somewhere close tend to find that their island has floated still further off into the fog.

Not finding what we went for is often the least surprising aspect of expeditions to inaccessible shores. Thinly populated coastal spots bubble with exciting possibility: diving gannets, curlews, spider crabs, guillemots. These are what the landlocked consciously come to see and hear, feeling privileged if such hopes are realised. More astonishing still are the rare glimpses of creatures only previously seen through books or screens – the shadowy silhouette of a sea otter or the clockwork call of what must surely be a corncrake. During one rainy summer in Ireland, our long, grey drive was suddenly interrupted by Rachael (aged about eight and not a great enthusiast of the wet and wild), who thought things might finally be taking a more promising turn: 'Look!' she exclaimed. 'Those crows have got red legs!' And sure enough, in the field beside the narrow lane a flock of choughs was stepping out. At the time, the children found my excitement more diverting than the choughs, but looking back, they remember the day and the place and the birds. The red-legged choughs, oblivious to our curiosity, had landed in their minds to roost quietly until the time was right.

A coastal quest can be full of surprises. Travellers determined to stand at the ultimate tip of southern Scotland make for the spectacular, soaring Mull of Galloway to survey the Irish Sea as it stretches away and away. On a clear day from the clifftop you can see across the Solway far into Cumbria or over the deep aquamarine to the Isle of Man, with the thin edges of Wales and Ireland lining the horizon. I like to imagine Fergus of Galloway surveying the salty domain for alien sails from this commanding precipice. It feels like the end of the world – and the beginning. But if instead of heading straight for the Mull or the beach, you take a turn off the road to Drummore, you arrive somewhere even more unexpected. After hours travelling, on trains or planes, buses, tracks and lanes to reach rock pools, cliffs and empty beaches, what you find is an exotic garden.

All of a sudden, you are in paradise, where windmill palms are fanning the sky and green feather-duster ferns cover the ground.

Gargantuan gunnera, leaves wide open, are too prickly to touch. Through the spring, magnolia flowers open like goblets of rosé and rhododendrons spill out in red and white. Crimson fuchsias and bright gazanias open for the summer, while in the autumn peeling eucalyptus rain showers of oval, scarlet leaves. The Royal Botanical Garden at Logan spreads over twenty-four acres, reaching almost shore to shore across the peninsula, so it is really too big for a secret garden. And yet, the surrounding woods mean it's easy to miss. Once inside, wave after wave of flowers remind you of what's just beyond the trees: as the heavenly blue poppies fade, kingfisher daisies surge up, before sapphire agapanthus spurt out like fountains from slim, unstable stems. Coastal light shines overhead, changeable and bright as the sea. This is a hidden world-within-a-world encompassed by the sea; an evergreen island that is not quite an island, but something very like it.

Though seemingly out of place on the rugged Rhins of Galloway, tropical gardens are a distinctive feature of Scotland's coastal character. Just above the western shore of Loch Fyne, I found myself stepping from the Highlands to the Himalayas. Reginald Farrer, a devotee of Jane Austen, rare plants and his aunt, Grace Campbell, saw Nepal in the natural falls at Crarae and set about conjuring Shangri-La through careful planting. A century on and the oriental bridge across the gorge is surrounded by sprawling shrubs and graceful acers that turn every shade of red as the summer fades. The Scottish burn runs through a world of giants under Himalayan firs and redwoods. The chambered cairn in the front lawn, pre-dating the planting by several thousand years, helps to settle the exotic trees into the lochside, but even here a towering evergreen dwarfs the resting place of an ancient Highland chieftain.

In cities, even the most modest green roof or window-box seems a breath of fresher air. A patch of green behind a terrace or maisonette is an outpost of nature, a place for birds, butterflies, caterpillars, bees. Great parks are the lungs of London, Glasgow, Liverpool,

Belfast. Odd, then, that in places exposed to howling sea storms, a garden can seem so much less *natural*. Wild or tame? Where do they fit into our binary ways of thinking? Parks and gardens burst with natural growth and yet they are planned and planted and pruned. They are quiet havens, too, protected and protective, perfect refuges for rarities. Out of place in over- and under-populated spots, gardens thrive on their own contrariety.

Scattered along the west coast of Scotland are slices of other continents. On the western edge of Argyll, overlooking Asknish Bay, is Arduaine Garden, laid out by Arthur Campbell on his return from the family tea estate. Like Crarae, it's bristling with plants from the Himalayas and East Asia, as well as Chilean shrubs and ferns, waterlilies and American aquatics. Further north in Wester Ross, among the heathery hillsides and brown burns, cold lochs in mountain clefts, sheep-bitten valleys and headlands battered by Atlantic breakers, is Inverewe. Aspirational Victorian landowners, bolstered by collective confidence and private fortunes, were rarely deterred by the absence of local precedent. If they wanted a garden of flowering camellias and rhododendrons in the Highlands, they were not to be put off by sceptics or storms. Osgood Mackenzie, Laird of Gairloch, inherited his estates at the age of twenty and set about transforming his wind-beaten promontory into a global garden. Well-placed woodlands had to be planted to create windbreaks, quantities of fertile topsoil shipped in, and then, with the help of seaweed fertiliser and the Gulf Stream, Inverewe would prove congenial to the most desirable flora on Earth. Mackenzie, though idiosyncratic, still had much in common with other men of his class and age, who imbibed the Imperial spirit from boyhood and were duty-bound to provide space for the treasures of the globe. Enraptured by the world's remarkable botanical wealth, they were able to express their wonder on a grander scale than most.

The thrill of botanical discovery can be felt in Frank Kingdon-Ward's account of a trek through Nepalese forests in search of unknown plants. From a giddy ledge in the Himalayas, he looked down over 'the wide waves of forest, beating against a cliff, where the magnolia blooms toss like wild horses, or lie like a fleet of pink water lilies at anchor in a sea of green turf'. Such visions of beauty inspired gardeners at home to be as adventurous as they could be in their plans and plantings. A magnolia, a rhododendron, a flowering cherry – all were symbols of global connection. Neither the mountains of Nepal nor the enigmatic society of Japan were completely out of reach. A home-grown grove of exotic flowers offered wealthy families the excitement of the Himalayas and the Andes, the river valleys of China, the American savannah, the symmetrical slopes of Mount Fuji – without the trouble or expense of travel. Some of the specimens brought back by nineteenth-century plant hunters were surprisingly well suited to Scotland. Asiatic magnolias turned out to be tougher than they looked and generally prefer a moist, acidic soil. Gardens on the west coast of Scotland are mostly very moist.

Plants introduced into the great Scottish gardens were often helped into place by their names. The *Magnolia campbellii* sounds as if it belongs to Argyll, but only because it was named after Archibald Campbell, a doctor born in Islay who spent most of his working life in India. He joined Joseph Hooker on a botanising expedition in the Himalayas and, though he was really more interested in the commercial potential of tea-growing, they got on well. Their friendship deepened after they were captured in Sikkim and inadvertently triggered the annexation of Darjeeling by the indignant British regime in neighbouring India. Hooker honoured his travelling companion by naming *Magnolia campbellii* after him, but somewhere in those beautiful pale flowers is a thin red tinge. The Scottish naming tradition continues more innocently at Logan, where the latest magnolia to be raised has been called after the curator's wife, Eileen Baines.

The Douglas fir, which grows tall and straight in many of the Victorian gardens, sounds as native as the Scots pine, but was introduced by the Perthshire explorer David Douglas after a long voyage up the western coast of America. The writer Ann Lindsay has traced his meandering journey from Scone to Hawaii, in search of unknown seeds and specimen plants. The hapless botanist's grisly demise in a poacher's bull pit only weeks after his thirty-fifth birthday brings home the occupational hazards faced by early plant hunters. A yearning for the wilderness proves less perilous for most of us, and yet Douglas's story reveals the darkness lurking around the roots of some seemingly settled and serene greenery. The exotic gardens in thinly populated peninsulas are not always as peaceful as they seem.

The Beara peninsula, or ring finger of Ireland's western reach into the Atlantic, boasts not only empty tracks and fields full of red-legged choughs, but also a tropical garden of its own – at Derreen. As in Highland Scotland, you can be crossing fields of sheep or scrambling down into deep, stony inlets one moment, only to find yourself amidst New Zealand tree ferns and rare rhododendrons the next. The gardens of Derreen House were masterminded by the 5th Marquess of Lansdowne, who liked to be at his Irish estate when not fulfilling his duties as Governor of Canada, Viceroy of India or Foreign Secretary to Her Majesty's Government. It is easy to see why he felt at home among his global collection. Although his country house was torched during the Civil War in 1922, the rare trees and flowering shrubs survived to rise and rampage through the fecund grounds. When I chanced upon the garden some years ago on my way around a small fishing harbour, it was like stumbling into another country. Out of place, and yet, with so many tangling creepers and overgrown palms, so much more rooted in the place than I could ever be. Derreen, now under the care of Alan Powers, is putting on a new face for the twenty-first century, which may make it seem more or less at home.

A sense of emptiness along certain coasts can quickly fill with thoughts of those who left there unwillingly, driven by desperation, dispossession or hunger. The ghosts haunting the shores make the extravagant gardens of great estates seem decidedly strange: unnatural other Edens, forced into bloom in spaces left by the displaced. The flourishing gingko, *Cupressus* and tulip trees at Drishane House at Skibbereen stand awkwardly in an area so deeply scarred by the Famine. Across Wester Ross and Argyll, too, the shells of deserted cottages speak of homesteads cleared for sheep and shooting. Still, the determination to recover paradise on the rocks of an exposed headland required vast teams of spade-wielding labourers – and perhaps they were able to share the wonder of what they helped to create.

Whatever the cost, there is something heroic about the vast gardens at Logan, Derreen or Inverewe – those monumental attempts to realise Eden in a decidedly recalcitrant world. The unlikelihood of these great sea-girt gardens is regularly brought home when winter storms lash the tropical plants. In late January 2022, Storm Corrie swept off the Atlantic, felling trees and flattening shrubs as it whirled through Inverewe at 90 miles an hour. Among the casualties were mature giants planted in the days of Osgood Mackenzie. He was no stranger to the force of the Atlantic, which is why his first step to a personal paradise included thick windbreaks. Not thick enough, it seems. In November 1920, Mackenzie, then in his late seventies, emerged from Inverewe House to the distressing sight of 2,600 trees, uprooted, beheaded, or snapped off by the devastating storm of the previous night: 'all of them 50 to 56 years old, and from 60 to 70 feet high, and all, I may say, planted with my own hands.' A century after Mackenzie's natural disaster, the walled garden at Logan was almost washed away by a February deluge which burst the ponds, flooded the woods and lawns and drowned rare trees. Richard Baines supervised the desperate recovery effort, but was left lamenting the loss of Logan's Vietnamese sub-tropical ginger plants. The moisture, on this occasion, had been 'excessive'.

Despite severe winter hazards, the North Atlantic brings special blessings, too. Since the Gulf Stream ensures milder climates along the west coasts of Ireland, Cornwall and Scotland, it is possible to grow plants there that cannot survive harsher temperatures – the palm trees that flourish in Cornwall would currently stand little chance in Aberdeen. The warmer waters that bring good growing conditions have brought ships from around the world, too. Maritime traffic crossing the Atlantic, from South America or Africa, from the Indian Ocean or the Mediterranean, has always approached the British and Irish Isles from the southwest. The ships might disembark in the deep harbours at Cork or Falmouth, head on for Dublin, Southampton, Bristol or London, or veer north towards Liverpool, Glasgow, Oban. Something of the international character of southwestern coastlines is caught, cultivated and commemorated in the exotic gardens just inland. What may now strike visitors as quiet, out-of-the-way spots were once the entrances to other cultures and international experience.

Falmouth's cosmopolitan character flourishes in the remarkable gardens that cluster around the Carrick Roads. From Bosahan, Glendurgan and Trebah on the Helford River to Enys, Lanterns and Trellisick House in the north or Lamorran on the estuary's eastern bank, plants from across the world take root and flourish. Cornwall abounds in harbours and plants. Whether you head up the steep hill from the fishing boats at Mevagissey to see the once Lost Gardens of Heligan, or just walk from the beach at St Ives to the Barbara Hepworth Sculpture Park, the vegetation is stupendous. I have a dog-eared pamphlet listing seventy-six Cornish gardens that are worth seeing and a feeling that before I get anywhere near the end, another ten will have matured and opened for visitors. Coming across a grand garden near the rocky coast of Cornwall is by no means as startling as in Beara or Wester Ross.

Somewhere beneath the desire to plant a perfect garden lies an age-old dream of heavenly islands, calm seas, sunsets, secrets and serenity. In the Ancient World the Hesperian Gardens were home to the nymphs of sunset, while the happy isles were imagined somewhere southwesterly in the warmer Atlantic. The magical islands were always beyond the reach of ordinary boats. In British and Irish waters, they float tantalisingly off the southwestern peninsulas – and if you can't quite get there, you can feel that you have in a tropical garden just inland. Warmed and watered by the Atlantic, the grey, stony extremities of Britain and Ireland are generous hosts to tender plants. Gardens and islands, lovely and self-contained, are ancient emblems of peace and order, surrounded by the unruliness of forests, cities and the sea.

Or so they seem in prospect. Gardeners and castaways often turn out to be equally prone to discontent: however beautiful their surroundings, they are still gripped with the desire for elsewhere. Andrew Marvell longed to retreat into a private Eden of ripe apples, peaches, melons, and luscious clusters of grapes. Once he got among the green shades his mind kept straying into 'other worlds, and other seas'. Even those most devoted to tending their plants need a break from time to time. Katharine Stewart, who spent many years bravely creating a garden near Loch Ness, took regular holidays in the Hebrides, topping up internally on the flowers of the machair and 'the sounds of the birds and the seals'. There's always another Eden.

At Caerhays Castle, camellias come out in every shade of pink, hydrangeas in white, mauve, blue, and magnolias in a delicate spectrum from bone white to pale pink, purple, magenta, deep gold, citric yellow and pale lemon. The efflorescence of natural colour results from years of hard work. Rare plants have been arriving here for over a century, ever since Ernest Wilson and George Forrest began unpacking their latest discoveries in John Williams's estate. Careful crossing of different species gradually led to hardier camellias and a staggering range of magnolia hybrids. Cornwall's gardens are sites for experimentation as much as escape. The kaolin industry left cavernous clay pits around St Austell, but in 2001 a new Eden landed in an empty crater as if from outer space, with great golf-ball globes for growing rarities from every continent.

With such various and voluptuous gardens, the whole of Cornwall might almost be one marvellous tropical island. Even the most modest houses are flanked by sky-blue hydrangeas and complementary crocosmias, all too often by rampaging bindweed, fireweed or Himalayan balsam as well. When my sister-in-law Helen and her husband Jonathan moved to the north Cornish coast, they found their new garden so exuberant that one of their first purchases was a chainsaw. A fertile retreat in a temperate county quickly produces abundant flowers, green leaves, generous fruit and a lot of hard work.

And yet, on the coastal path, with its steep dips and drops and sudden twists uphill, its cliffs and headlands bulking into the sea, the Atlantic has the power to blast away all thoughts of sheltered gardens. As the tide washes into the small coves over grey stones smoothed, rounded and rolled by the sea, stories of smuggling or memories of surfing surface more readily than thoughts of seedlings and secateurs. The panoramic expanse, heaving and shifting from slate grey to deep purple, dark blue and jade green, compels the eye and fills the mind.

The coast attracts thousands of walkers in search of wild places, hungry for a glimpse of Lyonesse. To reach the mythic land submerged somewhere just offshore means a journey through miles of grassy fields and scattered churches, along narrow roads with wind-warped hawthorn, through fishing villages and seaside towns, passing caravan sites, sailing clubs, night clubs, gift shops, restaurants, tea rooms, visitor attractions. Not quite Cornwall, nor the Isles of Scilly, Lyonesse is its own place, tantalisingly close but never quite within reach. Another Atlantis, just over the horizon, somewhere ahead of the long line of cars, coaches, vans and lorries.

As Wordsworth saw only too clearly, a yearning for the sea, for hearing the winds howling at all hours, is the obverse of an obsession with getting and spending – which often makes it difficult to separate the two. When he exclaimed that 'the World is too much with us', he was not setting himself apart but lamenting a shared capacity for distance from what really matters. The quest for Atlantis tends to be self-defeating, especially if everyone heads in the same direction. And so the search for elsewhere often ends in returning home. After a tumultuous decade of moving from place to place, taking long roads through hills and fields, villages, towns and great cities, beside mighty rivers and across mountains in Britain and Europe, Wordsworth returned to the Lakeland fells of his childhood. He found to his surprise that Eden was really 'the growth of common day' – it was just a case of looking more carefully at what was already there.

Red Kites

~

The tall oak reaches out above the scruffy hedge, as if stretching to wake itself each dawn. In the face of such poised magnificence, all other plant life is dwarfed or somewhat diminished. In nearby fields, other oaks tower over other hedges, scattering clumps of leaves, twigs or acorns, according to the season. They're the old guard, marking parish and farm boundaries; as their trunks have thickened with the passing years, they have taken on a proprietorial air of their own. The tall oak is unruffled by these sturdy rivals. Perhaps it's the rare symmetry of the central branches: beautifully balanced beams, spraying out evenly from the strong, straight trunk. Most of the oaks are more eccentric, with huge limbs wrenched to right and left, branches twisting up, down, across, and twigs flying everywhere. Each has its own unique silhouette: none quite as elegant as the tall, solitary tree at the corner of the hedge. In May, it is garlanded with bright rosettes, strung along the branches in bunched clusters of green. The tree with the iron-hard trunk and strongest boughs is suddenly arrayed in layers of spring frills. Above the canopy, two or three branches stick out, gaunt as deep scars on the pale sky. These are the favourite perches of birds uninhibited by an instinct to stay out of sight or mind. Usually, the oak rings with chatterings and trills, as crowds of finches, starlings, yellowhammers or fieldfares take up temporary roost through the colour-changing months. The thicket of busy twigs empties instantly when one of the larger residents arrives. A red kite swooping down to land on a dead branch, which, like a line under a signature, emphasises the universally acknowledged truth – the tallest tree belongs to the biggest bird.

From the ground, you might not spot it: a dark silhouette on a darker, leafless stick. The kite perches for some time, perhaps at rest, perhaps surveying the surrounding fields from the highest vantage point. A slight push from the springboard bough and it's away, not diving down, but up into the air, wings unfolding in slow, mesmerising waves. A kite in flight makes other birds look effortful. A crow cutting low across the fields has an air of determination, a flock of finches flits skittishly along an uncut hedgerow, while pheasants, flapping noisily from long grass, look astonished to be airborne at all. A heron does have a certain lazy style, but that low flight from pond to pond makes its purpose clear enough. Red kites, on the other hand, seem to relish every moment, spreading their huge wings for maximum fresh air and light. They float on air, as if the engine is turned off and there's all the time in the world to feel the breeze. Kites sweep through the sky, bodies motionless, surfing the waves, higher and higher, carried away with the currents and swirling out of sight. A single bird, a pair, a dozen tiny dark marks on the clear blue sky, high as kites.

On a clear morning, when the sky is an unmarked expanse of pale colour, you can have a distinct sense of being watched. Look up, not round, and there it is. Huge, hinged wings widening imperceptibly, stretching from an M to a flattened T, until a V-shaped tail fans out to steer into an updraught and away it goes. A single kite sends an invisible wash through vacant space. When three or four pairs are wheeling on the wind, their wings mark the airy territory in a language all living things understand. Not that they seem to care much for the rest, when scrambling and diving, gliding and swooping in mirrored swerves. Long, dark quills, spreading from a broad, immaculate red cape, roll back and forth in a rhythmic aerial dance. When kites are together, their sense of pleasure in each other's company is blazoned across the whole sky.

In bright sun, the dark outlines transform as they move closer, into beings with tiger-bright shoulders, glowing breasts of tawny-red and smoke-white plumes shooting out on either side. The rocket-launcher tails signal unburned energy, reminding onlookers of how quickly this relaxed mode can flip into action. Leisurely at lower altitudes, hanging on outstretched wings only feet above the earth, kites can drop without warning to the ground. A dead mouse, a blackbird, the carcase of a lamb: once in sight, it is only a matter of when. The wings suddenly tauten into a terrifying crossbow and down they go.

Sometimes, you hear a kite before it comes into view. A high-pitched mew, with varying levels of urgency. One morning I heard the unmistakeable call, but it wasn't the usual dawn greeting. The cry was intense and persistent, competing with a rougher caw. The red kite was meeting the challenge of a carrion crow. It was like coming across a prize fight or a pair of ancient warriors preparing for single combat, as the birds circled each other and swept up and down and around. A warning flap, a snap, a retreat, and then engaging again. Nothing like the playful swirls of kite with kite. Both stretched out their long, broad, sabre-tipped wings, and though the crow was smaller, it seemed utterly undaunted by the red enemy. This is the crow's customary patch and he was not about to give it up. The kite, startled from the complacency of sheer size, let out indignant shrieks, but stood firm in his space. A high-pitched skirmish: sweep, squawk, soar, circle, snap, swerve, ascend, and neither prepared to abandon their claim. Until at last, the kite seemed to tire of the contest and, with a flick of a wing, accelerated into a corkscrew spiral, leaving the crow bewildered in the sky. The kite dropped out of sight behind the hedge, the crow beat a retreat across the field.

These magnificent birds know where they stand in the local pecking order. In case any of their neighbours are in doubt, they hang out warnings from their high, messy nests. The skeleton of a crow with a few black feathers and one dangling wing serves as a signal to the corvid gangs of what might happen if they overstep the mark. Rooks will sometimes mob a single kite, banding together to hurry it away from their own nests and tree-territories, but the red kites are kings of the sky. The buzzards and kestrels gradually moved on as the kites arrived, though some have started to reclaim their old haunts. The lapwings are less inclined to call.

It is not so long since a red kite would have been an inexplicable sight above the fields of North Bucks. During much of the twentieth century, the only place in Britain where the species survived was Mid Wales. For the poet Gillian Clarke, the great birds were a precious secret to be cherished and shared only in love poetry. In her 1980s poem, 'My Box', 'rare red kites' are glimpsed in a secret garden along with goldcrests, wild heartsease and a golden tree. 'Red Kite' was a byword for rarity and hidden retreat.

On a family trip to the Welsh coast one summer, I remember stopping in the Brecon Beacons. The Red Kite Café sold coffee, tea, cakes, postcards, ice cream, Welsh flags and soft, furry scarlet dragons. There were paintings and photographs of the legendary kites, which were occasionally spotted in the remoter parts of the mountains. Our small son, Dominic, thought a little red dragon in the hand was worth any number of invisible red birds in the sky but tolerated the grown-ups' interest for a while. Needless to say, we saw no kites. But the trip was immeasurably enhanced by craning up at the grey heights in the hope of catching sight of the magical spread wings and forked tail. A few days later, my parents left us to a day of donkey rides and sandcastles, while they headed for Rhayader to continue the quest. They returned triumphant, after a thrilling sighting on a mountainside.

By the turn of the Millennium, red kites were already becoming a little less elusive. A century earlier, they had plummeted into the miserable condition of being among Britain's critically endangered species. Even in their last retreat, in the quiet valleys among the hills of Mid Wales, there had been fewer than a dozen pairs. The red, forked-tail kings of the air were going the way of the dragons, destined for a mythic realm, where they might assume magical powers, once bereft of their natural strength. If migrating birds were once thought to transport the souls of the dead, in the modern world it is often the birds themselves that are on their way to eternal darkness.

But, just as dragons are supposed to wake up one day, red kites have risen from their old retreats and returned in force. Whether they are the bold knights or the beleaguered victims, the wizards or the monsters, depends entirely on who's telling their story. For twentieth-century conservationists, red kites became a cause célèbre after catastrophic decline. As the targets of zealous gamekeepers and inadvertent casualties of poisonous pesticides, kite populations dwindled almost beyond recovery. The kite's increasing rarity only made their eggs more valuable to collectors, which then compounded the falling numbers. And yet, on the very brink of extinction, the red kite was gradually restored to life by the enthusiasm, expertise and dedicated efforts of ecologists, ornithologists, farmers and landowners.

In 1989, breeding pairs from Spain and northern Europe were reintroduced to special sites in the UK. The Black Isle on the east coast of Scotland seemed the perfect place to welcome red kites after an absence of more than a century. A few pairs were flown over from Sweden and set free to wheel over the Moray Firth. Five hundred miles south in the chalky Chilterns, Spanish kites were being released on John Paul Getty's estate at Wormsley Park – a location that certainly sounded promising, given the bird's fondness for earthworms. The surrounding woods offered nesting sites and protection from more hostile humans, allowing the kites to settle and to set about ensuring that their numbers increased. At about the same time, the M40 extension opened, causing an exponential increase in traffic through the Chilterns to Banbury and Birmingham. Drivers on their way through the enormous chalk cutting above Watlington were frequently distracted by huge birds of prey, high above the canyon, looking as if they had flown in from a Western. The giant birds were like something from another country, as indeed they were. Thirty years on, there are upwards of a thousand breeding pairs in the region. The red kite has recovered from rarity to the much happier state of mundanity.

Many still think of them as mountain dwellers nevertheless: 'Kite Country' means Mid Wales, not the Home Counties. These great birds evoke remoteness. High hidden valleys, known only to shepherds, with a few sheep, with rocks and stones: these surely are the kite's true home? Their soaring flight seems made for empty solitudes, their weird cry for whistling in the wind. And yet our sense of kites belonging to the wild places is really only a residue of relatively recent history. The Brecon Beacons were a refuge, an under-populated spot where the last kites could cling to life – Caractacus figures forced into doomed defiance. Our sense of what belongs to a place, or what's out of place elsewhere, can be surprisingly present-oriented. Now that we know red kites thrive in areas of pasturage and ploughing, with hedges, tall trees, mixed woodlands and villages, our sense of where they belong is changing.

Today, you might see as many as fifty kites soaring over a perfectly ordinary field or, more likely, just one or two sweeping by. They have little fear of humans (which is not always a help to them) and will sail along beside you if you're out for a walk. Local kites seem to recognise regular walkers, calling out with a high cry, perhaps to greet the morning or size up a small dog. They swoop down into open grass for breakfast, feeding on dead rabbits or nestlings, on barbecued chop bones or food laid out specially by kind, if misguided, well-wishers. Anything that catches those remarkably sharp eyes and proves light enough to carry is open game. Their nests are full of ragged old bags and ribbons, bits of bunting and tin foil, lost socks and tiny teddies. I've found dog toys in nearby fields, too, scavenged from our garden and then dropped, once a tasty-looking piglet turned out to be a disappointing beakful of cloth.

And yet for all their ubiquity, you can never quite get accustomed to these terrifyingly efficient creatures. Although their staple diet consists of carrion and worms and much of their day is spent cleaning up rotting prey from the fields, these birds still command immediate respect. The sheer power of their beaks and talons, the sharpness of their sight, the flaming red of their feathers and the spectacular agility of their flight always inspires awe. You can see a red kite every day and never lose the shiver of surprise.

Until very recently, it was hard to imagine how abundant these great birds once were. When Izaak Walton, in the aftermath of the Civil War, began offering advice to anglers on sourcing fish food, he suggested burying a dead kite to make a maggot farm. London, a rather less hygienic city than today, was full of red kites feeding on scraps and offal. They would swoop down into crowded markets, whisking food from people's hands like twenty-first-century seagulls in Brighton or St Ives. Since the Middle Ages, they had been recognised as rubbish collectors, flourishing where the human population was densest and dirtiest. As Mark Cocker has pointed out, it was London, not Mid Wales, that seemed 'the classic location' for kites. Once treasured – or at least tolerated – for their service to the community, however, urban kites gradually began to take on the less positive role of public nuisance, with unhappy consequences for their long-term survival.

So familiar were these large birds in the seventeenth century that when long-stringed sheets of paper or silk began to lift over Europe, the obvious name for a bright, light high-flyer with an eye-catching tail was 'kite'. (The novelty probably arrived in Britain from Java, via the Netherlands, after Dutch sailors saw Indonesian fishermen flying large flat leaves from long lines of plant fibre: a good game is rarely slow to catch on.) A home-made 'kite' is easy enough to make, as Benjamin Franklin famously demonstrated. In an age untroubled by Health and Safety concerns, Franklin encouraged the curious to take two strips of cedarwood, a silk hankie and a piece of twine, to fashion them into a kite with some wire at the top and then to thread a metal key onto the string, before sending it up into a lightning storm. Once drenched, the fizzing string conducted electricity into a glass jar, thus shedding light on one of nature's ancient mysteries. A home-made gadget capable of harnessing the power of the gods was an exciting discovery. But kites made very satisfactory toys, too. Just as wooden swords and hobby horses turned small boys into knights or cavalry officers, a silk kite on a string was a toy version of the noble art of falconry. While kites caught on in the playground, the raptors whose name they borrowed were in steady decline. As those made from paper, nylon or plastic became standard kit for seaside holidays, their name came to evoke the toy more readily than the bird.

Although red kites were once as common a feature of British towns as pigeons, they were never regarded as friendly companions. Thomas Bewick's *History of British Birds* was published in 1797, stimulating widespread interest in birds and inadvertently creating an invaluable record of eighteenth-century attitudes to different species. His remarkably well observed portrait of the kite shows the vast, folded wings and unmistakeable forktail, hunched over a rock and ready for take-off. Unlike many of the other birds, portrayed in attractive pastoral habitats with soft trees, bushes and winding riverbanks, the kite stands against a page pale and empty as a dull sky. What really distinguishes the kite from the rest is the sinister expression in its hooded eyes and the striking resemblance between the claw-like beak and the beak-like talons. Bewick's portraits of the sparrowhawk, peregrine, sea eagle, and even the buzzard look positively benign in comparison.

The kite's deadly magnificence is caught in words as well as being cut in wood. Awe at its ability to soar out of sight and then descend on prey with 'irresistible force' is balanced by a certain disdain for a raptor of such power that attacks only the smallest birds and animals. Bewick's admiration for the furious mother hen, defending her chicks against the depredations of the 'robber' kite, makes only too clear that the natural behaviour of hungry kites often dismayed human witnesses. These were birds with matchless strength and agility, naturally equipped with deadly weapons – yet their behaviour was that of lazy cowards, unashamed of stooping to prey on the defenceless. This was just what Shakespeare was evoking in Macduff's reaction to the murder of his wife and children: 'Oh hell-kite! All? / What, all my pretty chickens and their dam at one fell swoop?' The shocking discovery is extreme even by the standards of Renaissance tragedy, so Macduff's choice of words gives some indication of contemporary attitudes to kites.

To call someone a 'kite' in Shakespearean tragedy is very insulting indeed. Though Macbeth is in a league of his own, Goneril's behaviour to Lear provokes the same horrified expression: 'Detested kite!' Lear is not seeing his daughter as a murderer at this point, but as a thief and an abusive usurper. The power struggle of 'ravens, crows and kites' in the aftermath of Julius Caesar's murder signals similarly that the leaders who had pretended to be striking just blows against tyranny were nothing but self-interested cowards. Prince Hamlet, too, frustrated by his delayed vengeance on Claudius, reveals another aspect of the kite's unhappy notoriety when bemoaning his failure to fatten 'all the region kites with this slave's offal'. The red kite's character as bully, robber and murderer was lowered even further by its reputation as a scavenger, feeding off the carcases of the dead.

In 'The Braes of Killiecrankie', an old Scottish song about the fierce Highland battle of 1689, kites figure in the same grisly role. The soldier who faced 'the Devil and Dundee' only narrowly escaped falling prey to 'an Athole Gled' – or Atholl kite. While he may have been referring to the Jacobite troops based at Blair Atholl, the line more obviously recalls the local birds of prey. In the days of pitched battles, the red scavengers swooping down to feed on the flesh of the fallen were linked with blood and hell fire. Rudyard Kipling was joining a long tradition when he evoked 'Troops for Foreign Service' in a 'Birds of Prey' march:

The jackal an' the kite
'Ave an 'ealthy appetite,
An' you'll never see your soldiers any more!

Although British kite populations were in catastrophic decline in 1895 when the poem was published, their old reputation was still thriving.

Gledhow Lane in Leeds derives its name from the kite's northern alias – 'gled' or 'glead'. Since it runs between Oakwood and Chapel Allerton, once the site of the local gallows, the old street is another reminder of the tastes of the aerial scavengers. Kite's Hill, near the village of Selborne in Hampshire, was also once the location for a gibbet. The 'kites' in question may have been the criminals executed there, but the hill is more likely to have been named after the local raptors feasting on the dead bodies.

Such gruesome scenes inevitably inspired satirists, who sometimes took the red kite as an image for the tyrant, fattening on the sufferings of the poor, sometimes for the lawyer, scavenging on everyone. In the ancient fable of 'The Frog and the Mouse', an unsuspecting mouse asks a frog to carry it across a stream, only to be left to drown halfway, when the frog dives underwater. The floating body of the mouse attracts a passing kite, which swoops down and polishes off the frog as well. The moral is open to interpretation, but, once again, the figure of the kite is decidedly unsympathetic.

As red kites were driven to the verge of extinction and their plight became widely known, their image changed decisively. Something of the unappealing character attributed to them over the centuries may linger nevertheless, especially as these old associations were prompted by the birds' natural behaviour. Kites feed on carrion because their talons are ill-equipped to deal with living prey any bigger than frogs or mice, but this natural limitation wasn't what struck imaginative observers. It is easy to see how Aesop's fable was hatched, when you spend a bit of time watching a red kite circling slowly above, as if waiting for permission to land, and then suddenly swooping down with deadly accuracy on tiny prey. On a warm morning last May, I was startled to see a red kite looking very large indeed on the willow above our garden pond. Two crows were flapping about on the grass below, squabbling over the body of an unlucky rabbit. The crows flew off when they saw me, but a few minutes later the kite swooped from the tree whisking away the entire carcase without a sound.

As red kites have become more abundant, they have acquired a sense of comfortable familiarity, which may then seem at odds with their capacity for sudden destruction. It does not take much for the old suspicions to erupt – at once the special local bird is exposed as a 'detested kite'. Traditional unease based on interpreting avian instincts through human behaviour is not perhaps so far beneath the surface, which is why red kites periodically hit the news for all the wrong reasons. Cheering reports of successful breeding programmes are sometimes offset by stories about kites swooping, talons bared, into peaceful picnics. Worse still, they can be known to carry off family pets. The 'problem' from the conservationist's point of view is that if people regularly feed kites, the birds are unable to tell the difference between food intended for them and a child's cupcake. The 'problem' from the family's point of view is that a very large bird of prey has terrified their children or injured their pet. The old scenario of the kite as a traitor, biting the hand that has fed it, is still being played out – along with the darker fear of a false friendship that masks a cold-blooded intention of preying on the defenceless.

The anthropomorphic instinct that so often prompts the protection of non-human species can work in the opposite direction, if different birds are cast as friends and enemies, tyrants and victims. In a strange ironic reversal, the very perception of birds in human terms can lead to their persecution. During the lockdown months of 2020, three kites were shot in Mid Wales, and another two in Shropshire and Leeds. This may have been nothing more than casual destruction aggravated by boredom and frustration, but it is possible that the culprits saw themselves as saviours, protecting helpless chicks from powerful predators.

As species multiply, they often experience a corresponding drop in popularity. Once diminished to the point of extreme rarity and struggling for survival against impossible odds, even the fiercest creatures prompt pity more readily than fear. As soon as they increase beyond the safe boundaries of a protected site, they recover their wild and deadly magnificence. Where creatures posing no threat to humankind often retain their imposed character, fierce things are rarely seen as loveable and, though naturally powerful, are more vulnerable to clandestine attack from the deadliest creature of all. The poisoning of sixteen red kites near Dingwall in 2014 recalled the antipathy of Victorian gamekeepers to large raptors on grouse moors, which had done so much to destroy the species in the first place. Even among those with no particular interest in maintaining grouse populations, the close proximity of these great birds can provoke unease. A dozen pairs of kites perching in a stag-headed oak, hunched and alert, ready for take-off, might strike an unsuspecting rambler as a rather intimidating lookout patrol.

So much depends on the stories being told. A young sea eagle, reintroduced in the Isle of Wight, which flew north and joined the Chiltern kites, is the hero of a much more appealing tale than the one about the kite who scarred the head of a hapless (and hatless) picnicker in an attempt to snatch a sandwich. The headline in the *Daily Express*, 'Toddler attacked by red kite as she celebrates her birthday in park', did nothing for the raptor's modern reputation. Editors know that red kites are newsworthy, because of the strong and often polarised feelings they prompt in the human population. Awe and indignation can often inhabit the same breast. One of my neighbours, Martin Rogers, never tires of taking stunning photographs of these majestic raptors as they sweep through the fields at the back of his house. And yet, after he found his cat lying seriously injured in the garden one afternoon, his enthusiasm waned. The cat was bleeding from tiny punctures, which he assumed were caused by buckshot until the vet explained that they were talon marks.

The image of red kites has undergone more dramatic makeovers than most British species. From the routine refuse collectors of medieval towns, to ghoulish scavengers circling gallows and battle-grounds, to scarce mountain birds, to cherished endangered species, they have emerged as triumphant emblems of environ-mental recovery. While greenfinches have landed unhappily in the Red List of Conservation Concern, red kites are now nesting securely in the Green List. There are around 1,800 pairs breeding in Britain, with colonies in Yorkshire, Cumbria, Dumfries and Galloway, as well as their strongholds in Buckinghamshire, the Black Isle and Wales.

Horror, help or hope? The future of the red kite is anyone's guess. After the reintroductions of 1989, kites flourished in south-ern grasslands more vigorously than in the Moray Firth – whether because of the habitat, or because the Scottish birds have been more vulnerable to poisoning, or perhaps because of their old predilection for waste. The more people in an area, the more rubbish is left lying around. Picnics in parks mean easy pickings. Red kites may gradually recover their old role as refuse collectors, helping to clean up after fly-tippers and takeaway-droppers. There seems no danger of there ever being a shortage of rubbish. With more cars, the roads are strewn with carcases of pheasants, deer and badgers – good for the kites as long as they are nimble enough to avoid becoming roadkill themselves. But trees are on the increase, too, and as Britain's green canopy spreads, red kites are likely to spread with it. If there is appetising food and somewhere to roost, red kites are free to alight where they will. One day they may seem in place everywhere except the treeless wilds of high mountains and rocky isles.

Here Be Dragons

~

It is best seen on a morning in late September, when the sun's less high in the sky and dazzles early motorists without really trying. The light has a moister, tawnier air than in June, as if dyeing the hedgerow elms is just a matter of repeated immersions. Oaks and sycamores spread themselves to soak up the waning sunlight. Already odd leaves are deep yellow or auburn. Some have drifted down like discarded paper bags. Most of the hedgerows are still deep green, setting off the ripening clusters of scarlet haws, white tufts of old-man's-beard, gleaming purple sloes and shaggy, dirty gold hazelnuts. A greenfinch flashes out, followed by a hungry, twittering flock of mixed tits and finches.

The longer nights mean slower starts. In the dips of the long grass, gossamer exhalations of the sleeping earth lie still as if caught on camera, a moment of half-realised form before vanishing as if they'd never been. The warmth of the day sends night's secrets scurrying, scattering, sheltering, dissolving and disappearing. Everywhere there is a sense of spaces recently inhabited, dips rapidly abandoned, an only-just-emptiness. Life was here, life is still here, and yet now strangely absent. Everything is dissolving – ragwort melting from tough yellow petals into white seeds, willow-herb feathering and flying away, white trails scoring the blue before diffusing into tiny clouds, mingling with the lines of mist. Seas of hazy vapour make islands of trees – tall Scots pines become dark bushy outcrops in a luminous invisible valley where the ghostly poles of Lombardy poplars loom and the tufty tops of oak and ash float like the flotsam and jetsam of summer. Seven geese call out from above, as if to urge fuller consciousness. The familiar contours of the field are emerging, edges softened by wet September broad-leaves spread out for their last hurrah. And there it is. Rising like a vast submarine from the calm waves of waking green. A solid, angular, unignorable hulk, with a periscope that dwarfs the tallest tree, high enough to keep the whole area under surveillance. An amphibious invader, half camouflaged, half insistent on its unin-vited presence.

The white chimney is tipped with red lights to warn aircraft to steer clear. A tall lighthouse far inland, signalling the dangers below: not rocks, but a combustible, chemical hill. Puffs of poison-ous breath remind people of what's there. You can tell which way the wind is blowing by the direction of the smoke. Sometimes it's a northwesterly, blowing the gases gently towards the capital, occa-sionally a raw blast from the east sends them trailing cross-country towards Wales. On a still afternoon, when the air's heavy, the streaming cloud rises straight up into a clear blue sky, a smoke signal to be seen for miles around, though no one knows what it means.

The sleeping dragon hasn't been there very long. A decade ago its lair was full of Lilliputian protesters, arms lifted, cameras click-ing, signs brandished: 'No Incinerator! No Incinerator!' They marched through towns, massed into meetings, flooded public consultations, protested in the press, talked to TV crews, pleaded in council meetings. They tried to tell the world that their hill was under threat, their birds, their insects, their trees, their children. The dragon-keepers spoke calmly in village halls and primary schools, laying out perfect models with toy trucks and miniature trees and grass much greener than the real fields. They had maps and plans and projections and answers to every objection. The pop-up gallery showed photos of nesting wrens, early purple orchids and unrolled hedgehogs. Clean drawings of familiar horizons looking as if nothing had changed. It was all to do with the lie of the land.

When the talks and the models went away, the lorries that came were much bigger than anyone expected. In fact, they were hardly recognisable from the little layouts with the smiling figures and bicycles. They closed the roads and kept people away on Health and Safety grounds, or so the signs said. And then one day, the roads reopened and there it was. Huge, gleaming and armour-plated, taller than anything for miles around. It might have landed under the cover of darkness or erupted from the ground like a Bond villain's secret laboratory. There was nothing very secretive about it now. And it showed no signs of moving on. But the dragon-keepers were gone with their models and their pretty slides, leaving no trace of their explanations. They hurried away to tell people in other places about the kinds of lair dragons like and how well camouflaged they are. And there it is, five years on, as much in evidence as on Day One. Whether it's *noticed* as much is another matter entirely.

For the family who led the protest, whose windows opened right onto the site, it is no longer an obsession, nor even an intrusion. Maggi and Alasdair eventually managed to sell the family home and move to the Isle of Skye, where the fields are even emptier than those they woke up to every morning for many years. In the green valley they used to look across, the new incinerator remains difficult to ignore. As it does for miles in all directions. From the higher spots with the widest views of the vale, the dragon's tall white pipe and huge, sloping back stand out incongruously by day and night. When the low winter sun catches its sheer, plated sides, the dragon blazes red as a beacon. It has to be fed continuously.

What is mass-produced today is often thrown away almost as quickly. There is money to be made from processing the endless supply of rubbish. Odd shoes, empty bottles, electric cables, worn sofas, broken hoovers, unsupported IT, plastic bags and boxes and bubble wrap, punctured birthday balloons, bald Barbie dolls, ex-Xbox games, buckled bikes, yesterday's toys and takeaway trays have to go somewhere, whether underground or into the air or into new products. A wheelie bin is just a staging post in their long unwanted lives.

What was once someone's rubbish can turn out to be someone else's prize discovery. When we were about ten and twelve, my brother and I had an exciting afternoon exploring a mound of broken pots and plates in woods near a ruined manor house – not far from where we had recently moved. Best of all was a pair of delicate, mud-caked scales, which metamorphosed into brilliant brass when polished. They would, we were told, have been used for weighing letters, but despite hours of searching, we never found a single weight. Antique shops and museums are filled with the debris of vanished societies – washed and labelled and placed in cases. But what will survive of us? An ancient rubbish site is an archaeologist's treasure trove, a more modern one can furnish an auctioneer, but a contemporary tip is just a problem.

Incinerators are the self-erasers of modern consumer culture, though not always the most self-effacing. Over the last decade, growing concerns about carbon emissions, green belt land and increasing demand for new houses have made the expansion of landfill sites less and less attractive. Instead of hiding our rubbish and letting the methane ooze into the atmosphere, new kinds of incinerator combust waste under carefully controlled environmental limits, generating renewable energy in the process. 'Energy from Waste' installations have been rising across the UK at a surprising rate and in a surprising range of styles and colours. Some are no-nonsense budget blocks, but others are adventures in the aesthetics of refuse.

On the edge of the New Forest in the village of Marchwood, whose name recalls its sylvan past, a great dome of polished aluminium shimmers like a gigantic silicone implant on the shore. Further north, the new Millerhill Recycling and Energy Recovery Centre in Edinburgh is a slightly more modest, modernist construction, in great rectangular blocks of Bauhaus black and white. Some designers evidently attempt to minimise the impact of their enormous constructions: the curves of the Colnbrook incinerator in Slough and the solid block at Runcorn are encased in white to hide their heads in the clouds. Others are built to make a statement. In Leeds, the green high-rise plant, covered in real green plants, is saying something loud about the environment, though quite what that might be is less obvious than the 140-foot-high building. As a 'vertical forest', which looks rather like an inside-out greenhouse, the Recycling and Energy Recovery Facility (or RERF) is designed to reduce greenhouse gases and generate greenish energy. The Javelin Park in Gloucestershire on the other hand makes no bones about its raison d'être, with a design reminiscent of a mass collision of huge green and white dustbin lorries.

Enormous chimneys clearly pose an architectural challenge, though at Marston Vale, near Bedford, the new plant is meant to reflect the local heritage. A site once filled with brickworks inspired a design apparently in keeping with the old industry, but when it was finished the slim, glossy, scarlet pipes towered high above the four old, weathered-brick chimneys at Stewartby. Technological necessity is often the unlikely nurse of innovation. The Energy Recovery Facility at Exeter resembles a huge ocean-going container ship, while the Isle of Man's equivalent has a silvery, low-arched roof and stylish stack. This is meant to recall a Viking ship, but visitors could be forgiven for assuming it was modelled on a headless swan. As the island suffered severely from Viking raids at the turn of the ninth century, local people may well quail at the sight of the giant boat – but the Vikings settled in and so may the incinerator. Roman engineering projects built chiefly for practical purposes have now become World Heritage sites – just think of the towering aqueduct of limestone arches built to pipe water from the springs at Usèz to thirsty, low-lying Nîmes. Today's incinerators may not last quite so long as the Pont du Gard.

As more and more incinerators erupt across the land, new plans meet with more and more determined resistance. Despite a vision of a white outline indistinguishable from the clouds, proposals for an Energy Recovery Facility at Portland in Dorset have been vigorously opposed, as they have in areas of Greater London as soon as the news of what was approaching began to spread. In January 2022, protesters with placards urging urgent rethinking marched through Edmonton in the campaign to halt the plans for building a new incinerator there.

Protests can be successful. In Cambridgeshire, AmeyCespa's plans for an Energy from Waste plant at Waterbeach aroused the wrath of local residents who felt that the proposed building would be out of keeping with Denny Abbey, which has been in place since the twelfth century. In the open fenlands it is hard to see how even the most imaginative architect could convincingly conceal something 260 feet high. And, judging from the modern warehouse style drawn up in the plans, it appears that they didn't really try, recognising perhaps that it would be hard to compete with the intricately patterned, golden limestone of Ely Cathedral. At one point, it seemed likely that those who climb the 288 steps of the cathedral's West Tower could look forward to taking their bearings from the smooth white chimney of the new incinerator only eight miles away. But the proposed construction was finally turned down by the Secretary of State in June 2020, in the interests of national heritage.

Past, present and future co-exist uneasily in sites such as Waterbeach. As they often have. When the Benedictine abbey was built there in 1190, it was inspired by a different vision of the future and different ideas about how best to benefit the local community. When the abbey was closed three centuries later during the Reformation, the attitude of the prevailing powers had undergone another decisive change. Since then, Denny Abbey has been a private home, a working farm and an agricultural museum – and who knows what its future holds?

The arguments, at least, look set to continue. The case made by energy companies rests on limiting emissions and landfill, generating energy and profits, revitalising local economies through job creation and generally improving the area. Whatever its initial reception, the steel ship in the Isle of Man is saving the islanders from ever-expanding methane-breathing landfill mounds as well as providing renewable power. The case against draws on powerful counter-points concerning increased emissions, toxic air, light and noise pollution, environmental damage and aesthetic vandalism. Burning waste may seem cheaper than recycling, but there are different ways of counting costs. And rather than go to so much trouble incinerating waste – why not use up fewer resources in the first place?

And yet, the new-style incinerators are often repurposing old, industrial sites, like the disused coal-fired power stations at Ferrybridge or Skelton Grange in Yorkshire. Recycling and Energy from Waste facilities often replace earlier and perhaps less desirable methods of refuse disposal: the Isle of Man's Viking ship was built at the landfill site just outside Douglas, which had never been one of the city's main attractions. The Marchwood dome replaced a much less imaginative grey block. Although they sometimes seem to burst up unapologetically in remote rural areas, the dragons of the twenty-first century may be helping to disguise traces of an earlier and dirtier plant. As in Marston Vale, the armour-plated dragon nestling among the remnants of the Royal Forest of Bernwood in the gentle hills of Aylesbury Vale was built on a site previously occupied by the London Brick Company. Photographs from the 1960s show not one or two, but whole rows of tall, smoky towers, smudging the fields in thick, low-hanging clouds. Whether a past eyesore can justify a future stye is a perennial problem for the planners, but a minor improvement or a shiny new project can usually diffuse demands for more radical rethinking.

When might a fake hill emitting perpetual smoke cease to be an unwelcome intruder, an affront to the eye, a threat to health? Perhaps when worries about its dark secret interior are pushed aside by more pressing troubles? Or once it is in operation, because there's no longer any point in worrying about what can't be changed? Perhaps everyone gradually begins to accept that it provides jobs and generates income, security and satisfaction? And then they come to realise that it is not an incinerator after all, but a state-of-the-art development for creating energy from waste? It is even large enough to gobble up rubbish from further afield, cleaning up city streets and being paid for its trouble. Suddenly it rears up again as a friendly green dragon, devouring unwanted mountains and breathing enough fire to heat the neighbourhood. It may all depend on what you think about dragons. In Wales, plans for new incinerators have been firmly rejected.

What's new generally, and almost inevitably, becomes part of the landscape – even if it retains an essential out-of-placeness. From close at hand, the smoking, red-tipped dragon that drove Maggi and her family away soon ceased to attract much attention. Glimpsed through a hedge from a passing road, it might almost be the funnel of a steam engine just about to set off down the line.

Rain, steam, speed. Streaming hydrogen fluoride, nitrogen oxide. One day the incinerators of the young twenty-first century may be viewed as engineering triumphs of historic significance, with preservation societies protesting over their decommissioning or demolition. Belching chimneys among farms and villages which once marked the era of textile mills and iron foundries are now fondly regarded by many as remnants of a bygone age of manufacturing. As anything seen every day gradually becomes an unconscious element of home, people often only notice when it's about to be dismantled.

On an April morning of rough shining grass, of soft, pigeon-belly grey cloud, a whiter shade of pale smoke plumes over the heads of trees. It could almost be issuing from a farmhouse chimney, if the day were not so mild. The dragon's settled down to doze, now. Smoke rises daily and streams away, mixing with the morning mist until you can't tell them apart, it just seems that the morning cloud is a little thicker in places. The engines and the rubbish trucks are quiet on Sundays, but still the air is full of noises. Skylarks, calling, stepping up through the air above the meadow grass, chiffchaffs darting with urgent staccato, lemon green as the fresh shoots of the young willow. I wonder if they know what is under the hill?

Brick Lines

~

You can't always tell what is under a hill. The first time I saw the compact hilltop village of Brill, I thought it might have evolved from the site of a lost medieval village, because of the deep slopes and oddly shaped dips and hillocks around the windmill. Not that I was paying very much attention, with all the wide-open views across the plain to Oxford and Otmoor. The windmill was well placed on this exposed brow, but in spite of the strong breeze, the ice-cream man was keeping busy. The grassy crater below the mill was full of families. You can perch on weedy ledges or find a sheltered corner behind a hawthorn. The misshapen humps and bumps lend themselves to games of hide-and-seek or guerilla warfare, there are nooks for gingerbread houses and secret dens. Best of all (according to Dominic and his young friends) is to run or roll down the rough slides, though the nettles at the bottom are a major hazard. Windmill Hill became known as 'Hurtle Hill' – and then 'Hurting Hill'.

The way the earth mounds spread around the hillside reminded me of other lost villages – of Girsby or Stalling Busk – or the ramblers' church on the ridge of the Lincolnshire Wolds, isolated since the rest of Walesby moved down into the valley centuries ago. It was a few years before I realised that the lost buildings under Brill windmill weren't houses at all: they were disused clay pits.

And then everything made more sense. Brill is different from surrounding villages, not just because of its airy position and panoramic outlook, but because of its buildings. It is a very bricky place, with comfortable, weathered red houses, each different from its neighbours but entirely harmonious. The little market square, more like a tiny town than a village, is lined by cottages, minimansions, and un-uniform terraces, all built from similar bricks. Similar, but not identical – just like the houses. Once Hurtle Hill had been unmasked as a clay pit, I could see that the people of Brill had never had to go far for their building materials. And I began to think more about the place of bricks.

I discovered from Jean, one of my neighbours, who has lived here all her life, that her late husband, Hector, worked for the London Brick Company. He had grown up on a farm, but after years working as a cowman, he decided to take a job at the local brick works instead. It was a sensible decision for a married couple with a young family, because 'the pay was better and the hours were less'. As Hector was used to digging ditches and pitching hay by hand, ploughing heavy fields in November in a cabless tractor, or being up all night for the lambing and calving, the brick factory did not seem too daunting. Whatever the weather – hot, wet, cold or windy – he was out of doors, firing, stacking, grading, and loading bricks. It was not so different from working on the farm, except that mud and manure gave way to grit and brick dust. Jean, as always, took it all in her stride.

In 1966, the same year that Hector Crawford changed jobs, an American sculptor and former railway worker was busy with a large pile of Long Island sand lime bricks. Carl Andre was creating a series of different geometric arrangements using 120 bricks. He decided to call them 'Equivalents', which in a way, they were. But while Hector's daily productions were loaded onto lorries and sent off without much fuss, when Carl Andre's *Equivalent VIII* went on display at the Tate, there was national uproar. What was the gallery doing spending so much public money on a pile of bricks? While

Equivalent VIII had its defenders in the art world, the installation provoked furious headlines – the *Daily Mirror* ran the story under large letters: 'What a Load of Rubbish'. Cartoonists had a field day, with scenarios spinning on every brick joke in the book. The Giles cartoon in the *Daily Express* featured a builder at the top of a ladder, puzzling workmates on the scaffolding with his rhapsody on a brick, 'The repose and calm of this work reflects the simplicity and restraint of my earlier period, the symbolism remains personal and eludes exact interpretation.' The newspaper cartoon, an affordable, ephemeral artform aimed at the down-to-earth Brit, offered a perfect vehicle for ridiculing the rarefied world of modern art: minimalist materialism was hitting the brick wall of popular culture. But as Carl Giles was also revealing in his thoughtful cameo, modern art can surprise people into seeing things in new light. Once out of place, the most familiar object can seem rare and strange.

Carl Andre's *Equivalent* enraged or amused many who didn't bother to go and see it for themselves. It prompted some of those who did to contemplate the eternal truths of geometry or the multiple permutations of 120 cuboids. Others were more inclined to muse on the relationship between material objects, flat planes and empty space. Or simply to puzzle over why turning a wall into a floor – or a floor into a wall – was so troubling. Whatever else the work achieved, Andre's bricks raised questions about the nature of art. Andy Warhol's *Campbell's Soup Cans* had already demonstrated the art of the mass-produced, but Andre's 'Equivalents' were not even images of familiar objects. They were familiar objects in an unusual place. But who created the artwork – the man who arranged the bricks in the Tate or the men who manufactured the bricks?

Brickmaking was once a largely local matter. Brickmakers were independent artisans, moulding, firing and delivering their wares for local building projects. The distinctive character of an old wall is created partly from the shape and colour of the bricks and partly from the bricklayer's choice of bond. He might have opted for a 'Flemish' design, laying the bricks lengthways and then sideways to create a pattern of alternating headers and stretchers, or perhaps preferred the double-stretcher-single-header 'monk bond'. This distinctive style got its name because it was selected for many of the brick monasteries of northern Europe. I like the old herringbone that survives in buildings such as the Hospital of St Cross in Winchester. The narrow brick weave over the gateway has a wonderful 'Look at me' quality.

But it is the colour of the bricks that really sets them in their place. A Leicestershire vicarage is generally a richer red than its Suffolk counterpart, while the butter-coloured bricks of the Isle of Wight are paler than the smog-stained yellows of London squares. In Staffordshire you can see Victorian town halls and chapels built from dark blue bricks. In neighbouring Cheshire many of the older farmhouses are 'brindled' with mixed lines of rust-red, dark brown and black.

Different clays mean different cottages. Each brick might be roughly similar in shape, but their characters are formed by belts of local clay – Red Marl in Nottinghamshire, Etruria Marl in the Potteries, London Clay in the Thames Estuary. The colours are affected by firing techniques and sometimes by infusions of different elements in the process – if you want a redder brick you might need some iron oxide in the mix. Whatever the variations from brickmaker to brickmaker, the buildings constructed from handmade bricks now seem very settled in place.

Bricks are made from – and make – their particular places. In a striking watercolour map, Matthew Rice presents Britain in vibrant tiger stripes of tawny red, sand gold and white to show the sweeping lines of sandstone, brick, limestone and chalk. It is a work of art that makes bricks appear both natural and strange, creations and creators of place. Red marks the coastal areas of Cumbria, Somerset, South Wales and Hampshire, with longer stripes reaching deep inland from Lancashire and County Durham, across East Anglia and down diagonally from the Wash. Spots of grey granite bruise the extremities – at Land's End, Pembrokeshire, Carmarthen, the Hebrides and Aberdeen.

You don't need a geological map to find brick-making materials. Where there's clay there's probably a village with a claggy name. From Clehonger in Herefordshire to Cley next the Sea in Norfolk, from Clayhidon in Devon to Clayton-le-Moors in Lancashire, from Saxon settlers to modern gardeners, the local residents know very well that a defining feature of their home is very heavy soil. The site where Hector Crawford worked is surrounded by villages whose names point underground: East Claydon, Middle Claydon, Botolph Claydon, Steeple Claydon. As ever with place names, it is easy to jump to unwarranted conclusions, though. You might assume that Clayworth in Nottinghamshire or Great and Little Brickhill near Bletchley were inspired by the local soil, but in fact their names derive from ancient words for 'hill' – Old English *clawu* and the Celtic *breg*. Brickhill, like Brill, is one of those spots that seems especially conscious of location – combining *breg* with the Old English *hille*. And both long pre-date the use of bricks in Britain – except perhaps those made by the Romans, who took their building methods with them when they left.

It was the scarceness of bricks that gave them their cachet in the later Middle Ages. When Ralph Cromwell, the Lord Treasurer of England, commissioned an enormous red and cream keep for his castle at Tattershall in the 1430s, he was making an unequivocal statement about his soaring status and bottomless coffers. Out of place still in the flat Lincolnshire fenland, the tall, turreted keep with its glowing bricks made a striking contrast to the older earth mounds and stone barricades when it was finished, not to mention the homes of those dredging a living from the surrounding wetlands. From the parapet you still get a commanding view of the low-lying fields stretching away. It's as good as a drone, looking down on the nearby roofs and chimneys, tractors and cars, and you can see out past the church tower where the Cromwell family rest, to RAF Coningsby and on across the Fens. The jam sandwich layers of thin bricks and pale mortar have withstood the weather remarkably well.

Brick buildings were once rare and reserved for the rich. Why else would they have been the material of choice for Cardinal Wolsey when he was building Hampton Court Palace to impress England's new Tudor king? In Victorian Manchester, the reverse was true: the long, uniform red terraces rapidly built for the workforce and their families used what had by then become the cheapest, most easily available material. Manchester, out of place in the 1840s because of its bewildering growth spurt, rapidly became established as the quintessential Victorian city. As it struggled to support a burgeoning population of mill and factory workers, the city's appetite for bricks became insatiable.

Of all the various shades of British brick, the reddest of the reds is Accrington Red – a smooth, shiny brick moulded from the fireclay deposits of the Calder Valley. Manufactured in Accrington, but rapidly mobilised, these were bricks destined to go the distance. Tough enough to support the Empire State Building, strong, scarlet Accrington iron bricks were sent across the Atlantic to do the job. From 1887, when consignments of Accrington bricks were first loaded onto barges, boats and freight trains, the world began to redden. When the University of Birmingham was founded in 1900, the University Council was keen to demonstrate the new institution's progressive character and so commissioned buildings that would not be easily mistaken for the old grey Gothic arches of Oxford and Cambridge. The Chancellor's Court, round and red, is patterned in cream masonry and topped with grey domes. Beside the clock-shaped court, the Chamberlain Tower rises like a minaret in matching Accrington brick. These startling additions to the green, tree-canopied skyline of Edgbaston immediately assumed a distinctive identity, making Birmingham the reddest of the new 'Red Brick' universities. When David Lodge created Rummidge

University for his series of campus novels, its 'tall redbrick clock-tower' became an instantly recognisable sign of the modern university – pre-dating the Plate Glass, but more progressive than the Old Stone.

The high-fashion building material of Tudor England had gradually made its way to the high street. Demand for bricks was roughly in line with the growth of towns and cities. The Great Fire of London unsurprisingly fanned a desire for less combustible housing, while the accession of William of Orange two decades later brought more Dutch styles to Britain. As London swelled in the eighteenth century, bricks moulded from underlying and nearby clay turned into elegant terraces and squares. With the arrival of railways, freight-loads of building materials began trundling from north, south, east and west into the Victorian capital. Brickmaking was less a matter of handmade artefacts than of mass production on an industrial scale. As Annie Prangnell, whose small, family brickworks in the Isle of Wight kept going until the 1950s, reflected, 'They didn't want hand-mades when the machines came in.'

The foundations of the London Brick Company were laid at Fletton, near Peterborough, in 1877. An enterprising developer called John Cathles Hill saw a business opportunity and began shipping thousands of bricks manufactured from local clay along the Great Northern Railway line to London. As business boomed, the London Brick Company bought up more and more of the little independent brickmakers within an easy train ride of the capital. B. J. Forder's brickworks at Wootton Pillinge near Bedford became the London Brick Company and Forder's Limited until this rather unwieldy name contracted into the London Brick Company. At the same time, Wootton Pillinge itself disappeared under the smart, new cottages of Stewartby. Bricky spots no longer derived their names from the locale: as the woods that had inspired Wootton receded, the new model village was called after the Stewart family of brick magnates.

Stewartby was not a 'model' like Bekonscot or mini-brick-built Legoland, but a modern designer village in the tradition of Bournville or Port Sunlight: an embodiment of an enlightened employer's vision of sound, salubrious living quarters for working families. The broad, spacious streets and art deco brick-built homes were a living advertisement for the company whose chimneys towered over them like skyscrapers. The Stewartby brickworks became the world's biggest manufacturer of bricks with an annual production of 500 million. Across the level plain of the Marston Vale, 167 tall chimneys rose. From this smoking thicket of brick issued the building blocks of the new estates, schools, hospitals and shopping parades required by bomb-damaged cities to repair the scars of the Second World War and move forward.

Once the war ended, demand for bricks greatly exceeded supply – a situation not helped by acute labour shortages. In July 1951, the *Bedford Times* reported that local production had dropped by 10 million bricks a year, just when the industry was most needed. Southern Italy, on the other hand, was suffering from chronic unemployment. To address the problems at home, the Marston Vale Brick Company set up a recruitment office in Naples and, over the next ten years, more than seven thousand Italians left home to work in Bedford.

Half a century later, some of the men who arrived from Naples in the 1950s shared their memories with Carmela Byram. Both British weather and food had come as quite a shock. Raffaele Ariano had vivid recollections of sailing from Brindisi and a heat-wave in July 1955: 'When we arrived – *mamma mia bella!* Here the evening was so dark and there was so much fog. The day after it was raining and nearly every day it rained and rained. If you remember those days, it was like that, especially the Saturdays and Sundays.' The difference and distance from home condensed into one wet, miserable memory. For those who found themselves living in crowded hostels, cut off from family and old friends, unable to speak English or make themselves understood in shops, buses or pubs, the sense of displacement was acute. While some new recruits to the brick industry were disoriented and homesick, others recall the sense of elation at finding a job and a roof overhead and going to bed without fear of bombardment. Giuseppe Ritaccio was one of the first arrivals and, after traumatic wartime experience and post-war starvation, he felt as if he had landed 'in heaven'.

Bedford was a long way from Campania, but the Italian community gradually adjusted to the unfamiliar environment, especially after wives and families arrived to join their brickmaking menfolk. Within a few years, the town had its own Italian nursery and a new Catholic church on the Woburn Road, a few hundred yards from the statue of John Bunyan. If the tall concrete verticals and dove-grey façade of the 1960s church still stand out in a road of red-brick houses, St Frances Cabrini's is really a symbol of an immigrant community settling into place. Santa Francesca is the patron saint of emigrants and travellers, which is why Milan Central Station is also dedicated to her. In July, each year, the streets of Bedford come alive with Italian music, dancing, flags, gelati, pizzas and classic cars – Fiats and Lancias, Lamborghinis and Ferraris are all part of the Festa Italiana. What brought the waves of Italians to Bedford may be rapidly receding into the past, but the unlikely cultural legacy of the brickworks remains.

When the Stewartby brickworks closed in 2008, four of the tall, elegantly concave brick chimneys were preserved as a monument to the local industry. Whatever the speed of those passing on the A421, the name 'STEWARTBY' was clearly visible in long, white, vertical letters painted on dirty, faded brick. A few years later, Hanson, who took over the site from the LBC, lodged an application to demolish the old chimneys for reasons of safety. Despite a local campaign to save the gargantuan reminders of Stewartby's industrial heritage and Historic England's support for the preservation of these Grade 2 listed buildings, the days of the four chimneys were numbered. On 26 September 2021, a controlled explosion blew apart the base of the last survivor, causing a massive cloud of buff-coloured dust and seismic waves across the nearby lake. The final chimney crashed down before a crowd of spectators. Already a new estate is under construction. Those who lament the loss of the local landmark and all that it means to them are being appeased by the prospect of a replica chimney to tower over the new houses. Cloud Wing, the company masterminding the transformation of Stewartby, have adopted what is clearly intended to be a reassuring mission statement: 'Building communities, one brick at a time.' But there are residents who were under the impression that they already belonged to a community and remembered making bricks.

Dirty brick factories were not always popular in the neighbour-hoods they dominated, especially when these were rural. Huge, smoking chimneys emerge from grainy, greyscale photographs, amidst farms and scattered cottages, with spreading elms and oaks standing as dim markers along the eccentric lines of old pastures and cornfields. Brick lorries rattling round sharp bends on rural roads made a big impression on local children – as well as their mothers, though for different reasons. Chris Gassor, who grew up in the same village as Jean and Hector Crawford, recalls how they would spot bricks flying off the lorries into hedges and ditches and race to collect them in the hope of being rewarded with a sixpence from the driver.

Why would anyone lament the disappearance of something regarded as an eyesore, a health hazard and a danger to children? But the days of brick production are often remembered fondly. Those working in the factories might have to travel several miles by bus, train or bike, which made the plant an alternative centre of gravity. The brick factories had their own sports teams and social clubs, cafeterias and Christmas parties. Old photographs of sports matches and social get-togethers tell a very different story from those blurred by streaming smoke.

During the 1970s, it began to dawn on the London Brick Company that their quarries were more profitable than their bricks. As lorryloads of imported bricks began to pour into British building sites, rising costs made the market more difficult. Brick production was in decline, but rubbish production was not. Gaping clay pits were ready for refuse and the LBC soon realised the potential of landfill sites. Soon brick-shaped containers were chugging between London and Bedfordshire, under the LBC's new company name, 'Easidispose'. Since then, rubbish has become rather less easy to dispose of underground and the company has been renamed Shanks. From brickworks to landfill sites to incinerators: the claggiest spots have their own metamorphoses.

All along the clay crescent from the Wash to Southampton, old brickworks and empty pits have been repurposed. New community woodlands are being planted across Marston Vale. Already there are outcrops of young trees, with paths and picnic tables and promises of a woody future. The youngest saplings, little more than upright twigs in plastic tubes, look like tiny versions of the vanished forest of brick-red chimneys. From the country churchyard where Hector Crawford was buried in 2004, you can see the new chimney of the incinerator. On the pale green mound beyond the fields where he once herded the cows, the smouldering tip of a tall cigarette signals its presence. The last chimney at his brick factory was demolished in 1995, and since then, new houses have been built on the site and the huge clay pits transformed into a Nature Reserve. The sheltered lakes offer a safe place for inland sailing as well as for kingfishers, wild duck and geese (at least until the HS2 works began to destroy the old oaks and the surrounding woodland). Near Peterborough, the Forterra Brickworks still produces lorryloads of bricks. At its side is the King's Dyke Nature Reserve. What was once a cavernous clay pit has filled with water and reeds, with dragonflies, moths, frogs, newts and waterbirds. It is only a stone's throw from the lost Whittlesea Mere.

Red Caves

~

It was too early in the year for bluebells. A greyish, unremarkable morning, too light for rain, too dull for much colour. Still, I like to walk along the road, across the field, up the hill and into what is left of the old ash wood that divides the neighbouring farms. Before the woodland floor turns blue and the canopy light green, the tangles of bramble and ragged hedgerows are sprouting white clusters and the beginnings of spring leaves. The atmosphere in the wood is already different from last week and though the high, black buds on the ash twigs look the same from the ground, there's an air of swelling imminence. As the two dogs rootle about, heads down among sticks and dead leaves, a squirrel makes its way along a high branch before slipping away through the taller trees. I can just see it land and run along the hedge on the far side of the wood, before disappearing. Not much further along, the dark scruffy outline of the hedge turns lighter. It looks as if a large waft of old-man's-beard is covering the top, but, getting closer, I can see that it's thicker and much more solid. In a gap in the hedge, a sheep is stuck between the barbed-wire fence and an enormous bramble patch. It is shaking with agitation, eyes frightened and protruding.

Sheep, in my experience, are not usually good at reversing out of fences. I have often tried to encourage a sheep whose head is rammed into a wide-mesh wire fence to back out, but instinct always seems to drive them forward instead. This one was in a quite different and worse predicament. Its hind leg was caught between the top of the wire fence and the barbed wire, haunch wrenched upwards in what looked a very painful position. An instinct to move forwards in this instance would surely be disastrous. As my dogs were not helping to soothe its nerves, I tied their leads to a low-lying branch a little way off and attempted to calm the sheep. It was hard to know how it had got into quite such a position – or how long ago. Perhaps the sheep had tried and failed to clear the fence, landing heavily with one leg trailing. As it tried to break free, the wires must have tightened into an iron clamp. My attempts to pull them apart were too feeble to do much, though I hope the trapped, exhausted animal realised that I was trying to help. With no one else around, no obvious flock nearby and no idea of whose it might be, it was difficult to rally assistance.

By now my dogs, displeased by the disruption to their walk and disconcerted to find themselves abandoned under a holly bush, were making their presence known. Somewhere in my mind was an image of pulleys and levers, an idea that adding weight to a lever increased the force. Not far off, I found a strong and reasonably long stick, which could just be wedged between the wires and forced nearer to the sheep's trapped hind leg. With a slow see-saw and then as much weight as I could muster, the tight barbed wire was forced out a little and then, with a terrified jerk, the sheep lunged forward and the leg was free. Now it was in the bramble bush, but the thick fleece was a cushion against serious damage as panic propelled it forwards, sideways, round and out. In no time the sheep had charged through the undergrowth and come to a halt in a small grassy clearing. It was limping but alive and surprisingly mobile, so the best plan was to rescue my frantic dogs and take them firmly in the opposite direction.

We were all agitated now, though the dogs quickly reverted to their usual activities. I was scratched, shaken, but mostly worrying about whether the sheep needed a vet, water or, at the very least, the rest of its flock. But it wasn't at all clear where it had come from, so all I could do was go home and try to find out which farmer to phone. After a few calls to friends and neighbours, including the nearest sheep farmer, I got a call back from Jason, who usually knows these things, telling me that he would let the likely owner know. There was nothing more to be done, though when I walked up to the ash wood a few days later, a fat, contented sheep was grazing happily in the grassy clearing, with no sign of distress or ailment.

The question of how a stray sheep finds its way back to the right flock continued to puzzle me. There are plenty of stories and poems about hardy shepherds setting off in all weathers to ensure the safety of their flock, or of trusty sheepdogs sniffing out ewes buried in snowdrifts twenty feet deep, but it hadn't really occurred to me how farmers recognise lost sheep as their own. It was something to do with ear tags or marks on the fleece – most of the sheep in the field next to our garden have smudgy red blobs on their haunches. My rescue sheep had nothing obvious to set it apart from any others. Admittedly, I had not examined it very closely, and even if I had, it wouldn't have helped me identify its owner. A sheep in the wrong place turned out to be another red door, unexpected because of its ordinariness and proximity to home.

I found myself thinking of hillier country, of stone walls running up the steep side of fells, of Herdwick sheep roaming across the high slopes, and sometimes sitting on the tiniest mountain tracks, impervious to oncoming cars. The stray sheep caught in the wire could not have come very far in a countryside chequered with hedges, fences and roads, but how do the hill farmers keep tabs on their roaming flocks?

An old *Shepherd's Guide*, unearthed from the bowels of the Bodleian Library, shed light on the mystery. William Hodgson's *Guide*, published in Ulverston in 1849, began with a set of 'rules', reminding us that 'the duty of every person . . . when he sees a stray sheep' is 'to take care of it' until, with the help of the *Guide*, the sheep's owner can be found. The need for such a manual was reinforced by a further warning: those hanging on to a stray sheep for 'too long' risked prosecution. How long was 'too long' is unspecified. The *Guide* itself consists of pages and pages of small engravings depicting sheep in profile, with red spots painted on by hand to indicate the distinctive marks used by different farmers. In the Millom area, Myles Tower's sheep were distinguished by two red strokes over both shoulders, John Whineray of Sled Bank's by a large red cross on the far side, and Joseph Wood of Birk Moss's by a red pop on the shoulders and another on the short ribs of the near side. Shepherds in Bootle, Eskdale, Wasdale, Ennerdale and Crosby Ravensworth all had their own systems of noughts and crosses, and all were carefully recorded to keep them in place. I have seen sheep with red marks many times, without stopping to think about why. I'd never thought of the red smears as a code of ownership, a language legible to the initiated. A 'pop' or 'stroke' of something red certainly sounds preferable to a red-hot iron brand, as far as the sheep were concerned.

There are more up to date authorities on marking sheep, but I like being led through the fells and farms of the southern Lakes by these red-spotted Victorians. William Hodgson knew his Cumbrian villages and his audience. 'Twinters', he announced at the start, were 'generally reddled on the back of the head'. Twinters seem to be two-year-old (or two-winters-old) sheep, but what exactly is reddle?

An imaginary hill walk through the Lake District took a sudden turn towards Dorset, as memories of *The Return of the Native* began to stir, throwing up an image of the reddleman, Diggory Venn. Hardy was at pains to point out that there was nothing too mysterious about Diggory, while also revelling in the old suspicions surrounding the solitary figures who plied his trade. A first encounter with a 'blood-coloured' Wessex reddleman was enough to strike fear into the stoutest heart. Generations of mothers kept their broods in check by whispering, 'The reddleman is coming for you!' The men who earned their living travelling from farm to farm with supplies of reddle were usually coated from head to foot in the bright red powder. Their customers mixed it with oil to make a thick, red paste for applying to fleeces. During the mating season, tups – or rams – have reddled chests, too, which means the ewes they encounter are left carrying tell-tale posterior smudges (this also explains the red-smudged sheep-rears in our neighbour's field). But where did the reddlemen pick up their wares? Hardy speaks of the 'pits' where men like Diggory Venn fill their carts, but he was more interested in the fate of their trade than the source of their stock, as railways steadily took over the ancient supply chains. The last reddle pedlar in Dorset was probably Mary-Ann Bull, whom Hardy and his friend Hermann Lea described in 1913, alone 'with her ancient pony and still more ancient vehicle . . . selling silver-sand, peat, reddle' across rural Dorset and neighbouring counties.

Reddle, or as it is also called, raddle, ruddle, or red ochre, comes from the earth. In the Forest of Dean, they know all about the treasures underground. Here, reddle has been dragged up to the surface for some seven thousand years. And yet, though so deeply embedded in place, the red veins running through the forest take a little time to find. I've driven through the Forest of Dean many times, admiring the tall oaks and the way the roads wind through wooded valleys, but not always thinking about the local industries hidden within the trees. I've walked here, too, through the trees, over rocks, along the banks of the Wye. Once I spent a night under canvas – or rather nylon – in a campsite near Symonds Yat. From the commanding stone, you look down on the swaying layers of mixed green treetops, on the river flecked with kayaks and canoes, curling its way through the trees. It's better to be closer to the forest floor, however, if you want to find red ochre.

On a fine July day, it is hard to match this summer-holiday site with William Camden's description of the 'wonderfull thicke

Forrest . . . so dark and terrible, by reason of crooked and winding ways'. In his day, those who lived in 'the grisly shade' had a reputation for being 'fierce, and bolder to commit robberies', though even in 1637, the woods were beginning to thin out as iron mining moved in. As the forest has grown older, it has gradually shrunk and shrunk. The thick bristles on the brows of the hills have thinned, the wooded valleys lightened. The shade no longer seems grisly. This makes it easier to glimpse the trunks of tired brick chimneys among the trees, leaf-covered lines of iron tracks leading nowhere. A half-submerged tunnel opens in the undergrowth, but the mouth has been silenced by a rusty grid. Each year, the leaves dry, drop, and muffle any echoes from below.

The Foresters, as people who grow up here are proud to call themselves, are not in a hurry to lose their ancient identity. As the traditional local industries have disappeared, their value has come into sharp focus. In 1983, the Dean Heritage Centre opened at the old scrap metal yard at Soudley. Before the scrap metal merchants arrived, the site beside the brook had been a sawmill and, prior to that, a leatherboard factory. The nearby streams and ponds previously powered a corn mill, which in turn replaced an iron foundry. Past lives still congregate in places that have been working for centuries. The Centre holds recordings of interviews with people who worked in the Forest of Dean: sheep farmers like Tom Preece; Mike Hinton from the tin plate works; Pat Harper and Pam Stratford, who worked at the pin factory; and several retired miners. Mervyn Fox was eighty-eight when he shared his vivid recollections of working in an iron ore pit with Jonathan Wright and Jason Griffiths. Old stories are now being dug up and preserved for future generations, oral deposits to be shaped into new meaning.

The tall pithead at Hopewell Colliery stands proud against a sweeping bank of spruce and chestnut trees, reminding motorists that this is mining country. Drivers on the road from Cannop to Coleford can hardly miss the high wheel at the top of the wooden tower. Another solid iron wheel, fixed vertically on the ground below, invites them to stop and find out more. The Freeminers of the Forest still work the old gale (a mine which is theirs by ancient right) and, for a small fee, will take curious travellers down into the tunnels to see the coal seams. Beside the car park, the café has books and maps and mining helmets, as well as home-made scones.

Not so far from Hopewell, a narrow lane leads downhill to the village of Clearwell, passing steep, grassy slopes with black sheep and saddleback pigs. Before reaching the village, the lane runs beneath a low stone building, surrounded by rusting engines, metal troughs, girders, oil cans, iron wheels and hazel bushes. On the grass just above, a worn brick chimney, set on a stone plinth, is set off by the falling copper leaves. It would all be quite easy to miss, were it not for the signs pointing to the Clearwell Caves.

There's something about the name that gives the place an inherent elusiveness. The alliterative words run off the tongue like a spell, conjuring natural magic. It's not difficult to imagine Merlin asleep in such a place. Deep in the forest, the ancient caves hold their secrets. But their claim to fame is mineral rather than magical. This is Britain's last working iron ore mine. And where our ancestors found iron ore, they also found red ochre.

A grey stone arch, round like a railway tunnel, frames the no-nonsense metal door. This is at once an old industrial site, with disused chimneys and bits of railway track, and a modern museum, with lights, tickets and instructions. Instead of rough caverns, the door opens onto clean glass cases. Carefully chosen objects, diagrams and explanatory labels are good for orienting visitors into the site's special geology and history, less so perhaps for its enchantment. Hopes of Merlin seem forlorn, though the search for reddle is successful enough.

In one of the cases, there are glass jars filled with bright powders, colours ranging from burnt sienna to scarlet. Ochre, yellow, red, brown, purple are arrayed like an apothecary's wares, or rather a paint-maker's ingredients. On the shelf below are the glowing iron oxide rocks, with the picks and scrapers that prised them from the ground. Once unearthed, rocks like this are smashed and washed, crushed and rinsed, until only pure oxide is left for grinding into powdery pigment. The substance put to practical use by Victorian sheep farmers had been prized by artists across the globe for millennia. Over thirty thousand years ago in the limestone caves of central France, artists were using these natural colours for murals, while on the far side of the world, indigenous Australians at Wilgie Mia had been working with red ochre even longer.

In gifted hands, images made with red ochre become eternal. From the cave paintings preserved in underground caverns to the drawings in galleries around the world, red ochre is the long lifeline of art. Both Leonardo da Vinci and Rembrandt rendered their bearded faces immortal with red ochre: *sanguine*, the blood chalk, transfused from the veins of the earth. Michelangelo took hold of *sanguine* to translate his vision of the Creation into awe-inspiring forms for the rest of us. Wise men and women have always mixed magic from these gifts of the earth.

A case of Celtic faces stares out. Carved stones with lozenge eyes, long noses and mouths that might be muttering to a friend are displayed on thin, steel spikes. One might be a woman. Her large, blank eyes would not look out of place among Picasso's *Demoiselles*. And yet her hair stands up like the canopy of a tree, which turns the great eyes into branches, the straight nose into a trunk. A depiction of an ancient earth goddess, perhaps, or an early version of Wittgenstein's rabbit-duck? A tree-woman, either way. Like all the stone heads, she is reddened with ochre, a blusher that has kept its colour for more than two thousand years. The stone tablets come from Littledean, a few miles east of Clearwell, but their purpose is less than clear. Pilgrims may have carried them as votive offerings for a shrine, or tributes to a river goddess. They might be prayer tablets or protective charms, or perhaps people just liked carrying images of their loved ones wherever they went. These odd little stones would fit neatly into an Iron

Age pocket or pouch. But, apparently, they may not be from the Iron Age at all.

There are rocks and stones on display, too. Unsculpted, but much more strangely shaped, the mineral deposits found in the caves might do well in a contemporary art competition. Creased and pleated, catching whatever light could be folded into its being, a cluster of calcite crystals encrusts a stalactite. A lump of brush ore resembles petrified iron filings, bristling towards an unknown lodestone. A small, petrified red-brown sponge, called *Michelinia*, lurks beneath a cluster of translucent yellow crystals on crease limestone. Shiniest of all is a crimson stone, with a hard, smooth, bubbling surface. Its official name is 'botryoidal haematite' and it is covered in red ochre. I can see why the miners called it 'kidney ore'. The Clearwell mines are crystal caves, running with blood.

Small, battered boots, soles caught at the point of flapping free, are suspended in the glass time capsules. Worn by children, they probably passed from brother to brother, to cousins and on to young sons. I wonder what happened to the last feet, the last fingers that pulled them on one morning before following the men into the mine.

As the objects come to an end, the ground and the temperature begin to fall. A tunnel, lined with long ladders and grey pipes, laid with rails and lit by a spotlight, runs straight down into the mine. Luckily, there is a gentler descent. The footpath, leaving daylight behind, roughens and drops down through spaces hollowed from rock. Low lights throw shadows high into the uncertain rocks and reveal a path pitted by what look like paw prints. Should we follow the tracks of an unknown pack or the discreet signs to deeper churns?

The path descends into the earth, which gradually opens into a large cavern. Above the space is a small, limpid lake. Perhaps this is the water which gave these caves their name? It looks rather muddy from above and turns out to be a tiny reservoir – clay walls rather than clear wells, crafted by miners who needed fresh water during dusty ten-hour days underground. Their way through the caves was lit by lights clamped between their teeth, clay pipes stuffed with candles instead of tobacco. No wonder they needed frequent drinks. Red dust coats the rocky walls and the gravel stones underfoot. Picking away at the rich seams hour after hour released clouds of gritty powder. By the time Mervyn Fox was working in the mines, carbide lamps offered a stronger light, but the smell of the gas brought its own challenges. The caves no longer smell of gas and the lights are low but reliable. If the air is dusty and unfamiliar, no one is breaking rocks or staying below ground for more than an hour or two.

Although it's November, there are a few other visitors, who appear at the far side of the bigger caves or emerge from behind a stalagmite. I can hear human voices, though the words are muffled. There are signs of activity everywhere, as if men are at work nearby, but not quite in the same cavern. A rusty truck is waiting to be filled, a length of steel rope coiled for use, a winch firmly sited on level ground, ready and waiting. A steel cylinder stands poised on four angular metal feet, as if for take-off. It is there to offer shelter in case of a sudden fall of debris: the small cavity is just big enough for a miner to take cover should the roof collapse. Chains lead up through a crevice in the cave roof, but the dusty tools at the bottom have been laid down. It is an odd mixture of the arranged and accidental, the old and impending.

In one of the bigger caves, a large red figure spreads across the ceiling, long arms and legs bending with the natural cracks and protrusions. 'The Ochre Man' was painted in 2022 by the street artist known as STIK. He made his red giant with ochre mined at Clearwell. It's quite a step from the Sistine Chapel.

The caves get quieter as you move further into the ground, but there is no sense of vacancy in the empty space. In the darkest recesses, horseshoe bats cling to the rock, wings folded round like black beechnuts, sleeping through the winter. Bats don't like to be bothered. They can rest easily in the underworld of caves, flying through the black spaces guided by the echoing darkness. There are red spiders down here, too, with long spindly legs. I am happy not to be able to see them.

I've never felt at ease underground. I'd always rather be in the fresh air, high on a mountain, out on a stretch of beach, in a field or wood. In the Catacombs in Rome, the weight of centuries hung heavily on the narrow winding paths through the dead. I couldn't wait to be climbing up and out into Italian sunlight. The world beneath the forest is different. Caves and churns spread like roots, pushing through the rocks, swelling into high caverns, squeezing into low tunnels. There's no telling where they might end. Some of the orifices are narrow, as if about to close, others open wide like the mouth of a giant turtle. The underground channels have grown over millennia, working their way deeper and wider, following the mineral seams. Mervyn Fox preferred coal mining to iron because the seams were level and predictable, whereas 'iron ore runs everywhere. You have to follow the lead. You kept going and it would open up.'

Red vaults run with white veins, crimson tunnels bulge with darker arteries. It is like being inside the belly of a dragon. Masses of large, reptilian eyes, red-brown with dark instead of white sclerae, stare from the wall of the cave. The rusty wheels, iron-rimmed with six curling spokes, are piled high. Somewhere water is dripping and there are faint, scrabbling noises. Alone in a tunnel, treading through a stony throat, I have a strong sense of someone walking silently behind. No other visitors are anywhere close, no voices or footsteps. But still there's a sense of someone watching, someone just around the last bend, or about to come into view. I don't feel threatened as much as watched over.

A little further on there is an iron door in the cave wall. It is firmly shut. The low-lit path continues round the bend, and I have no wish to stop and try opening the door into the red rock. The world on this side is strange enough. The quiet is deep, and different in character from the stillness of the November day. Clearer and older, somehow. It's as if time is held beneath the ground, immune to the regular cycles of night and day. Where no sunlight falls, the dark day is eternal. The caves are their own place, forever out of time. I have entered a parallel world governed by different rules. I don't know the rules and feel profoundly out of place.

As the path ascends slowly into the day, I touch the rough, stony walls to see whether my hands have turned red. Humans have been picking up stones from these mines for thousands of years, but it hadn't even crossed my mind to take home a loose pebble. In the small shop at the top, I can't see any reddle for sale, but among the pencils, pamphlets and postcards is a bowl of rocks marked 'Iron Ore'. The perfect memento of Clearwell Caves. I have it beside me now.

How our ancestors worked out that a lump like this could be refined and melted and moulded and cooled into strong, workable metal is hard to fathom. You could easily miss this stone completely. And yet, on closer inspection, I can see that this is no ordinary rock. From one side, it looks like the model of a mountain pike, except for the rough, powder-pink dust and pale speckles. If you turn it under bright light, the dull rock glitters, patches of rouge and white shining like ice against the dark, creased stone. On the other side, thin charcoal lines of rock cluster together like basalt columns scaled down for gnats and midges. It could almost be a miniature Staffa, if only it had a magic cave.

Fingal's Cave

~

The bar of luxury milk chocolate on my desk should have been eaten by 5 March 2015, so it's not a very tempting treat. I bought it for the cover rather than the contents. The golden foil is wrapped in paper printed in the subtle colours of an oil painting, with the title of the exhibition where it was displayed: 'Turner and the Sea'. The painting shows the evening sky in shades of dark blue and grey-green, seeping into the softer reds surrounding a sinking sun, as the sea below glows wine dark. In the foreground, you can just make out a pair of swooping seabirds above the surface of the surging waters. Along the hazy line where sea meets sky, the brown silhouette of a steamboat, funnelling coal-coloured smoke into the night air, is heading west. The vertical design of the chocolate wrapper accentuates the boat's tall chimney and parallel mast, while the stream of dark smoke signals the invisible fire harnessed in the hull. From this small slice of Turner's painting, the sea, the air and the whole world seem strangely warm. The original painting from which the confectionery designer tore a strip gives a very different impression. *Staffa, Fingal's Cave* is four feet across, with only a third of the canvas occupied by the sun and steamboat. The rest is a homage to the Hebridean island, where Fingal's Cave is visible through the haze and spray.

Although the sun has almost set in the right-hand side of the picture, Staffa is brightly lit from above as if by heavenly powers, while the mouth of the great cave seems to be vomiting out any dirty smoke from the boat's engine. The island is iridescent in opal pink and blue, rising from shining spume, while the cave itself is bright with white light. Turner's painting offers the natural wonder that is Fingal's Cave and the man-made wonder of the steamboat, but it's not difficult to see which awed him more. The boat, slinking off into the night, is dwarfed and dazzled by the island cavern. For those who saw the painting on its first public outing at the Royal Academy in 1832, the steamship was the very image of their progressive, reforming age, cutting through the mist and leaving the rough, old cave far behind. When I stood in front of the painting in the National Maritime Museum, on the other hand, it was the steamboat that seemed old-fashioned because the cave has changed very little. Each time I've been to Fingal's Cave, the sense of natural magnitude dwarfing human endeavour has been inescapable. Turner's painting amplified the feeling: a luminescent, natural arch opening into the unfathomable past.

When Turner embarked for Staffa, steamboats were a byword for innovation – proud products of an age of science, engineering and technological achievement. It was largely the launch of steam ferries in the Western Isles that made Turner's Hebridean expedition feasible. During the 1820s, people started to take day trips from Glasgow to Arran and Bute or Loch Lomond. Others were setting off from Oban to Mull and Iona, the Small Isles and even Skye. The new *Steam Boat Companion, and Stranger's Guide to the Western Islands and Highlands of Scotland* told them where to embark and what to see once aboard. By 1825 the guide was recommending new trips as far as Staffa direct from Glasgow: as Nigel Leask points out, it was now 'only a hop, skip and a jump from the Broomielaw to Fingal's Cave'.

By the time of Turner's arrival at Staffa in 1831, he was a seasoned traveller in his mid-fifties, but for most of his life, boats had moved with the winds. As the main purpose of his trip was to gather material for illustrating a new edition of Sir Walter Scott's poems, the noisy, steam-driven, tourist-laden ferry was a rather unlikely vehicle for imagining the merrily, merrily bounding bark in *The Lord of the Isles*. Scott's poem travelled back in time to the fourteenth century, long before the invention of steam or tourism. The new Scottish steamers, including the *Maid of Morven*, which carried Turner up the Sound of Mull and across to Staffa, had masts as well as engines – a belt-and-braces approach to the natural and manmade conditions. In Turner's painting of Fingal's Cave it is the power of steam that emphatically drives the boat, not sail. For better or worse, this was the technology of the future.

If Turner's picture hasn't changed since he finished it, attitudes to steamships certainly have. The cutting-edge engine gradually lost its sharp modernity and was rendered redundant by oil and electricity. The last surviving passenger steamboat in Scotland is called *Sir Walter Scott*. Lovingly polished and preserved for tourists in the Trossachs, she has been making trips up and down Loch Katrine since 1900, becoming more and more romantic as the years passed. What has been softened by nostalgia is now hardening once more. As the darker side of coal power dawns on the twenty-first century, Turner's atmospheric sunset has taken on a new complexion. That giant vomiting mouth was not perhaps reactionary after all, but prophetic.

The first time I saw Fingal's Cave directly was from the deck of a CalMac ferry. It was a day trip from Oban to Staffa and Iona – just like Turner's. We took the same route, admiring the bulk of the Ardnamurchan skyline to the east, remarkably unchanged from the drawing he sketched from the deck of the *Maid of Morven* in 1831. The ferry took us along the north coast of Mull with views across to Coll and Tiree and the open sea, before turning to head south for the Treshnish Isles. On a long summer day in the Hebrides, the sun was high and so was the general mood. The ferry was packed with passengers straining to spot whatever the

wide sea might have to offer. Gulls, seals and storm petrels, cormorants, gannets and terns, something that might have been a whale.
The waves were calm, the winds kind, the cameras and coffees to
the fore.

It was a bright, open-air kind of day for seeing Staffa, but even
so the island's ancient strangeness cast its spell across the water.
Admittedly I had come prepared – hoping – to be transported.
This is the stronghold of Fingal, the legendary hero, father of the
ancient Celtic bard, Ossian – Oisín, as he is known in Ireland.
When Turner was here, Fingal's Cave was even more famous than
it is today, thanks to a whole host of Romantic artists, writers and
musicians. I had been enchanted by proxy long before I saw Staffa.
I was following James Macpherson, whose creative translations of
the ancient legends of the Highlands had entranced late eighteenth-century Europe and made the names of Fingal and his
warrior band familiar to everyone. Napoleon, gripped by the
heroic deeds of old, had his grand palace at Malmaison adorned
with huge Ossianic paintings, but nothing could compare with
Nature's oceanic hall in the Hebrides. The CalMac ferry could not
take us right into Fingal's Cave, but we were close enough to see
the famous basalt pillars with the water chopping and churning
inside. The door into the dark was yawning open, yet there was no
chance of entering the great cavern. When I saw Turner's painting,
I could hear the Staffa sirens and knew that I had to go back.

Not so long afterwards, I set off for the Highlands and Islands
once again, this time in the footsteps of John Keats, who visited
Staffa in 1818 with his friend Charles Armitage Brown during a
very, very long walk from Lancaster to the Moray Firth. The
steamboat companies had yet to be invented so they were travelling on foot, with occasional carriage rides and sailing trips. They
had tramped across Mull through bogs and bare moorland, soaked
and famished, but imaginatively undiminished. Heading west
across the island by car from the Oban ferry, I couldn't help reflect-
ing that however much it might rain, travel in the twenty-first

century was plain sailing compared with what Keats experienced.

You can tell you are on the right track when you finally reach Fionnphort, a hamlet on the west tip of Mull, looking across to Iona. There's a one-storey building, with one door and one window, and a sign running right across: *Fingal Arts and Crafts*. The shop is on a rather smaller scale than Fingal's grand sea cave, but it's good to see him still doing his bit for the island economy. The green sign carries a faint hint of his Irish alias, Fionn MacCumhaill, and matches the bright grass of nearby fields when the sun is out. The name of the village means 'white port' in Gaelic – the same adjective that inspired blond Fionn/Fingal's name. The sand is as white as the shimmering beach on nearby Iona. In the Hebrides people inhabit the co-existent worlds of Gaelic, Scots and English, of land, sea and air. At the harbour, the name *Iolaire of Iona* is carved in the wooden prow of a small boat – the eagle of Iona. With only a few passengers, embarkation is quick. Within minutes the *Iolaire* is off, if not exactly flying, chugging from the quay to carry us to Staffa.

For the *Iolaire*'s skipper, Davy Kirkpatrick, the waters around Mull mean more than a workplace. He knows the tides and the currents, the rocks and the weather signs. He's been taking visitors out to the islands for years and knows all about the birds and marine life, the local boats and boatmen, and the history of trips. Two hundred years ago, before steam ferries and timetables, tourists had to rely on the local sailors. A small boat might wait for days until the wind was in the right direction for sailing to Staffa. Keats was lucky – a break in the dismal weather allowed a crossing from Iona and landing in Staffa, which is impossible in rough sea. As he was exhausted and not awash with cash, it was just as well. Crossing the open stretch between Iona and Staffa, I wondered how it might feel in a small sailing boat when the wind rises and the sea heaves and the rain gushes down. We were generously supplied with voluminous yellow oilskins, while a small open cabin kept a few passengers a little drier than the rest. The experience of moving between the islands is somehow fuller, more intensely felt, out on deck, drenched by the rain and saltwater.

Staffa is so odd that it can never cease to startle. Unchanged for millennia, it is still – and forever – out of place. Rising bolt upright from the sea, the small island is surrounded by strange floating shapes. Bac Mór, a huge grey-green submarine of an island, is known as the Dutchman's Cap, though which giant Dutchman dropped his hat here seems unimportant. Beside the broad back of emerald Lunga is the low line of Fladda, even flatter than the rest. The minke whales that surface here might easily pass for new volcanic islands, erupting momentarily from their own element before disappearing again. A land-and-seascape without trees, with little shelter except for big, bald rocks or the ruins of a shieling.

Basalt Staffa, jutting from the waves, mocks the bare horizon with mysteries of its own. Its face changes with the light. As a dark silhouette, it could almost be a giant crab rising from the deep, but at times the sun catches the concertina cliff, warming it golden brown. Suddenly Staffa's a tight forest of strong, straight trunks with a bushy canopy – as if a secret wooded island has been turned to stone. It almost looks as if it might sail away or dive down into the depths of the ocean: if you came on the wrong day, it seems, there would be nothing there at all. Sea caves crack Staffa's sides like secret doors leading down to the centre of the Earth or up into the clouds. The great cave on the southern side troubles the tight regularity of the basalt columns: an inverted heart, or an old, creased, Cyclops eye, staring out to sea. The shape-changing cavern grows and shrinks, lighter and darker, inviting and repelling as the tide swells and falls. A flat, black infinite mirror, hanging by a tarry thread and promising refuge from the present, whenever the present might be.

Since the huge hexagonal pillars of Staffa have been standing up straight from the waves for at least two million years, we might have got used to them by now. But wherever rows of basalt columns survive, they demand attention. Ancient volcanic eruptions across the world have left vast columnar outcrops, from Moses Coulee

Canyon in Washington State to the Deccan Traps in India or the Svartifoss waterfall in Iceland. Often these striking formations inspire some trepidation, judging by names such as Devils Tower in Wyoming or Devils Postpile in California. Much closer to Fingal's Cave is the Giant's Causeway in County Antrim, little more than a stone's throw across the Irish Sea, if you happen to be a giant. Where the Causeway is part of Ireland, reachable by car and mediated by the modern visitor centre, Fingal's Cave keeps its secrets far out at sea.

Those who told tales of Fionn building a Causeway from the Giant's Chimneys to his Scottish island cave were clearly familiar with both. They recognised the geological resemblances and made sense of them in their own way. The unaccountable appearance of Ailsa Craig was also put down to Fionn's heroic feats of strength. We are now more inclined to believe that the hard, hexagonal rocks were once hot, fluid extrusions of the volatile Earth. As molten lava, hurled into the air by shifting tectonic plates, cooled, contracting, cracking and re-erupting over millions of years, the black, even columns of basalt were left exposed in their perfect symmetries. It is no wonder that people coming across them far out at sea assumed they were the work of a great Designer – whether Giant or God or Devil, or goodness knows what.

Modern geological theories on the origin of hexagonal basalt only increase the frisson of fear at the site of primordial cataclysm, however far in the past. If you are unaware of the science, the instinctive unease over something so strikingly unusual may be even stronger. Drawing closer to Fingal's Cave in a small boat, I felt as if we were about to be sucked into the gaping, striated jaws of a vast basking shark. Davy, less over-awed by a shoreline he'd seen a thousand times, simply swung the *Iolaire* round to take the eastern seaboard. We moored soon afterwards in a narrow inlet where the ridged rocks are scooped and stretched like a gigantic petrified shell – the perfect entrance to a magical marine kingdom, soaked by rain and sea spray. Davy, conscious that his passengers might not necessarily notice what was there, pointed out the dim features of a bearded man in the rock formation above the dark entrance of Clamshell Cave.

To reach Fingal's Cave means a walk along the cliffside on the tops of truncated columns, hexagon after hexagon. On a stormy day, the sea below hurls against the rocks, warning all comers to tread very carefully. This was not a moment to be overly rapt by the poetry of the place – a careless step could be fatal. The path to Fingal's Cave offers raw experience, felt on the wind and under-foot. My abiding memory of Staffa is of standing on the narrow path along the wet cliff edge as the wind whipped off the sea, hoping that a stumble didn't send me over the edge. As it is so bare and hard, there's no risk from a crumbling stone or the slippery deception of long grass, but the nearness of the wild sea is enough to prompt a wobble. The bleak, black rocks and breakers below seemed all too close. Keats's cheerful description of the very same path as 'convenient stairs' is rather chastening.

On the day I was there, the noise of the rain and the wind and the waves was too insistent to catch the uncanny pauses that calmer weather might allow, but still the vast space filled with salty air and unfamiliar sounds. The roar in the cave echoed and rebounded, as the waves rushed against the rocks and fell into themselves. All around, and above, black pillars amplified, intensified, disappeared into the strange darkness. All was wet and unfamiliar. Nothing prepares you for Fingal's Cave.

Myth and memory ebb and flow. Sea caves echo with the sounds of waves, with gusts that carry human voices away and bring them back, if at all, chopped and changed. Keats imagined Lycidas sleep-ing here, on cold, bare marble in the 'cathedral of the sea'. But how to describe the experience? He thought of Aladdin's Cave, of Merlin's magical powers, of the Revelation of St John, but none were remotely right for Staffa. A place out of time, out of place. Fingal's Cave leaves people lost for words, subdued and scoured by overwhelming natural forces.

Not everyone sees like Keats. The practically minded Vikings on their way to sack Iona in the ninth century called the island 'Staffa' because of its most obvious physical distinction – the tightly packed pillars. In the right light, they bear a strong resemblance to bundles of gigantic wooden poles or 'staves'. The island reminded them of home, where buildings were constructed from pine-pole palisades, like the medieval church at Urnes in Norway. Place names accumulate meanings, just as places do. I like to think of 'Stave Island' as the vertical lines of rune-staves, with the angled rock fissures forming runic letters up and down the cliffs. Gannets perch on the illegible messages left by the ancient Earth for future millennia.

As the Vikings receded into legend, 'staves' tipped from vertical poles to horizontal lines, creating structure for music – which is just what Fingal's Cave does. Among local Gaelic speakers, it was sometimes known as the musical cave, *Uamh bhinn* – an idea that would have been congenial to many of the bewildered visitors who braved the short, choppy crossing from Mull to listen to the sounds of the sea cathedral. The music of the Cave, where 'mighty waters play / Hollow organs all the day' made a profound impression on Keats and everyone else who went to listen. The straight, even columns in the dark interior seemed to be the pipes of a mighty organ rising from the deep and played by the invisible wind. What could be more compelling than this grand phenomenon, creating music for the sheer pleasure of music-making? Here was a natural emblem of divine Creation.

Or so it seemed to some. The German diplomat and writer, Karl Klingemann, who visited Staffa with his friend Felix Mendelssohn, was deeply unsettled by finding himself inside this 'immense organ, black and resounding, and absolutely without purpose, and quite alone, the wide grey sea within and without'. Here, in a remote stretch of wild water, was a natural phenomenon mightier than any of man's achievements, sounding out its strange, unworldly music – for whom? The disconcerting concert in Staffa had the power to make listeners feel out of place and internally at sea. For Mendelssohn, violently seasick on the voyage across, it was all a churn of unfamiliar sounds and unwelcome sensations.

While visitors were thrown off balance by the unexpected experience of Fingal's Cave, the puffins nesting in the Treshnish Islands, the porpoises flitting between Tiree and Iona, the fishermen sailing the Hebridean waters knew all about Staffa. The island has occupied the same spot for millions of years, but it only moved into the world's spotlight after Joseph Banks and Daniel Solander stopped there on their way to Iceland in 1772. Banks had recently returned from exploring the South Seas with Captain Cook, laden with botanical treasures and full of remarkable tales about plants, people and countries unknown to Europeans. After such eye-opening global adventures, the British Isles seemed a bit tame. He was only anchoring off Mull for a few days before setting off again, north across the Atlantic. When Banks heard about a nearby island, which the locals claimed was as remarkable as the Giant's Causeway, it seemed worth taking a quick look. At the time, the 40,000 basalt columns in County Antrim were subject to intense scrutiny by contemporary geologists working on competing theories about the formation of the Earth. To find similar rocks in a remote Scottish island might potentially be of interest to the scientific community. Curiosity, as so often, paid off. Banks was staggered by Fingal's Cave – 'Compared to this, what are the cathedrals and palaces built by men!' When he got round to sharing the 'discovery' with the world a couple of years later, Staffa shot to international fame.

The guide who told Joseph Banks that this was Fingal's Cave may have been mistranslating *Uamh Bhinn*, 'the melodious cave' (as the Gaelic *bh* sounds similar to an English *v*), or he might have called it *Uamh Fhionn*, 'the cave of Fionn' – especially as the legendary Fingal was now well known thanks to Macpherson. Places make poems and poems make places. Where and when do local associations begin – with the hero of Gaelic folklore or with a bestselling poem in English about the hero of folklore? It is often hard to tell when the stories that 'everyone knows' were first told. Stories of Fionn and Oisín survive in the manuscripts of medieval Ireland, but who knows what was told around the fires on long winter nights in the islands? A sense of empty remoteness reflects very recent times: the population of Mull and Iona in 2021 was 1,800 people – a drop of some 9,000 since the early nineteenth century. The ruins of Lunga remind passing travellers that the island was once a living community. Even Staffa has had its homes and inhabitants. It had already been abandoned to the deer by the time Keats landed here. As people move, old stories can get left behind, especially when tied to a place now deserted. A burn, a cairn or a boulder on a beach shed much of their character when human companions of longstanding depart.

Joseph Banks put Staffa on the map. In Martin Martin's *Description of the Western Islands*, published only half a century earlier, a hand-drawn map unfolds from the front page to show the Outer Hebrides running north to south down the left side of a somewhat distorted Skye and shrunken Mull. Iona floats off Mull's northwest coast. Each is more reliably identified by the neat copperplate names than by any recognisable outline. You can spot the tiny islands of Gometra, Lunga, and even Bac, but search in vain for Staffa. Nor does Fingal's Cave get a mention in Martin's book. He may not have got as far as the west coast of Mull, because even Iona gets fairly short shrift. Perhaps the men and women he chatted with in Tobermory were more interested in the Spanish ship blown up in their harbour than in small, underpopulated islands off the coast.

It seems strange, now, that a natural phenomenon more remarkable than the ruined castles or standing stones that attracted serious antiquarian attention should go unnoticed for so long, but even the fame of the much more accessible Giant's Causeway only really took off in the 1740s. Fionn's Irish stronghold, with its own set of stone organ pipes, had always been there, too, but it took a skilful artist and a host of entrepreneurs to turn the volcanic formation into a visitor attraction. Curiosity about the Antrim coast was piqued by Susanna Drury's success in a Dublin art competition. Her remarkably accurate renditions of the corrugated rock face, towering above a party of Lilliputians in hooped dresses and frock coats, lent themselves to becoming very saleable prints. Almost at once, the Giant's Causeway was attracting widespread interest – and many visitors. In Drury's west-facing view of the basalt columns, tiny sails are just visible on the pale blue horizon, while the soft early morning light catches people crawling over rocks that resemble huge stacks of golden guineas. Her intricate water-colour is very different in style from Turner's swirling oil painting of *Staffa*, but just as prescient in its way. Keats planned to trek as far as the famous Giant's Causeway on his northern tour, but ran out of time, energy, cash and enthusiasm. Having failed to reach the geological wonder of Antrim, he was more excited than ever to be landing at Staffa.

Fingal's Cave was so famous by the early nineteenth century that many of those who made long, arduous journeys to the 'Cathedral of the Sea' were often disappointed – not by the natural wonder, but by having to share its magic. Poets, artists and musicians found their long-anticipated island inspiration somewhat stymied by all the other sensitive souls making similar creative pilgrimages. Wordsworth finally managed to visit Fingal's Cave at the age of seventy-three, only to find that he couldn't quite get the full experience with all those tourists milling about:

> Not one of us has felt the far-famed sight;
> How could we feel it? each the other's blight,
> Hurried and hurrying.

Like Turner, Wordsworth took a steam ferry, so should not have been quite so surprised to find fellow passengers at Fingal's Cave. Keats, arriving in a much smaller sailing boat twenty-five years earlier, had a little more reason to be put out by the 'fashion boats ... cravats and ... petticoats' he found when he finally arrived. Both had to admit they were themselves tourists, stopping for an hour or so in the age-old sea cavern. Both nevertheless felt compelled to compose poetry *after* the event.

However discombobulating, Fingal's Cave matters. The power of the island extends far beyond the moment of immediate experience. Once Mendelssohn recovered from the seasickness that ruined his rough crossing from Argyll, Staffa's ancient staves inspired the otherworldly pitch and atmospheric surges of his *Hebrides Overture*. And it was after Keats returned to Hampstead that the haunting sounds and shapes of Fingal's Cave rose up through cold winter days to take form in his epic, *Hyperion*. Like Turner's great painting of Staffa, the *Hebrides Overture* and *Hyperion* were created from mental sketches and memories of a place felt rather than understood. Each expresses the privilege and fear of being at the mercy of mysterious forces, of things beyond easy comprehension. An ancient site, permanently out of place for those who seek out its secrets, Staffa sinks into the mind to surface in its own time, taking shape in dreams during the dark hours of half-consciousness.

Red Springs

~

When John Keats returned from his trip to Scotland, he had more on his mind than Staffa. He was physically exhausted and suffering from a chronic sore throat. His younger brother Tom was desperately ill. With painful irony, the brothers were renting an apartment in Well Walk, Hampstead, less than half a mile from the Vale of Health. The road which runs from the High Street along Flask Walk and down to the Heath takes its name from a natural spring. The well is still easy to find, a few yards from where the Keats brothers once lived, opposite a house John Constable moved into some years after their departure. Classical in design, with its oval crest and sculpted botanical panels, the dove-grey stone fountain over the small arch looks rather like an altar, or a tomb. Flights of solid steps on either side invite ascent from the road below. A pink granite plaque on the plinth reminds passers-by to give thanks to Susanna Noel, the Countess of Gainsborough, and her young son, Baptist, for donating six acres of land, including the well, for the benefit of the poor:

Drink Traveller and with Strength renewed   Let a kind Thought be given
To Her who has thy thirst subdued   Then render Thanks to Heaven

Susanna made their generous gift in 1698, but the monument was raised almost two hundred years later, when a small village of some 600 souls had burgeoned into a Metropolitan Borough of over 45,000. In the great age of sanitation and sewers, the days of old wells were numbered, while magnificent drinking fountains were springing up everywhere. The new installation in Hampstead was not quite on the scale of Manchester's triumphant Jubilee Fountain, but it belongs to a similar wave of freshwater philanthropy.

I have always been intrigued by the 'well' in Well Walk. Years ago, when tracking James Macpherson and Ossian, I made trips across the Highlands and Islands to Speyside, Kingussie, Skye, Glencoe, and Staffa, but I also spent many days in Hampstead, where a very elderly Clan historian kindly allowed me access to his private archive. Regular visits to his house took me along Well Walk, past the pale monument with its enigmatic letters carved into smooth stone: 'Chalybeate Well'. What did it mean? I didn't even know how to pronounce it, where the stresses should fall in this mysterious name. Chalybeate, chalybeate. It is not a word that slips away easily: once noticed, the word remains inscribed in the mind, the clean incisions softening with the passage of time, but somehow leaving an indelible mark.

I re-encountered 'chalybeate' more recently, when staying in Yorkshire. I have now found out that chalybeate is a natural mineral water infused with iron, and that the name was inspired by the Chalybs, who were once famous for making steel. They lived and worked along the northern coast of Anatolia and were known to the Ancient Greeks as iron merchants and metalworkers. The *ch* in 'chalybeate', being Greek in origin, is not soft on the tongue like Charlie, but crisp and hard, as in Christopher. Strange that English springs should remind anyone of ancient ironsmiths on the Black Sea, but when the adjective was coined in the seventeenth century, scientists were almost as immersed in classical learning as in modern experiments. The Hampstead water fountain, with its gleaming grey stone and cold, rose-coloured granite, makes a suitable memorial to the old chalybeate spring and its iron-tinged waters. Though I didn't realise at the time, the 'well' in Well Walk was another of my red doors – it just remained unopened for many years.

Lady Gainsborough's far-sighted attitude to her spring, on the other hand, had immediate – and profound effects. Almost overnight, her gift transformed the boggy ground on the edge of the Heath into a booming health resort. A chalybeate spring in Kent had already demonstrated a highly beneficial influence on Tunbridge's invalids – and income. Mr John Duffield of Hampstead was quite sure that their own chalybeate waters were every bit as efficacious as those in Tunbridge Wells and rapidly set about developing a Pump Room, a Long Room and Assembly Rooms. Since apothecaries from London had been coming up to the Heath for years to collect medicinal plants, and many wealthy Londoners had retreated here during the Great Plague, it did not take much to convince people of the special healthiness of Hampstead. The red-brown water was bottled at the Lower Flask Tavern in Flask Walk and what wasn't sold on the spot would be loaded up for the City. The iron-enriched waters were at once a magnet and an export – while carriages carrying well-to-do patients rode up the hill, cartloads of well water went trundling down. In Fleet Street, Mr Philps the Apothecary offered threepenny flasks of Hampstead water for sale at the Eagle and Child, with a delivery service for those too ill or too rich to visit his stall.

Money flowed with the mineral water, and for a few decades, Hampstead Wells became as fashionable as Tunbridge and handier than Bath for the London trendsetters. But after George III began to favour the spa in Cheltenham, Hampstead's Chalybeate Well lost some of its lustre. Health, fashion and fortune seekers were now heading west once again. The springs in Well Walk were still flowing, but the income stream was steadily drying up. By the late nineteenth century, when the old spa buildings in Hampstead were demolished, the Chalybeate Well was fast becoming a detail of local history – quaint and out of place in the modern metropolis.

Health has its fads and fashions. A couple of centuries can witness the same natural springs turning from exciting discoveries to defining features to tourist attractions to yesterday's news, before disappearing entirely. The chalybeate spring at Scampton was well known during the Middle Ages but no longer features as one of Lincolnshire's 'Things to Do'. It lies buried somewhere in a field just outside the village, roughly in line with the end of the long runway across the road. Had it not been for the Rev. Cayley Illingworth's interest in the old Holy Well, it might have vanished entirely without leaving a trace. Illingworth did not explain why the spring was called after St Pancras: the story was probably long lost when he mentioned the well as an antiquarian curiosity in his 1808 village history. And when medieval pilgrims were refreshing themselves at the well dedicated to St Pancras, an early Christian martyr beheaded on the orders of the Emperor Diocletian, the Roman villa beside the spring was already buried in oblivion. Unknown to the pilgrims, the ground beneath them hid the remains of a bath house enjoyed by people who had worshipped different gods. And who might have flocked to the red spring before the Romans arrived? Natural phenomena can be found and lost, lost and found by successive generations, in place throughout, but not always part of the place. Whether old wells will ever again be recovered, or revered, may depend on summer temperatures in years to come.

The chalybeate well at Scampton never caught the eye of spa-inspired speculators in the eighteenth century, perhaps because it had always been there, perhaps because its old superstitious character no longer appealed, but more likely because no one spotted its potential. The springs that burst into the limelight were those seen as fresh discoveries – features of the landscape that surprised curious observers. Their wider fame then depended on how soon the report spread, on which businessman realised that rusty red spring water might turn into gold. The well that made Tunbridge a royal destination was first spotted by Dudley, Lord North, when he was convalescing in Kent. The tart spring water seems to have worked wonders for his various ailments, because he hurried back to court to tell his friends, who soon followed suit. In Cheltenham, it took the entrepreneurial spirit of Henry Skillicorne to seize on William Mason's initial discovery, enlarging the well, building the Pump Room and promoting the local spring-loving pigeons as a symbol of the growing town.

Harrogate's chalybeate waters caught the eye of a local gentleman called William Slingsby when he was out riding in the Forest of Knaresborough in 1571. As he had travelled on the Continent passing through the famous city of Spa, he recognised the distinctive, acidic taste of the natural spring. A few decades later, Edmund Dean, a successful doctor from York, followed up the story of Slingsby's discovery. One day in 1625, he set off into the forest with his friend Michael Stanhope. After crossing a 'rude and barren Moor', they found the spring, scummy brown with a metallic sheen, which did not immediately seem very appetising. Undeterred, Dean tested the peculiar qualities of the water by mixing it with crushed galls: instantly the phial turned deep claret. Stanhope was astonished: 'the water changed colour, and seemed to blush in behalf of the Country, who had amongst them so great a jewell and made no reckoning of it.'

The chalybeate spring quickly put Harrogate on the national health map – not least because the identification of one healing spring led to many more. Harrogate turned out to be a very leaky place, running with sulphur wells, chalybeate waters, hot and saline springs. In Bog's Field, which is now part of the peaceful, shady Valley Gardens at the heart of the town, there were as many as thirty-six natural springs. This was not entirely news to those who lived near 'Sour Acre', though the idea that such a smelly spot should be the place for health-giving dips and drinks was rather surprising. When Celia Fiennes visited Harrogate, her horse refused to go near the 'Sulphur or Stincking Spaw' because on top

of the overall smell of brimstone, it exuded 'an additional offen-
civeness like carrion or a jakes'.

In spite of the smells, the small, scattered moorland village steadily grew into a bustling town, with new buildings, ballrooms,
hotels, houses, assembly rooms and gardens around the spa. The
original spring, known as the Tewit Well after the lapwings that
flapped about it, continued to hold its own. For Celia Fiennes, the
chalybeate spring was the 'Sweete Spaw', reminiscent of Tunbridge,
and an altogether pleasanter experience than the wells of Lower
Harrogate. The barren moor in the forest was steadily turning into
an elegant promenade on the edge of Harrogate, ideally placed for
visitors approaching from Leeds. The old well is still surrounded
by grass and scattered trees, and a more immediate rotunda of
neoclassical columns – a modest temple to health and to Harrogate's
prosperity. The path across the Stray near the Tewit Well is lit by
spring cherry blossom, blushing annually as if to recall the centuries of neglect before the doctors arrived.

Well-watered Harrogate's unrivalled position as the Spa of the
North did not last very long. While Edmund Dean was doing his
investigations in the great Forest of Knaresborough, the ferrugin-
ous waters that filter through Yorkshire limestone were also quietly
dripping away into the sea. In the same year that Dean and
Stanhope rushed into print with their news of Harrogate's healing
water, the newly widowed Thomasin Farrer was taking regular
walks along the beach beneath her home in Scarborough. One
morning, her eye was caught by the colour of the cliffs. At the foot
of a long crevice in the cracked sandy limestone was a red stain. It
looked as if the cliff were recovering from a wound, blood mixing
with water as it oozed and spread. When she went to investigate,
she found coloured water spurting from the rocks. It tasted rather
odd – neither pure as freshwater from a mountain stream, nor as
salty as the sea. There was something tart about it, slightly acidic,
almost metallic. But not unpleasant. In fact, she liked it rather a lot.

Whether Thomasin Farrer had read about Dr Dean's discovery

or was simply an observant woman with an enquiring mind is unclear, but as a wealthy widow, she was in a better position than many to please herself. She started collecting the cliff water for her own decanters to sip and share with special friends. Gradually the water's reputation spread, until another York doctor, Robert Whittie, hearing so many of his patients swear by Scarborough Spaw, decided to investigate. He was not disappointed and left an excited description of the well 'at the foot of an exceeding high cliff, arising upright out of the Earth like a boyling pot'. It flowed constantly, 'affording above twenty-four gallons of water in an hour'. Once identified as a chalybeate spring, Thomasin's red door in the cliff was open to all.

It was only a matter of time before the old fishing port of Scarborough, variously a Viking settlement, medieval fairground, friary, Royalist stronghold and Parliamentarian prison, became better known as a spa. When Celia Fiennes rode into Scarborough during her great northern journey of 1697, she was delighted by the 'very pretty Sea-port town' with its high hill jutting out to sea and the great expanse of firm sands. She was happy to abandon her side-saddle and walk along the shore, watching ships sailing south towards the Humber or north to Newcastle. What diverted her most, though, were the well-dressed ladies and gentlemen who tripped across the sand twice a day at low tide to reach Scarborough Spaw – not least because, as far as she could see, the water sold there was just seawater and no different from what came bubbling out of little springs all over the sands. Visitors might be told that the Spaw water was tinged with mineral salts, 'vitriol, alum, iron, and perhaps sulphur', but Celia remained unconvinced.

Whatever a few sceptical visitors might think about the waters, the good fortune bursting from Scarborough's springs was in full flow. By the time Francis Nicholson was born in nearby Pickering in 1753, it was obvious that for any aspiring Yorkshire artist, Scarborough was the place to be. Nicholson knew how to turn out delicate watercolours for wealthy tourists at a remarkable rate: during the longer hours of the summer, he could finish six in a day. His many watercolours of the South Bay show the Spa at the foot of the cliffs, set apart from the rest of the town by the curve of the rock face and the wide V-shaped valley that cuts through the cliff. The beach is packed with busy figures, servants with bags and boxes, and horse-drawn carriages for those who worried about getting their silken skirts sandy or their buckled shoes wet. A view from the rocks further round the bay shows determined tourists descending steeply down a broad, zigzag path from the clifftop. Everyone is heading for what looks like a simple farmhouse with pantile roof and a stable block beside. It is the town's main attraction in its Georgian heyday: the famous Scarborough Spaw.

Once doctors began to prescribe sea bathing as well as mineral waters, Scarborough's success was firmly afloat. Unlike Harrogate or Hampstead, Tunbridge, Bath or Cheltenham, Scarborough had a spa and a beach. It was one of the few resorts in the whole of Europe to offer such a double dollop of health. Brow, near Annan, also had a chalybeate spring beside the sea, but never grew to more than a few houses and an inn. Whether people were wary of the Solway's unpredictable tides or because no entrepreneur had spotted the business opportunity, Brow missed the boat when it came to the seaside spa boom. The well is still there, walled in by bare, red stones in a grave-like hole in the ground, serving as a modern shrine to Brow's most famous patient. Neither the iron-infused waters nor the sea could save Robert Burns.

Scarborough's fortunes, on the other hand, remained buoyant. The town featured, along with Harrogate, in Tobias Smollett's comic novel *The Expedition of Humphry Clinker*, but Matthew Bramble, its central hypochondriac, made a much more memorable stop at the seaside spa. Nicholson's Scarborough watercolours are generally bathed in soft sunlight, while members of the gentle sex are transported discreetly into the sea in bathing machines. In Smollett's more rumbustious creation, Matthew Bramble descends from a bathing machine into the freezing sea and lets out a shriek at the cold, which prompts immediate rescue from the waves by his devoted servant Humphry Clinker, with the ultimate embarrassment of total exposure. Everywhere he goes from then on, Bramble is pointed out as 'the monster that was hauled naked a-shore upon the beach'. As a medical man, Smollett was well aware of Scarborough's appeal to wealthy patients – as a writer, alert to the comic potential of hydrotherapy in all its glory. Richard Brinsley Sheridan, whose pen warmed to the variety of life in Bath, was just as quick to see the rich possibilities of transporting parties to a northern spa on the beach. When he took over the Theatre Royal in Drury Lane, he dusted down Vanbrugh's old comedy *The Relapse* and sent Lord Foppington north for his wedding to a Yorkshire heiress, daughter of Sir Tunbelly Clumsey. Once repackaged as *A Trip to Scarborough*, Sheridan knew London audiences would come flocking to his stage spa as eagerly as the pigeons at Cheltenham's chalybeate spring.

A walk through the elegant streets above the South Cliff, with their tall, white terraces and straight flights of iron steps running up to the front doors, makes it easy to imagine Scarborough in the days of crinolines, petticoats and periwigs – though how the silk-clad sojourners coped with the sand is more of a puzzle. From the finely proportioned Esplanade on top of the cliffs, the sea lies outstretched, with small boats chugging past the lighthouse at the old harbour mouth. On the horizon, the silhouettes of trawlers and ocean-going tankers hardly seem to be moving. The sun catches the white triangular sails of small dinghies and surfboards against the deep aquamarine of the sheltered bay, where tiny swimmers, almost as white, strike out into the deeper waters. The castle sits on the great rock above, commanding the coast despite broken walls and gashed towers.

Across the valley, the elegant iron walkway takes you high above the road to the seafront. Although the view of the town has changed since Smollett's day and the noise of the traffic rises from car engines rather than carriage wheels, the castle, the lighthouse, the bay and the outstretched headlands sweeping away to the south are much the same as ever. The outline of the great, flat castle rock, sloping into the sea like a basking sperm whale, landed in my mind long ago and the memory resurfaces with every re-encounter. I came here on my first school trip at the age of five. All I can remember is the castle on the headland, the lighthouse, the sand, and a cold wind – and constant fierce commands from the teachers about keeping together and not going into the water. For a small person used to paddling, it was all a bit puzzling. A long bus journey to the seaside and then – no sea.

Between the Esplanade and the road below, vigorous sycamores cover the limestone cliffs in thick green leaves through the summer. Walks to the sand meander gently through the sloping gardens: down and down through an open-ended maze. The sandy beach is still full of children, picking up shells, splashing into the shallows, surfing on rollers, staring into rock pools, riding donkeys, flying kites, playing frisbee, football, French cricket, or wielding buckets and spades for building castles. The harbour jostles with small yachts and fishing boats laden with lobster pots and weathered nets. In August, the smell of fish, fresh seafood and salt hangs over the beach, blending with candyfloss and fizzy drinks. The rock shops sell sugar-shells and cerise-coated sticks, with Scarborough's circular name legible in the shiny white sugar. Above the beach is a string of arcades, fish and chip shops, kiosks, cafés, outdoor tables hidden under big brown teapots, gargantuan ice creams and slices of cake as big as the plates.

In bright sunlight, the arcades are dark at first, but the flashing lights and virtual car chases create a place open to all and yet oddly removed. Luminous soft toys lie in seemingly accessible heaps, though the overhead hooks and claws move unpredictably, disappointingly. Copper mountains teeter on the brink. If only you have the patience to time the drop of a coin, a happy crash adds a percussive crescendo to the electric squeals, pot shots and gasps that play over bursts from a Sooty and Sweep mechanical band. A miss doesn't matter – you can always have another go. If the mechanics of the games have changed over the centuries, the principles – and the prevailing sense of fun – are much the same.

It's different in January. The arcades and the cafés are mostly open, but the town is quieter. A winter wind is ripping across the bay, whisking the breakers and propelling the gulls. And yet, the broad sweep of the beach gleams just as brightly, as the tide retreats and a few hardy donkeys stand waiting for riders. Scarlet and citric puffer jackets on the prom send long reflections across the wet beach, tinting the sand beneath the transparent sheet of water with primary colours. When the tide is not too high and the wind drops, the beach is scattered with dog walkers, joggers, elderly couples, determined parents with cocooned toddlers and the odd out-of-season tourist. There are even a few wild swimmers braving the waves, though not for very many minutes.

Towards the Spa, across the firm sand, below the cliffs, below the promenade, the salt water runs out through shallow channels, filling deeper pools before flowing down into the sea. Low ridges of shining sand run horizontally, between blurred, dissolving foot-steps, broken razorshells and driftwood. Seawater spreads across the beach with slow-moving shapes of fluid white. Standing in thin surf, you look down to the tawny sand through a miniature archipelago of flat, floating islands, shifting and reshaping, trans-formed by a bubble or the movement of a boot. Jura, Islay, Rum, Canna, Mull, stretching into Skye or Lewis or Shetland, before breaking into Soay, Raasay, the Orkneys, until the next white breaker chases them all away. The waves wash across the beach, swilling away former lives. There's no trace now of the bathing machines, the horse and carriages, the velvet gentlemen or the long-skirted ladies and their maids. *Begin again, begin again*, the whisper of the waves backs the calling gulls.

The Spa still sits at the foot of the South Cliff. From a distance it looks somewhere between an ambitious sandcastle and a modest French chateau, round tops shining on each corner and at the centre, a larger dome. The base, rising above the beach, is pitted with dark cavities. Beside the main hall, a low colonnade stretches out, white as the line of the tide. A low glass dome catches the light, lying ready to reflect the morning sun or shine on a moonlit night. At the far end, before the vertical chessboard wall and the brightly painted beach huts, glass stairways and towers join the colonnade to the Ocean Room, with its rows of croquet-hoop windows. This is a place in perpetual transition, it seems to say, proud to change with the times.

Beneath the Spa buildings, between the beach and the car park, a flight of weathered steps curves down the solid sea wall. In a small arched alcove towards the bottom is what remains of the original red spring, trickling over dark bruised stone, with a dull red gash in the middle. It is easy to miss the spot from which everything started. There is nothing on the scale of the Chalybeate Well in Hampstead to remind all comers of Thomasin Farrer's fortunate find. But the Spa has long since assumed a life of its own – and has always been ready to move forward. Thomasin's name is remembered in the building above, where you can buy a drink in Farrer's Bar.

Along the shore a low wall stretches as sinuously as a basking sea serpent, its concave curves sending stronger waves crashing back on themselves with a resounding hiss. On a fine day, it's exciting to balance on the edge, waiting for a big wave to rush in, rear up and drop back into the sea. When the North Sea is battering the coast, it is rather too exciting to stand here.

The lofty white hotels and houses along the top of the cliff, the glassy Spa and the bright beach chalets at the foot, are all at risk from the crumbling stone, as the winter rain, wind and sea pound away. The rock above the Spa is currently barer than the stretch nearer the valley. A massive engineering project designed to strengthen the limestone by driving in steel piles has left it exposed

– and fortified for whatever lies ahead. The elements that combined to secure the Spa's success have periodically joined forces to threaten its survival – water, earth, air and even fire have done their worst, and yet still, the Spa survives.

At the height of its early fame, Scarborough Spaw was brought low by huge waves hitting the cliffs, sweeping away the wooden staithe and weakening the building. Not long afterwards, rocks rolled down on top of it. Luckily the first owner, Dickie Dickinson, was an irrepressible character, who soon had a bigger and better Spa ready for summer visitors. Within a year, the wharf was damaged again and the red springs disappeared. Once recovered, a new staithe was built for the new Spaw House, which sat high above the beach on a two-level stone platform, offering protection from the waves and an extra challenge to frailer visitors attempting to reach the water cure from the sands.

A century later, after the great storm of 1808 swept everything away once again, the breakers in the South Bay went hurtling towards a gloriously castellated Gothic spa, with turrets and flags and battlements designed to tease the old stone fortress on the hill across the bay. By now the Spa was celebrating its sandcastlery – resigned perhaps to regular destruction and rebuilding. It was more or less washed away again in the 1820s, before being utterly destroyed in an even worse storm sixteen years later. And yet, within months, a new Spa was under construction and Victoria's reign saw extensions, improvements, destructions and new starts. Architects come and go – the Spa goes on for ever.

The long life of the Spa by the sea is epic in character. Not for Scarborough the quiet decline of the Chalybeate Well in Hampstead. Fred Casano's portrayal of a great winter storm in the South Bay shows people packing into the Prospect Tower at the Spa to watch a schooner being overcome by hurling waves and swirling breakers, high as the dance floor. The spectacular blaze that destroyed the Grand Hall in 1876 was witnessed by a young artist called Alphonse Neumans, who caught the horror and helplessness of the crowd on the beach in dark silhouettes against a huge conflagration. Thick scarlet and yellow paint explodes over heavy brown clouds, as lines of dark smoke burst from the windows. The cliff glows weirdly in dusky orange behind the Spa, as the Grand Hall is reduced to a skeleton in the blaze. In John Atkinson Grimshaw's view from the clifftop, the same fire is a more distant detail, the flaming red Spa set off by a wide, limpid, moonlit sea and empty sands. There is no crowd, no panic, no sense of the voracious roar; only well-dressed figures on their evening walk looking down in surprise, or disapproval even, in keeping with Grimshaw's austere title, *Sic transit gloria mundi* ('Thus passes the glory of the world'). The Burning Spa is a world away from Francis Nicholson's tranquil watercolours, or the luminously calm atmosphere of Turner's painting of the boats in South Bay at low tide.

Whatever setback, natural or human, has confronted Scarborough Spa, sooner or later it has recovered and carried on. The buildings have changed through the centuries since Thomasin Farrer took her historic walk beneath the cliffs, but the spirit of the red spring remains. When German battlecruisers bombarded Scarborough in December 1914, shattering windows across the town, smashing the walls of the Grand Hotel, the harbour lighthouse, the castle, and the promenade, the spa buildings astonishingly escaped the devastation. But with wreckage all around and sombre recruiting posters urging everyone to 'Remember Scarborough', any thoughts of entertaining visitors were gone. For four years, Scarborough battened down the hatches as sporadic raids damaged the town and destroyed the fishing fleet.

But the end of the Great War saw the old ebullience returning. The deep blue cover of a *Souvenir Guidebook* for the National Teachers' Conference of 1924 features ships in full sail, ploughing through the waves against a radiant rising sun. Delegates are introduced to 'the spirit of Scarborough' – rugged, warm-hearted, indomitable. And of all the attractions, the spa takes first place, as 'the most select' and 'most beautiful resort in the town'. Famous for music, sea views and romance, the spa's old therapeutic reputation still mattered. The generation recovering from life-changing trauma and unimaginable losses might be too modern for 'taking the waters', but a chalybeate spring long famous for stimulating cheerfulness was never more necessary.

As the red spring ceased to satisfy twentieth-century tastes, its old influence was re-channelled into music. When the teachers arrived in Scarborough, the Spa had re-established its own orchestra, whose symphonies went on wafting across the bay for decades to come. The repertoire at the Ocean Room has gone on altering with the times and now offers a mixed season of music festivals, comedy, burlesque, tribute bands, children's shows or Coffee Dances with Howard Beaumont, 'King of the Keyboards'. Among the highlights of 2023 was Showaddywaddy's Fiftieth Anniversary Concert. The range of drinks has widened, too, since chalybeate water fell from favour. Anyone in search of a spa treatment is now more likely to head to the Crown Spa Hotel at the top of the hill.

Although Britain's eighteenth-century taste for taking the waters has long since receded, its spirit lingers among the beautiful town houses and colonnades of the old spa towns, its memory in museums and monuments and place names. Bath, Leamington Spa, Bristol Hotwells, Tunbridge Wells, Sadlers Wells all hold their history in their names, running off the tongue like staging posts on Matthew Bramble's tour. In Liège, the ancient city of Spa still retains the name that inspired them all. After my family moved from Yorkshire, we lived in South Limburg for two years and would sometimes cross the border to visit Spa. I could never understand why we had to drive so far to see somewhere that sounded just like the local Dutch grocery shop. But I knew nothing then of chalybeate waters, even though I now see red springs bubbling up throughout my life.

Not far from our home is a small wood. I might hardly have noticed it in an area scattered with odd remnants of the Royal Forest of Bernwood, clumping at field corners, along the ridges of hills, dividing farms. But its name caught my eye: Spa Wood. A path leading downhill from the village of Brill runs close to this small copse, but the trees give little away. There are a few fallen branches and tangles of brambles but no obvious sign of buildings – and no access. The modern owners are evidently less keen on visitors than their Victorian predecessors. Edwardian photographs of the wood tell a fuller tale. Here you can see the shell of a building in the trees, a pale dome against a paler sky and a semi-circular portico of Ionic columns. Young trees spring from disused steps, lithe trunks and slim branches burst across the iron railings, the neoclassical order. What might be the remains of a grey arch is dimly discernible. There is very little left of the spa now. No sign of the pump room that once stood beside the chalybeate spring. You can imagine the pleasure gardens in the open field, but the buildings have vanished from sight. A few fragments may still stand in the woods, the stump of a column poking up through the undergrowth. Out of place among the trees, the old spa has been abandoned, the spring deserted.

The Waves

~

A crossroads in bright sunshine, where two small, straight, hedged roads meet. No signpost. Perhaps it doesn't matter whether you turn left or right or just carry straight on? This is the sort of junction at which anyone arriving would normally know which way to go – why would strangers ever find themselves here? Not for the first time in rural Ireland, I felt a little disoriented and foolishly out of place, not least because my phone was out of battery and Malcolm, who was driving, had left his behind. The massive bulk of Ben Bulben was somewhere behind us, but where? It is less easy to get lost in the century of Google Maps than before, but once off the main routes in unfamiliar country, where little roads run away in all directions, you can still lose your way – perhaps yourself.

If you're not going anywhere in particular, just heading for the coast because you need to see the sea, it doesn't really matter which road you choose. Where the sea rolls all around the headland, left or right or straight ahead will surely take you there. You can taste the salt in the air, breathe it in the light. Everything is clarified, so any road towards the clear horizon is the right road – though after a few moments' deliberation, the one on the left won. I'd like to say that we took the one less travelled and it made all the difference, but the difference on this occasion was an unnecessary addition of about twenty minutes. The chosen way wound on and on and around and away from the sea, looping back so far that a reunion with the main road began to seem unavoidable. The only thing to do was to find a field gate and turn around. On the way back, retracing the journey with only one or two uncertain forks, the unsigned crossroads never re-appeared, but a small rough track through an open gate looked promising enough to stop the car and walk.

The mud track was hard-dried, half covered in grey stones and tough grass, and dropping away below pasture fields and barbed wire. A grey pony, not overweight by any means, stood and stared. The lie of the field and the track meant he could look down his narrow nose at any visitor, but still he seemed unnecessarily scornful of the handful of grass held out in what I hoped would be understood as a gesture of friendship. His eyes were not so much sad as suspicious.

The field stopped, the barbed wire carried on, above what turned out to be a steep drop into a small inlet. Across the narrow channel was a tufty slope, rising into smoother grass pocked with sporadic tufts of long, arching leaves and blood-red flames of crocosmia. The stony track led in the other (and only realistic) direction. Eventually the path crumbled into rubble and openness and an expanse of flat grey slabs. Across a large bay, jagged with rocks and ragged promontories, was a line of distant mountains. To the northwest, the sea was spreading out as far as the bright horizon.

The grey stones were smooth and surprisingly warm underfoot. Bright sunshine made it hard to tell how high the tide might rise at this time of the year, while at the same time drying up any worries on that score. A little way off, the sea was unthreatening and very inviting. Slabbed stones stretched away, offering long steps down, with occasional pockets of seawater and a few proper rock pools. The waves were almost as flat as the rocks, swelling gently, breaking into thin streaks of white spume, bursting only over the rocky outcrops offshore. The surface glinted in the sun. There were no boats, no anglers, no dog walkers. Only gulls and cormorants and guillemots, floating and diving, bobbing up and flying off. Along the shore, oystercatchers were stepping and piping, quick, busy, purposeful. The water gleamed silver, white gold, diamond bright against deep aquamarine. A perfect image of ordinary, unachieved peace. At least initially.

There were darker spots, too. Not far from the shore, three craggy, uneven rocks cut through the swelling surface. They made convenient perches for the cormorants and created a narrow, sheltered sea pool within the bay. Between the rocks, floating in the pool, were small shapes, lighter than the rocks, darker than the bobbing gulls, dipping about in the light, quick waves. Perhaps it was a pod of porpoises or dolphins. I couldn't tell how far away the rocks might be, nor the size of the shapes. They weren't moving as fast as porpoises often do, but perhaps they, too, enjoyed basking in the warmth of the day. I have seen photos of sleeping sea mammals, hanging in the water before surfacing for a breath of air. It was hard to think that the water could be deep enough, but without being able to gauge the distance it was difficult to know. That watery gap between the rocks might be just the deep, secure spot for feeling at one with the world. Could there be a seal colony rising from the waves to scan the shore? Or stretching out on smooth, flat slabs just below the surface, where the shallower water would be warm and calm? It must be a large colony, with so many dark shapes emerging. Somehow the calm of the day was being disrupted by a distant circle of stones in the sea.

How distant was difficult to judge, but the harder I looked, the less like a seal colony it seemed. So many dark patches moving in the water. It must be a trick of light on waves rolling and breaking gently over submerged rocks. The sky was cloudless, the gulls moved too quickly to cast such consistent shadows. Then I realised it must be seaweed. I could see the dark forms rising above the water – the fronds being thrown up in the spume. The surface of the sea looked smooth from the beach, but the currents through the rocks were evidently strong. More and more shapes or shadows were bobbing up, more and more fronds rising from the deep.

The whole panorama of the circling bay and the blue-grey hills and the bright Atlantic shrank away, as that small, spotted area of seawater by the rocks became the intense focus of it all. I wanted to know, had to know, what they were – the shapes that kept floating up and down, perpetually moving and yet staying within that same patch of sea. Though the oystercatchers were as busy as ever and a rock pipit hopped quite close, nothing could compete with the mysterious dark forms in the water. At once, I felt an urge to wade in, to swim out and get closer, and a counter-impulse to retreat from the shore, to get as far away as possible. The pull of the sea was strong – and strange.

And then, suddenly, it all became clear. The shapes were not dolphins, or seals, or birds. Neither were they any kind of seaweed. They were hands. Many, many hands. Eighty, ninety, a hundred or more, open hands, rising from the waves. The fronds were not fronds at all. They were fingers. The outlines were becoming clearer and clearer, more and more compelling. They were drawing me into the water. Beseeching or beckoning? Mesmerising, either way.

Malcolm was some way off photographing the contents of a rock pool. When he realised how agitated I had become on this fine, sunny day, he was a bit surprised. After looking out to see what it was that had caught my eye, even more so. There was nothing out there except rocks, waves and a few seabirds. Perhaps it might be time to head back?

The sun was still bright, but the morning no longer felt as warm. The sea, though more urgently inviting, was strangely repellent, too. And the tide was rising. Turning away, the stones were cooler and harder, the terraces above towering rockfaces to be scaled. The little track, the grey pony and the car were all a long, long way away. Malcolm was still taking shots of the changing light across the bay, but I didn't want to look back, not out to sea. The hands might still be there.

Later, I tried to track our trip, retrace our steps and locate the beach on a map. Not knowing which of the little roads we'd taken off the N15 made it quite difficult to be sure. The most likely place was Streedagh. I began to look up local legends of Sligo and Drumcliff. I searched books about coasts and ghosts. There were many tales of mermaids, phantom horses, grey men, flying ships, and sea-people who live beneath the waves, but I couldn't find anything about masses of hands reaching out from the waves to lure people into the sea. The reflections of water and light play tricks on those ashore, so surely such a striking optical illusion had been seen before and made into a story? In the end Wikipedia gave me a bigger start than all the enchanting collections of maritime folklore. A desultory search of 'Streedagh' threw up 'The *Streedagh Armada wrecksite*'.

In 1588, three of the ships returning from the Spanish Armada foundered off the coast of County Sligo. *La Lavia*, *La Juliana* and the *Santa Maria de Visón*. Estimates of the human cost suggest that over a thousand people were on board, of whom perhaps fewer than three hundred survived. The sea's endless ebb and flow rinses prints from the sand, whirls away wreckage, erodes rocks, grinds shells, and washes memories clean, but at times the marks of human misery are too deep to disappear entirely. Places are changed for ever by extraordinary, unwished-for events. What's out of place overwhelms the customary and leaves the place somewhere different from before.

All around the coast of Ireland and Britain are sites where ships have been wrecked. So many have gone down over the years that it is impossible to compile a full list. The Royal Navy has documented its losses in detail, but countless small boats and merchant vessels have also disappeared, leaving bereft families and fishing communities but few official records. A quayside plaque, a fading photograph, a poem, a song or a local story may be all that remains of the fatal storm.

In Ireland, the National Monuments Service has now developed the 'Wreck Viewer', an interactive map plotting the exact location of some 4,000 Irish shipwrecks and recording what is known about a further 14,000 sites. As each wreck is identified by a scarlet spot, Ireland appears to be spewing drops of blood from every conceivable inlet. Strange that such extraordinary disasters should begin to look like a norm. Streedagh Strand is submerged under three red points, signalling the sixteenth-century Spanish wrecks, and then a fourth, marking the grave of another vessel two hundred years later.

The ships that went down in 1588 came from Venice, Naples and Dubrovnik, before being requisitioned for King Philip of Spain's campaign to conquer England, restore Catholicism to Elizabeth Tudor's Protestant nation and eliminate an international rival for global markets. From the Mediterranean to the English Channel, the Armada sailed in the service of Spain. As the Spanish king's grand project scattered in disarray, many vessels carried on northwards up the east coast of England and Scotland, rounding Orkney and the Western Isles before sailing on to Ireland, where three finally foundered in Donegal Bay. What can the whole enterprise have meant for the unlucky captains and crew? Or for those ashore, who witnessed three great ships heave into view, only to be smashed onto the rocks by the winds and waves?

Remarkably, we have a partial answer to one of these questions. A lucky survivor of the shipwreck left a graphic account of his experience at Streedagh and the aftermath, in a long letter to His Majesty King Philip II of Spain. The horror of being caught on board a sinking ship is vividly conveyed in Captain Francisco de Cuéllar's memories of the 'boisterous waves' and 'terrible hurly-burly'. As the ship broke beneath the terrible storm, men were swept to their death or threw themselves into the sea. Cuéllar couldn't swim, making his plight especially desperate. Only by gripping one of the ship's scuttle-boards was he carried ashore, where he lay, soaked, severely injured and silent witness to the looting and butchering of fellow sailors as they staggered from the waves. Ironically, his life was saved by the injuries sustained in the water, because the looters who stripped the bodies for valuables dismissed his blood-covered clothes as beyond recovery. He was left on the shore to die of his wounds.

Traumatised, but still alive, Cuéllar set off on the long journey home. The next few weeks brought bewildering waves of confusion and clarity, hope and disappointment, brutality and kindness. Often a single encounter involved extremes – the Englishman who attacked him with a knife was restrained by a local man, who in turn took Cuéllar's clothes and gold, while his beautiful daughter pleaded for kindliness, supplied herbs to treat the wounds and yet still kept her patient's valuables.

If his reception in Ireland left much to be desired, the prospect of encountering English soldiers under orders to execute any Spanish invaders who crossed their path was even worse. Shared dislike of a common enemy, together with Cuéllar's evident charm, intelligence and ability to speak Latin to priests, helped him on his way through County Sligo. He went in search of protection from families such as the O'Rourkes, who remained fiercely resistant to Elizabeth I's Protestant rule and whose castle on the shores of Lough Gill was not far from the shore where his ship was wrecked. After a series of narrow escapes and distressing encounters, the fugitive Spaniard was offered temporary refuge at the MacClancys' island stronghold further north in Lough Melvin.

In his dramatic account of what followed, Cuéllar emerges (unsurprisingly) as the hero of the hour, defending the castle with a tiny force of fellow countrymen from the onslaught of a large English army, while the resident chieftain fled to the mountains. The siege was finally abandoned in the face of blizzards and snow-drifts, with the army slinking back to Dublin and the band of Spaniards in triumphant possession of the castle, ready to welcome back the rightful owner. MacClancy returned the favour by detaining Cuéllar, who managed to evade the unwanted hospitality and head for the coast. Helped by a sympathetic, though still to be reliably identified bishop, Cuéllar was finally able to make his escape from Ireland. He travelled across to Scotland and, with the help of a network of Catholic families, finally boarded a boat for Flanders. The letter to King Philip of Spain was written in Antwerp on 4 October 1589.

Since Cuéllar had already been stripped of his command and only narrowly escaped execution several weeks before the shipwreck, he was understandably keen to attract royal favour. He had been found guilty of disobeying orders during the Armada campaign and may have been travelling as a prisoner on the unlucky galleon. As there were few survivors to contradict his version of events, it was an excellent opportunity to send home a winning report. Whatever embellishments may have been inspired by hopes of a royal pardon, Francisco de Cuéllar's extraordinary account still offers rare insight into the experience of a shipwrecked mariner, washed up on an unknown shore. It is impossible not to feel pity for the terrified Spanish sailors in the storm and horror over what they experienced.

In the days when voyage by sea was the norm and reliable lighthouses were not, shipwrecks were a very real hazard for any traveller. Despite the relative frequency of maritime disasters, their brutality is, and always has been, shocking. Fishermen risked their lives daily, seamen regularly embarked on voyages knowing that each quayside farewell might be their last. This did not make wrecks any less momentous. The commonplace can still be forever out of place.

What's deeply feared inevitably demands psychological defence strategies, which may account for the abundance of marine superstitions. In the case of the wrecked Spanish sailors murdered on Irish shores, Robert Hutchinson has pointed to the local belief 'that it was downright unlucky to save a man from the sea'. Similar beliefs in the sea 'taking its own share' washed around the shores of Britain and Ireland, making those on the coast fearful that one rescue from the water might somehow lead to one more drowning.

The shipwrecked sailors at Streedagh suffered from another common belief: since the ships of the Armada were known to be laden with gold, their unlucky crews offered easy pickings. The sheer preponderance of wrecks meant that many of those living on a hazardous coast were accustomed to salvaging booty. Valuable cargoes attracted operations of varying degrees of legality, making it difficult now to disentangle fact from fiction. Coastal folklore is full of hair-raising stories about the fate of ships deliberately wrecked – as well as strange kinds of retribution. The tale of the Otway family of Chambercombe Manor in Devon is a case in point. Sophia Kingshill and Jennifer Westwood tell how the Otways were thought to lure richly laden ships towards the shore with false lights, until one night their own daughter, returning home unexpectedly from Ireland, fell prey to their crimes. Her body was hidden in a secret room when her remorseful father abandoned the family home, where it remained for two hundred years before giving a later owner a grisly surprise. Tales like this swirled around rocky headlands, across seas and time, though there is little hard evidence of sabotage. Wrecking may be just another maritime myth, an age-old coastal conspiracy theory, or perhaps a dark fantasy of the get-rich-quick kind. Opportunism, on the other hand, was widespread. When ships went down, some of those ashore risked their own lives to save others from drowning, some rushed to care for traumatised survivors, while others were more interested in the valuable cargo.

In the case of the stricken ships at Streedagh, any impulse to save the lives of drowning men collided uncomfortably with a competing impulse (or order) to despatch intruders. Reading Cuéllar's version of events, it is easy to forget that the Spanish sailors belonged to an invading force, making them objects of terror to both local residents and English soldiers. The Dingle peninsula in the west had seen Spanish and Italian troops landing in support of an Irish rebellion only a few years earlier, followed by conflict, defeat and serious repercussions. The Armada of 1588 was a much more concerted attempted at conquest by a major foreign power; those on board the Spanish galleons were a would-be conquering army. First-hand accounts of any early invasions are sparse, those written by the defeated, even sparser. But it is not unlikely that if an enemy ship ran aground, those ashore would have been more inclined to fight or flee than to fish the feared marauders from the water.

I've often wondered what it was like for scattered communities in the centuries before long-distance communications, when the first news of an invasion arrived with a fleet of men bent on seizing land and silencing any opposition. It is hard to imagine the shock sustained by the tiny ancient community living beside the quiet beach at Bosta in Great Bernara, when Viking ships sailed into the bay one day. Evidence of such raids on the west of Ireland and the Outer Hebrides, on the Northumbrian or Yorkshire coasts, on the Isle of Man or the Solway, conjures up scenes of quiet lives shattered by boats coming out of the blue, as if from outer space. It is not surprising that stories of flying ships are common across the world. And yet an encounter with injured, half-drowned and traumatised victims of a sea storm always speaks as well to human instincts deeper than the defence of territory or national distinction.

Though news of the Spanish Armada travelled more rapidly than the Viking conquest, relative to the global immediacies of today it was glacial. Along the south coast of England, blazing beacons raised the alarm, but it took time for reliable details to reach other regions. In Fair Isle, people were rather taken aback when survivors of *El Gran Grifón*, a large Spanish supply ship, washed up on their shores. In Orkney, the surprise was probably even greater, as boats from Fair Isle arrived with cargos of Spanish sailors who were attempting to make their way home. This was as nothing to the unexpected appearance of Spanish troops in the

Small Isles of the Inner Hebrides, Rum, Eigg, Canna and Muck, in the wake of the Armada. In 1588, the formidable chief of Clan Maclean, Lachlan Mór Maclean of Duart, was embroiled in a bloody feud with Clan MacDonald and quick to seize an advantage. When he allowed the battle-battered, storm-struck *San Juan de Sicilia* to anchor in Tobermory for a few weeks of rest and refurbishment, the soldiers on board were swiftly redeployed for less peaceful purposes. The Small Isles were attacked, and Mingary Castle, the rock-solid MacDonald stronghold on the coast of Ardnamurchan, besieged. The havoc in the Islands and the Sound of Mull was soon matched by that inside Tobermory harbour, when the Spanish galleon was blown up, killing most of those on board – though the explosion does not appear to have been retaliation by the MacDonalds.

Over a century later, when Martin Martin visited Tobermory, he saw 'fine brass Cannon, some Pieces of Eight, Teeth, Beads and Pins' from the by then legendary ship and chatted to people whose older relations remembered stories of the explosion. Local opinion pointed to a man named Smollett, from Dumbarton, who was probably an agent of Francis Walsingham. The story recounted most often related to Dr Beaton, 'the famous Physician of Mull', who was unlucky enough to have been on deck when the gunpowder ignited. As the *San Juan* blew up, Dr Beaton flew up, but landed remarkably unscathed. His survival, little short of a miracle, immediately entered local legend. Eventually, some of Lachlan Mór's Spanish soldiers returned home, but what they had experienced and what they inflicted during their northern mission can only be imagined. The wreck of their galleon remains buried deep in the mud of Tobermory harbour; the stories it released continue to bob about.

Martin's record of his visit to Mull reveals the deep impact on the islanders of the chance arrival and destruction of a fugitive Spanish galleon. It also shows how telling and retelling the story helps to settle difficult events into a place. The Armada left an immediate trail of broken ships, drowned sailors, bereaved families and traumatised survivors, and a longer-lasting legacy of personal, local and national memories. While historians and archaeologists excavate and analyse whatever evidence survives, the stories slip in and out of place, revived, rewritten, repressed, processed, discarded and refashioned by successive generations.

The fate of the Spanish ships that disappeared off the coast of Britain and Ireland in 1588 is still under investigation. Some were wrecked, some scuttled, some vanished seemingly without trace, but many of their stories rapidly acquired a life of their own. Memories of the *San Juan de Sicilia* began to prompt salvage operations in the 1630s: decades before Martin arrived in Tobermory, the Earl of Argyll had sent diving bells down into the harbour to see what might be rescued from the seabed. Since then, sporadic attempts to find buried treasure have been spurred by the occasional appearance of tantalising gold coins, silver bells, pewter plates, and even brass cannons. As the diving equipment has grown more sophisticated, the lost ship has become more deeply submerged in sand.

The three Spanish ships at Streedagh lay undiscovered for hundreds of years. Then, in 1985, almost on cue for the Armada quatercentenary, a team of divers came across three cannons. More expeditions followed, buoyed by science and local stories of strange flotsam and jetsam. Thirty years later, winter storms reminiscent of those that had wrecked the ships in the first place began battering the northwest coast of Ireland. Bigger pieces of debris started to wash ashore, bringing a team of marine archaeologists hurrying from Dublin. Karl Brady recalls how carefully they explored the bay, examining some thirty locations until, at last, in an unlikely area of shallow water, they spotted some 'dark patches in the water'. Excitement mounted as a cannon became visible, and then more and more signs of wreckage. Although this site had been explored before, the recent storms had disturbed the seabed so violently that the churning sands spewed up heavy armoury long since buried and forgotten. Guns cast in 1570, adorned with dolphin-shaped handles, decorative flames and figures of saints, had failed in their purpose of protecting the sailors. The enormous cauldron once filled with tar for keeping the ship watertight is equally poignant. The objects, startled from quiet centuries of stasis, evoke the lives lost: all hands on deck, then down below the waves. The lifeless treasures, once lifted from their watery beds, risk disappearing again, so they were quickly submerged in underwater tanks for desalination and conservation.

The discovery of the legendary Armada wrecks diverted attention from the eighteenth-century 'Butter Boat' that has lain at Streedagh since sinking there in 1770. Since the worn ribs of its wooden carcase have been emerging from the level sands at low tide for as long as anyone can remember, it just seems part of the beach – and yet its true identity has only recently been established. The ragged wooden teeth that are bared when the sea goes out belong to the *Greyhound*, a Whitby boat that foundered in winter storms a long way from home.

For years, people dived, swam, paddled and played on the beach at Streedagh, untroubled by the wrecked 'Butter Boat', unaware of what else was lying beneath the waves. They have continued to do so, since the identification of the Spanish wrecks and the *Greyhound*'s history. If anything, the transformation of an 'unspoilt' into a 'historic' beach just adds to its interest, while the thought of wrecks and hidden treasure gives it an air of romance. It was all so long ago. In Tobermory's Canadian namesake, at Lake Huron, wreck diving is a popular leisure activity – boats have been especially sunk to extend the attractions of the Fathom Five National Marine Park. If this seems a novel attraction for holidaymakers in search of excitement, it is only a simulated version of older pastimes. In the age of Nelson, the new enthusiasm for sea-bathing was not dampened by the prospect of having to share a beach with a wrecked ship. As the 1805 summer season started at Weymouth, people rushed to the beach as usual, undeterred by the topmasts of the *Earl of Abergavenny* poking up through the waves. The tall ship had been wrecked only a few months before with a loss of 260 lives.

Gradually the waves close over shipwrecks, the sand steadily submerges the debris. Time washes over sites of disaster, scouring and smoothing the broken pieces, until whatever is left is almost illegible to later generations. A favourite beach may hide a long history of untold tragedy, but the sand and the pebbles are still flat and inviting. A day out at the sea means a day of immediate physical intensity – the barefoot sensation of wet sand, the sound of gulls and dogs and families, the taste and smell of salty air, the mind-emptying plunge into cold water. Why give a thought to what may have happened there yesterday, let alone hundreds of years ago? Yet still the sea can turn unpredictably. A winter gale may suddenly rip through the seabed and release what has been lying there, decently buried, for centuries. In a matter of hours, a familiar haunt is changed utterly, as the past surges up and what has been safely hidden in place all along resurfaces.

The Long-Armed Armada

~

The so-called 'Armada Portrait' of Elizabeth I is astronomical in design and ambition. The resplendent queen, smooth face encircled by a dazzling ruff, domed forehead adorned with round mounds of red hair, right hand resting on the globe, commands the viewer, just as she commands the seas around her island nation and, by implication, the world. Her pale, puffed-out sleeves are almost as spherical as the pearls in the spangled brocade and the multiple strands of her necklace. This is a monarch with aspirations to be Queen of the Heavens: sun, moon and stars all rolled into one. With such power at the centre, the seas visible through the windows seem mere servants of her will. Her back is turned on the scene outside as she fixes the viewer with a cool eye and carefully controlled smile. But we can see what is going on. On her starboard side is the nimble English fleet preparing to face a square formation of lumbering galleons. Over the port shoulder, the chaotic remnants of the Spanish fleet labour beneath the waves and an angry sky. Whether the dark rocks are in Fair Isle, the Hebrides, Antrim or Donegal, the rough tides are rising to engulf the enemies of the realm. For Elizabeth, the failure of Spain and England's former king (as widower of her half-sister, Mary Tudor) was a propaganda bonanza. Such victory against the odds was a sign of divine favour – and the stuff of legend. Medals were quickly cast, pamphlets printed, commemorative coins minted for scattering among a grateful, loyal people. For the nobility, the Armada Portrait said it all.

The moment of national triumph was not to be forgotten. Here was an event of such magnitude that its after-effects would be felt long after those involved were no more. While Elizabeth was deified by her portrait-painters, the fame of her naval commander lived on in stories. Sir Francis Drake, already lionised for circumnavigating the world, came to epitomise a peculiarly English sangfroid in his wish to finish a game of bowls before finishing off the Spanish foe. (The story has also helped in diverting attention from the human cost of the Armada, and other activities such as shipping slaves from Africa to the Caribbean.) Such deadpan derringdo and heroic defence of the queen's realm retained strong appeal in the age of Victoria. The tercentenary of the Armada inspired an outpouring of patriotic pride. John Seymour Lucas's painting *The Surrender* depicted a moment of symbolic capitulation, in which Don Pedro de Valdés, whose ship was captured by the *Revenge*, bows politely to a magnanimous and magnificently pantalooned Sir Francis Drake. The legendary admiral, jaunty in doublet and hose, was commemorated in his hometown of Tavistock with a commanding statue and series of bas-reliefs retelling the tale of the bowls in bronze. A replica of Joseph Boehm's Drake was erected at Plymouth Hoe in time for the tercentenary celebrations. Though centuries had elapsed, the Armada stories were speaking to a new generation, prompting them to mark the relevant dates and places.

At the height of Victorian Imperial expansion, Elizabeth I's victory over Spain seemed among Britain's proudest moments. The anniversary of Drake's death in Panama eight years later offered another opportunity for commemorations. In 1896, Sir Henry Newbolt, keen to stir a sense of patriotic duty in the hearts of schoolboys, was moved to compose a rousing ballad about 'Drake's Drum'. By now Drake had grown into a legendary figure of almost Arthurian stature, ready to rise again in defence of the realm:

'If the Dons sight Devon, I'll quit the port o' Heaven,
An' drum them up the Channel as we drummed them long ago.'

Although his body was buried at sea, Drake's impressive drum was brought back to Devon to be treasured by his descendants at Buckland Abbey. The grand old instrument is meant to start beating if ever England is under serious threat. During the Napoleonic Wars, when fears of invasion were running high, fishermen from Brixham reported hearing the sound of Drake's drum, but in later conflicts it began beating far beyond Devon. Sailors heard the drumbeat during the Battle of Jutland and at Scapa Flow. When the armada of small boats was evacuating troops from the beach at Dunkirk in 1940, Drake's drum could be heard beating the retreat. The ominous sound was amplified in the ears of young men who had learned to chant Newbolt's poem at school: with pounding hearts and a racing pulse, no wonder their minds filled with a throbbing beat. The battered drum is now housed in a glass museum display in what is hoped to be permanent retirement in Plymouth.

Beyond the paintings, the poems and the public memorials, the Spanish Armada left traces less obvious, but no less enduring, in places many miles from Buckland Abbey – places such as Tilbury and Tobermory, Antrim and Orkney, Skye and Streedagh. Memories of the ill-fated campaign are scattered around the shores of Britain and Ireland, just as the Spanish galleons were in 1588. Some place names, which now sound like attractions at a theme park, derive from these half-forgotten catastrophes. The seaside resort of Spanish Point in County Clare was named after the *San Marcos* and *San Esteban* were wrecked in the treacherous waters, and the surviving crews hanged. Port-Na Spaniagh is a steep stony inlet close to the Giant's Causeway, lying deep below the Giant's Chimneys. Its name changed when the lost Spanish galleon *La Girona* dared to arrive uninvited by Fionn MacCumhail and foundered on his deadly rocks.

The wreck of *El Gran Grifón* left permanent marks on Fair Isle in the row of Spainnarts' Graves along the south coast, though whether those laid to rest succumbed to illness or foul play depends on which of the local legends is more reliable – or which you prefer to believe. Some of the desperate Spaniards were said to have been crushed to death as they slept, or thrown over the cliffs by islanders worried about the strain on their winter provisions. But if the graves are those of an Armada crew, they may just have died from illness or exhaustion. When a number of their companions arrived in Anstruther during an attempt to return home, they are known to have been treated with kindness, so why not in Fair Isle? Over the centuries, stories take on a life of their own, coloured by storytellers and their audiences, so whether shipwrecked Spanish sailors were welcomed, tolerated or reviled is now difficult to assess with any certainty.

In Orkney, the Spanish were welcomed with open arms by at least some of the residents, judging by the traditions of local families who claimed descent from survivors of the wrecked galleon. The island's late nineteenth-century folklorist Walter Traill Dennison left a vivid description of the Westray Dons, whose lively intelligence, dark hair and tendency to wilder gesticulations marked them out from neighbouring families. It is possible that Dennison absorbed some of his era's Armada enthusiasms, because when Peter Anderson was assessing the Spanish influence on Orkney and Shetland in 1988, he found people who still regarded themselves as Dons, without being convinced that their forefathers arrived with the Armada. Personal histories may be more affected by contemporary concerns than is immediately apparent.

Down the east coast in Lincolnshire, similar stories traditionally account for the dark hair and finely chiselled features noticeable in a number of long-established families. The Addisons and the Sleights, who have been farming in the Lincolnshire Wolds for generations, are widely believed to owe their distinctive looks to survivors of the Armada. As in Westray, the story goes that some of the Spanish sailors who abandoned ship got on so well with the locals that they settled in Lincolnshire instead of travelling home. According to long local tradition, the flat sands at Donna Nook were not always renowned for seals or bombs, but for a ship beached on a sandbank there in 1588. I have not come across any record of an Armada shipwreck on this stretch of coast, nor a 'Donna' in the Spanish fleet. But *donna*, or 'lady', might once have meant 'Spanish ship', and it is not unlikely that a galleon ran onto a sandbank at low tide during the Armada's desperate northerly retreat. Given their disastrous encounters with Drake's fleet and the storms at sea, Spanish sailors might well have chosen to take their chance ashore. As herring fleets in later centuries moved up and down the east coast, it is also possible that the tales told by Orcadian Dons inspired more southerly equivalents.

Romantic stories of exotic encounters may have arisen in many areas over the years to account for potentially embarrassing differences within families. Anywhere close to the coast can claim contact with the Spanish Armada, an event too distant in time for awkward detail. The Armada fulfils a dream of mysterious ancestry, a chance to be just a little bit more interesting than others might think. When I asked John Purser, who knows Hebridean tradition better than most, about Armada legends in the Scottish islands, he replied with his usual energy, 'Legacies of the Armada? God help you! There must be an Armada story for every black-haired, olive-skinned person on the Western seaboard. It is true that the best way to get a half-drowned mariner to survive hypothermia is to strip him naked and shove him between the sheets with a well-endowed lady. How far this charity was extended is, however, open to speculation.'

John was also sceptical about the supposed connections between Skye terriers and Spain. The island's silky, long-haired terriers have often been described as the descendants of Spanish dogs, kept aboard ships to control the rats. Whether any of these little dogs swam ashore in Raasay in the aftermath of the Armada is open to doubt, especially as a competing lineage suggests Viking stock. The early history of canine breeds is notoriously uncertain. Since Lady MacDonald of Sleat was a keen breeder of Skye terriers, her home at Armadale Castle might have strengthened the Spanish association. 'Armadale', meaning an arm-shaped valley, is part of the rich Viking word-hoard, but imaginative dog enthusiasts might well have been reminded of the Armada – especially as Lady MacDonald was breeding dogs there in the late nineteenth century when demand for Armada memorabilia was at its height. In the well-kept grounds of Armadale Castle, a pair of bronze terriers, drop-eared and prick-eared, look eagerly across the lawn. Georgie Welch's sculpture, commissioned by the Skye Terrier Club, is called *The Homecoming* – and there is no question of home being anywhere other than the Isle of Skye. And yet the gardens remain hospitable to international arrivals, as the tall monkey puzzles and silver firs testify.

After Queen Victoria chose two Skye terriers as pets, their fortune for the duration of her reign was assured. Edinburgh's famous statue of faithful Greyfriars Bobby gave a further boost to the breed's reputation for loyalty, although it now seems likely that the model for the bronze sculpture may have been Bobby's successor, secured after his demise by local retailers, who had spotted the story's value in attracting visitors. The original Greyfriars Bobby, who guarded his master's grave for so many years, was probably a terrier cross. Since the Skye terrier is now the most endangered breed in Britain, these perky dogs are in danger of entering their own legends. In 2020, Kennel Club registrations dropped to a mere twenty-seven. Although there were a few more in 2022, unless their fortunes continue to improve, the happy pair unveiled at Armadale in 2013 to raise awareness of their plight may become an unhappy monument to the last of their kind.

The Spanish Armada has offered rich inspiration to storytellers down the years – as well as a way of explaining anything unusual or out of place. Herdwick sheep may seem an unlikely ovine counterpart of Skye terriers but have been honoured with a similar legendary origin. The Cumbrian coast was rather less wreck-strewn than the Scottish Isles, with little hard evidence of Armada casualties, but still the idea of Herdwicks arriving with the fleeing galleons has taken hold. A Herdwick sheep poised on a steep ridge in the Lakeland fells seems far removed from sinking ships and drowning – though their disregard for a cold drenching is obvious enough. They are such an integral part of the Lakeland scene that to suspect them of being other than indigenous seems odd. Their smooth, snowy faces and rough, grey fleeces are at one with the rocks, their strong, agile, white-stockinged legs well up to the tough terrain. Hardy Herdwicks are as happy on high mountain-sides as on slaty lake shores, untroubled alike by driving wind or rain. I'm always impressed by their even-handed imperviousness to sleet, steep screes and wet walkers in crackling kagools. Their local attachments have been recognised for many years – as evidenced in the formation of the Herdwick Sheep Association in 1899. Canon Rawnsley, founder member of the Association and keen defender of Cumbrian traditions and treasures such as the Rock of Names, saw the Lake District as the land of the shepherd, the Herdwick as the Lakeland shepherd's special breed. His interest in the mountain sheep may have been strengthened by his first name – a man who had been christened Hardwicke and was affectionately known as 'Hardy' perhaps felt a special obligation to the almost synonymous breed. But the question of *why* the Herdwick is so distinctive has prompted speculation.

Geoff Brown has dismissed the widespread story of Herdwicks swimming ashore from a Spanish galleon wrecked off the Cumbrian coast in 1588 and then settling in Wasdale. He is similarly uncon-vinced by the rival claim of their Viking ancestry, arguing instead that 'breeds are made by people'. Herdwicks, in his matter-of-fact view, developed their distinctive characteristics over a couple of centuries of selective breeding. The more colourful explanation has nevertheless been thriving for at least as long as the Herdwick came to be recognised as a unique breed. In his *History of Westmorland*, Richard Ferguson recounted the widespread legend of the Herdwick's Armada origins but, as his book was published in 1894, the 'legend' may have had a boost from the recent tercentenary celebrations.

The Herdwick's supposed Spanish origins perhaps make more sense when we remember the thriving Renaissance wool trade. Fine merino wool from specially bred Spanish herds was highly prized across Europe and so helped to create links between sheep and ships. Medieval Spain was a pioneer of elaborately patterned knitting, too, which may shed light on the tradition surrounding Fair Isle sweaters – another supposed legacy of the Armada. The intricate designs and bright, distinctive colours that mark out a Fair Isle sweater from more muted woollies have long been linked to the Armada ship that sank there. The idea of Spanish castaways teaching the islanders how to cast on is much cosier than the tale of their being cast off the cliffs. Unusually intricate knitting patterns also have a practical purpose in old island communities, such as Eriskay, where each fisherman had his own individual sweater. It is easy to imagine mothers, sisters and wives spending winter evenings knitting special designs for their men, but the domestic scene darkens with the thought that one day they might be called to identify a body by the unique pattern of the drowned fisherman's sweater.

The many Armada legacies show how stories of strange origins thrive and grow through telling and retelling. What was utterly alien on first encounter is gradually absorbed into a place, in a long process of mediation and assimilation. It's not a question of nonsense prevailing over sense: origin myths carry their own authentication. Foundational stories often trace an entire community to a handful of brave survivors arriving from a ravaged land. Just as Aeneas escaped the burning city of Troy, enduring countless trials before finally founding Rome, Herdwick sheep left a sinking ship to find their true home in Cumbria. The hardy survivor, unbowed by storm and destruction, arrives in unknown territory and goes on to triumph over adversity. It is an age-old story of redemption from the wreckage. If generations of people have been ready to believe that Fair Isle sweaters, Herdwick sheep, Skye terriers and even their own ancestors have Spanish heritage, they have also been demonstrating a deeply felt need for a distinct – and complicated – local identity.

At Croft Castle in Herefordshire, the magnificent lines of Spanish chestnut trees are now a defining element of the old estate. These full-figured, spreading veterans were planted somewhere between 1580 and 1650, supposedly from chestnuts seized from the Armada. What's more, they are laid out in battle formation as if to resemble a line of stately Spanish galleons. Whether this was the original intention is now hard to tell, though the story is in keeping with the political leanings of the castle's sixteenth-century owner, James Croft. Active in an uprising against the Catholic Queen Mary Tudor, and later an apparently loyal subject of Elizabeth I, James Croft might well have enjoyed recreating the moment of national triumph over Mary's widower, King Philip of Spain. On the other hand, his grandson Herbert, who inherited the estate, converted to Catholicism, while his great-grandson, also Herbert, remained a Catholic until 1630, but then joined the Church of England. An arboreal naumachia might have been conceived as a victory parade that would grow larger and larger as the years went by, a living inspiration to a long line of heirs – but exactly when it was planted, and whether in celebration of England or Spain, is rather hard to determine. Four centuries on, the chestnuts have fulfilled the vision of steady expansion, even if the original rationale for their planting has become a hazy memory. On a sunless autumn afternoon, when the wind snatches away the last gold leaves, making the carbuncular trunks creak and the twisted boughs sway like broken masts, it is easy to imagine that a great fleet of grotesque galleons is dropping anchor before nightfall.

As the trees have grown and expanded and contorted over the centuries, so has their meaning. Even the most powerful landowners cannot control how their monuments will come to be viewed. Planted in triumph, maturing into harmony, supremely beautiful and sustaining, Spanish chestnut trees may have done more to soothe old enmities than diplomatic initiatives or political alliances. The magnificent row of veteran chestnuts on the slope above Hope End in the Malverns is the most awe-inspiring and yet oddly endearing group of trees in the entire estate. Even the least likely tree-hugger feels drawn towards their enormous, upright, twisting trunks and generous, open-handed leaves. The problem with the story of the old Croft Castle trees is that chestnuts of this kind, *Castanea sativa*, were not generally known as 'Spanish chest-nuts' until the eighteenth century – and then only by specialists.

Whether planted in 1580 or 1650, or any time in between, trees of this kind would have been known as sweet chestnuts – or merely chestnuts. They were also widely regarded as indigenous – or at least long naturalised into British landscapes. Since a famous old tree such as the monumental chestnut at Tortworth in Gloucestershire was large enough at the time of the Norman Conquest to merit a mention in the Domesday Book, later antiquarians assumed, not unreasonably, that these trees were natives. If the vast chestnut in the grounds of Rydal Hall was some four hundred years old when Wordsworth walked past it on his way to Ambleside, it would already have been a mature tree at the time of the Armada. So the chestnuts planted at Croft Castle in the wake of the Armada, like those at Hope End, would most likely have been regarded as indigenous British trees. If they were connected with the Spanish campaign, it would have been as defenders of Elizabeth's Protestant nation through the provision of timber for parts of warships. Among the many alarms triggered by the Armada was the fear of axe-wielding invaders: the Forest of Dean was awash with rumours that the Spaniards were under orders to destroy their trees. Since chestnuts were also valued as nut trees, the rationale for their planting may have been more mundane altogether. But this need not get in the way of a good story.

Over the course of their very long lives, ancient chestnuts, like the stout old inhabitant of Rydal Park in the Lake District and its slightly younger counterpart at Balmerino Abbey in Fife, have become Spanish. They are local characters, cherished for their eccentric shapes, extraordinary longevity and faintly exotic ancestry. Out of place by virtue of their age and girth, they remain supremely in place.

Once, trees of this kind were a rare sight in Britain for other reasons. William Gilpin, an influential arbiter of arboreal style and careful observer of Britain's tree canopy, was puzzled by the contemporary dearth of chestnut trees. By the time he published his *Remarks on Forest Scenery* in 1791, chestnuts, though once abundant, had been 'almost totally exterminated'. If these had been relatively unfashionable trees in the seventeenth century, the planting plans at Croft Castle seem even odder. As chestnuts only became widely known as 'Spanish' during the nineteenth century, their 'historical' associations may well have grown then, too. High Victorian pride in Britain's fighting past conferred a strange Spanish ancestry on certain families, woolly sweaters, sheep and dog breeds – so why not trees, too?

Monkey Puzzles

~

There must have been twenty at least. Lined up in pairs, jostling for space, a seething mass of green spiky limbs, positively pulsating with life. If you turn your back on them, they will surely be on the move: a bright battalion ready for action, small bayonets fixed to every extremity. The bomb-blast bursts at the end of their branches were almost audible. Who would have expected such an encounter, after trays and trays of pansies and petunias, salvias and snapdragons? The red-coat army of annuals was utterly over-whelmed by the young monkey puzzles.

The bristling emerald brigade dwarfed the dank tanks of bedrag-gled pond plants that decoyed a few unsuspecting browsers to this far-flung corner of the nursery. If from a distance, they looked like great green thistle-heads, no one on closer encounter would suspect them of softening into thistledown and floating away. The strong, barbed, polished-leather plants were ready to put down roots and grow – the botanical version of a Great Dane puppy, all sharp teeth and enormous claws. When fully mature, the *Araucaria araucana* – or monkey puzzle, as it is better known – can reach over a hundred feet in height and ten to fifteen around the trunk. These may be perfect trees for landscaped gardens like Armadale, but not for a small frontage in a city street. And yet, what seemed so star-tlingly out of place in the small garden centre was once a common sight in suburban roads. I remember seeing them on the way to my grandparents, strange towering trees with their dark contorted heads and narrow trunks. There were so many of these extraordinarily formed evergreens that they ceased to seem extraordinary at all. The arrival, celebration, domestication, habituation, repudiation and rehabilitation of the araucaria is just as strange as the Armada legacies, though in this long story, the Spanish dimension has often been downplayed.

Such prickly trees are an odd choice for neatly trimmed gardens. Their formidable spikes spiral outwards, layer upon layer, needle-sharp. Even the hungriest squirrel might hesitate before venturing onto such an inhospitable branch. It is hard to imagine a less approachable tree – which is just what struck Charles Austin when he saw his first young araucaria. It was being planted at Sir William Molesworth's Cornish estate in 1834. Not that space was the problem here.

Austin's host, a keen collector of specimen plants, was ambitious to create a global woodland at his family estate at Pencarrow, a few miles inland from Padstow. Collecting rare trees was fashionable among status-conscious gentlemen, the Victorian equivalent of bagging a Banksy – except that, unlike artworks, exotic trees carried the extra thrill of gambling, given their uncertain chances of survival in a cold, blustery northern climate. As Cornwall offered warmer, wetter ground than much of Britain, the Pencarrow garden offered a safer bet than many. Molesworth's latest arrival was quite an acquisition. At a cost of £25 (the equivalent of about £3,000 today), the araucaria merited a planting ceremony surrounded by a circle of suitably appreciative guests. Charles Austin couldn't resist stepping forward to stroke the striking branches, needling his hand and his wit: this prickly newcomer 'would be a puzzler for a monkey'. From then on, it was known as the 'Monkey Puzzler'.

The whimsical name suited the age of pinetum-planting and Nonsense Botany – it wouldn't sound out of place among Edward

Lear's 'Piggiwiggia Pyramidalis' or 'Manypeeplia Upsidownia'. Gradually, as the Monkey Puzzler became more familiar, it turned from active subject to inanimate object – shedding its final *r* as surely as its lower branches. The popular name probably owed something to the tree's unusual habits, too: as proud gardeners watched their prize trees grow, they were puzzled by the way those straight spiky branches broke free from the perpendicular and began to curl like monkeys' tails.

The monkey puzzles at Pencarrow now rise above nearby birches, young chestnuts and ailing ashes. From the grand, top-heavy avenue to the single specimen set in a spreading lawn, the stately araucarias give every impression of owning their space. The old estate is full of hidden presences. Under the long grass and flourishing shrubs the visible rings of an Iron Age hill fort ripple out. Thick, bright moss softens the log piles, offering a velvet bed to toads and beetles. Brambles, ferns and creepers bury wartime Nissen huts. The rampant undergrowth merely serves as a launch-pad for the rocketing evergreens, explosive, effervescent, and yet, exuding a strange air of lofty stillness. Their great cylindrical rope-coil trunks scorn the ivy's efforts to absorb them into the Cornish woodland. There is something defiantly out of place about the araucarias, however well suited to the soil and local weather. Still Pencarrow is known as the home of the monkey puzzle: Charles Austin's reaction to a pricked finger was an unlikely gift to the estate's future marketing team, but today's gardeners are busy maintaining the tradition. Carefully distanced from the feet of the tall, textured trunks are bright green saplings, small branches held out straight and ready for the century ahead.

Pencarrow may boast the first tree to go by the name of 'monkey puzzle', but not the arrival of Britain's earliest araucaria. This claim to fame is jointly held by Spring Grove in Isleworth, where Sir Joseph Banks had a large garden full of floral surprises, and the Royal Botanic Gardens at Kew. The story goes that during Captain George Vancouver's explorations of the Pacific coast of the Americas, the

Scottish plant hunter Archibald Menzies found himself at a dinner in Santiago given by Ambrosio O'Higgins, the Viceroy of Chile. Intrigued by the unusual-looking nuts on the table, Menzies pocketed a few to take back to Britain. On the dangerous voyage around Cape Horn and northwards across the Atlantic, Menzies was under arrest for insubordination (or in his version, unfairly detained by a misguided captain), which allowed plenty of time for studying his botanical curiosities. Under sail, battered by storms, becalmed in the doldrums, the voyage lasted long enough for the strange Chilean pine nuts to germinate and turn into even stranger seedlings, which Menzies presented to Banks on his final re-entry into London in 1795.

Whether the seeds were unhealthy from the start or discouraged by months on board ship, the two seedlings planted at Kew and Isleworth failed to thrive. A handful of other survivors did better under glass, and so a decade later, they were planted out in Kew Gardens, where one lived for almost a century. This was a cause for celebration among British horticulturalists, but as these trees can last for some two thousand years in their native environment, it was really a sad case of infant mortality. Since araucarias are mountain trees, happy at a thousand feet in the Chilean mountains, their initial dismay at finding themselves in a flat, low-lying garden next to the Thames is perhaps unsurprising. But in the Age of Empire and global gardening, effort against the odds was a matter of pride, so it was not long before more seeds began to arrive from South America followed by more determined planting and nurturing.

Menzies was proud of his pine seeds and dined out on the tale for decades. Joseph Hooker, Director of the Royal Botanic Gardens at Kew, told his friend Henry Elwes the story of the strange nuts at the Santiago dinner, which he'd heard directly from Menzies himself. Though well aware that the araucaria had actually been 'discovered' by Spanish explorers in South America long before Menzies got there, Elwes enjoyed Hooker's enjoyment of Menzies's tale enough to include it in his magnificent multi-volume study of

The Trees of Great Britain and Ireland. Again the chain of anecdotes shows how, under the right conditions, stories about trees grow just as well as their arboreal subjects.

David Gedye has devoted years to researching the lives of the first British monkey puzzles. Childhood curiosity and family loyalty led to a lifelong personal passion for these mysterious trees: his great-great-grandfather was Philip Frost, the Head Gardener at Lord Grenville's Dropmore estate in the Chilterns and one of the earliest nurturers of an araucaria in England. Gedye is rather sceptical about Menzies's dinner in Santiago and more interested in the role played by the naturalist James Macrae, who brought healthy, viable araucaria seeds and seedlings over from Chile thirty years later. Macrae's young specimens were then raised by skilled gardeners in various nurseries and botanic gardens and from there, the young trees began to find their way into great estates – including Lord Grenville's at Dropmore and Sir William Molesworth's at Pencarrow. Victoria and Albert, keen on setting trees and trends, had one of the earliest at Windsor, though it wasn't as happy or long-lived as the monkey puzzle planted near their new home at Osborne in the Isle of Wight to celebrate the queen's mother's sixtieth birthday in August 1847. In the Royal Collection, a striking photograph from the 1870s shows how quickly the Dowager Duchess's sapling flourished into a wonderfully well-balanced pyramid of a tree, with strong, pipe-cleaner boughs, tips uplifted to the heavens.

The first British araucarias were botanical sensations. Any new arrival able to survive – and even thrive – in British soil always causes a flurry in the world of plant science. Unlike some of the trees introduced by explorers in the eighteenth and nineteenth centuries, the araucaria had the further distinction of being instantly recognisable. No other tree curls quite so memorably. As the first right-angular-boughed saplings began to turn into graceful trees with innumerable green tresses flowing groundwards in long, loose ringlets, Victorian landowners were all agog. No wonder the araucaria became a tree of choice for young men bent on giving their grand gardens a money-regardless makeover. In the era of arboreta, when fortunes were judged (and spent) on ever-greens from across the globe, the araucaria stood out among all the exotic cypresses, firs and redwoods. Nothing could match the Chilean champions for the sheer magnificence of their silhouettes. These were statement trees (though what exactly they stated, apart from the owner's extravagance, remained to be seen).

By the end of the queen's reign, soaring monkey puzzles were de rigueur for any self-respecting tree collector – from the Duke of Wellington's fine, upstanding trees at Stratfield Saye to the giants at Tortworth Court or the great, green forest at Beauport Park on the south coast. In the grounds of Hafodunos Hall in Wales, a stately avenue of araucarias seemed set to rival the vast ancient yew in the churchyard at nearby Llangernyw. Monkey puzzles flourished in Ireland, too, adorning the gardens of big houses such as Mount Stewart or Kilmacurragh. The strange living legacy of Victorian tree tastes survives in the Woodstock Gardens at Kilkenny, though a mature, if rather top-heavy, monkey puzzle in Cork was finally toppled by Storm Ellen in 2020. The Gulf Stream and abundant rain washing the shores of Dumfries and Galloway inspired James Maxwell to plant two hundred araucarias at Monreith, across the bay from the Logan Gardens, while a few miles north at Castle Kennedy, the monkey puzzles link the White and Black Lochs with deep emerald. In the Armadale Gardens in Skye, an enormous araucaria stretches up above the well-kept lawns and rhododendrons, a big friendly giant watching over the Skye terrier sculpture and across the sea to Knoydart.

In a matter of decades, rare Chilean conifers became familiar monkey puzzles, standing companionably beside castles and carriageways, city streets and country churches. A magnificent specimen lifts from the garden of a tall townhouse in Bath, poised to send great round pine cones raining down Lyncombe Hill. The butter-coloured city spreads below, offering a classical background

for the bold botanical newcomer, as it teases the Georgian architects with an exuberant Victorian answer to Rome's cypresses and
stone pines. I'm sorry Jane Austen lived too soon to see it.

Far away in the tiny Yorkshire hamlet of Stalling Busk, the
monkey puzzle by the Edwardian church of St Matthew's is now
taller than the pitched slate roof. An Arts and Crafts alternative to
the traditional yew, the dark branches have now curled into
demonic shapes which wouldn't look out of place in a medieval
carving. There is something inherently playful about the form of
these evergreens, which may be why the popular name has stuck
and why the cryptic crossword-compiler John Graham, recognising a fellow puzzler, chose 'Araucaria' as his pseudonym.

As monkey puzzles settled in and fell in price, they became a
fairly common suburban tree. Ask anyone who grew up in a small
town or city street in the 1960s or 1970s whether they remember a
monkey puzzle and the chances are they will. The memorable tree
on Humberstone Avenue in Grimsby marked the last but one street
on the journey to my grandparents' house in Bargate Avenue. These
are, after all, the easiest of trees to recognise. Someone hard pressed
to tell an ash from a sycamore, a spruce from a Scots pine, would
have every confidence in their ability to identify a monkey puzzle.

Children who grow up with monkey puzzles in the garden or
nearby park often become very attached to them. This is the Curly
Wurly tree – a mass of prickly curls and whirls on a lolly stick. As
they grow in height, they shed their lower branches, leaving a
totem pole of towering eyes. The familiar figure of a huge monkey
puzzle tree in his parents' garden loomed so large in Robbie
Blackhall-Miles's infant mind that he has now become a conservation horticulturalist, fostering endangered species in his Welsh
garden. For Michael Viney, on the other hand, growing up on the
outskirts of Dublin, memories of the monkey puzzle were of a
'jagged, overpowering' tree towering above small front-lawns: 'A
dreadful stillness seemed to hang over every monkey-puzzle house,
as of the death of an argument that had everyone exhausted.'

All too often, what began as a little piece of abroad in the front garden soon became a rather big piece of abroad. Aspirational gardeners planted their monkey puzzles and then stood back in satisfaction to see them grow. And grow. And grow. By the later decades of the twentieth century, small semi-detached houses across the British and Irish Isles were becoming hidden by their dark, twisting conifers. Heavy shade and dried-out soil did nothing for other garden plants, while the lower branches of the huge trees had an unhappy habit of losing vim and vigour, turning sickly brown, flopping down and finally dropping in a rotting heap. The fear of a massive trunk crashing through the roof disturbed the dreams of those in the beds below. Would-be homeowners could hardly be blamed for avoiding properties dominated by these dark, towering trees. Unsurprisingly, the monkey puzzles began to come down again.

As monkey puzzles began to disappear from the streets of Britain, a new breed of plant collector emerged to track them down. Although ageing araucarias in tight spots can sometimes look a little moth-eaten or bereft, as their crowns thin and lower branches turn from vibrant sweeping tails of green to dangling, soggy brown cables, they still retain their magnetic allure. If the new journeys of exploration and discovery remain much closer to home than the old Pacific expeditions, they can still prove exciting – and obsessive.

Sarah Horton, an independent funeral celebrant from Liverpool, spent three years in pursuit of British monkey puzzles. Her quest to track down every surviving tree in the country soon took her far from the parks and gardens of Merseyside to North Wales, Cornwall, Northumberland and beyond. This was amateur plant hunting, twenty-first-century style, with micro-camera at the ready and a website for sharing the findings. Sarah soon realised that the task was too much for a lone Monkey Puzzler and began recruiting agents to the cause. From Agent John in Fife to Agent Dragonblaze in London, the Monkey Puzzlers were out and about and on the case. As hundreds of araucaria photos flooded in, the red spots on the Monkey Map deepened from a mild rash to multiple outbreaks of crusty clusters. Central Cornwall disappeared altogether under the layers of scarlet marks. The project spread beyond Britain to Ireland, the Netherlands, Belgium and Germany, with reports and photos arriving from America and New Zealand. When the overall count was running at 3,000 trees, Sarah Horton decided that her project had done its work: in May 2016 the open invitation to send in your latest sighting was politely withdrawn.

Once you've thought about a monkey puzzle tree, you will start spotting them, whatever the size. I've been watching a couple in the next village for about five years and was pleased to see they had just grown tall enough for a few lights at Christmas. I must have mentioned this to my nephew, Tom, because he arrived some time later with a rather bedraggled monkey puzzle in a large container – it was outside his new house and he thought we could give it a better home. So far it has shown no sign of growing another centimetre, but neither has it turned any browner than when it arrived. I'm hoping it might flourish one day, though perhaps not too vigorously.

If monkey puzzles have seemed out-and-in-and-out-of-place in the British Isles, largely depending on tree tastes and garden space, their fortunes in South America have fluctuated even more. Long before they became known as monkey puzzles, these trees were called Chilean pines because they have been growing for millennia in great bristling forests high in the Andes. *Araucaria araucana* grows wild in the Araucania region of southern Chile. But its real name is Pehuén, as it is known by the local Chilean people. Their tribal name Pehuénche comes from the pine nuts harvested from the tree's enormous green cones. Traditionally, the Pehuénche depended on the Pehuén: not only were the abundant nuts their staple diet, but the fibrous bark furnished rope and textiles, the gummy resin remedies for wounds and ulcers, the huge trunks a generous supply of timber, firewood and paper.

The Pehuén forests support a rich and rare ecosystem of animals, birds and reptiles, too. They are home to small furry marsupials known as *monitos del monte*, to long-haired grass mice and miniature deer called *pudu*. Bright green parakeets split open equally bright pine cones with their tin-opener beaks to feast on the rich nuts inside. In spring the soaring trees fill the air with golden pollen, while their deep green branches swarm with hosts of rare insects. Many of the species living among the old Pehuén trees survive nowhere else in the world. No wonder this is Chile's National Tree, as celebrated by Pablo Neruda in his 'Ode to the Araucaria Araucana'.

Warm, volcanic regions offer the perfect environment for araucaria. I have yet to see them in their native mountains but gleaned some idea of their natural magnificence from Dominic when he was trekking through South America. After the jagged peaks and glaciers of Patagonia his sightseeing standards were raised to quite a height. But the astonishing spectacle of dense clumps of monkey puzzles growing among live volcanoes in the Andes comes high in his list of world experiences. Eruptions of dark smoke and spitting fire alternating with the explosive green canopies of skyscraper trees – surely one of the natural wonders of the world.

The extreme antiquity of araucarias should offer assurance of the tree's long-term prospects. The huge, blank eyes of lenticels peer from the rough bark, as if staring into the past and the future. The ancestors of these trees were coeval with Jurassic life, witnesses to the tyrannosaurus and triceratops. The Pehuén outlived the dinosaurs and Neolithic man. They saw the extinction of the megafauna – those magnificent creatures that struck Homo sapiens as a bit too large and close for comfort. And yet for all the longevity of the araucaria, their fitness to survive humankind is now just as doubtful. Pehuén pine cones, round as woody ostrich eggs and as full of potential life, are regularly snatched by poachers, the long, strong trunks chopped down by illicit loggers.

In their old home in the Chilean mountains, the fading eyes in the tall trunks frequently stand and stare as fellow araucarias are felled for timber or cremated in forest fires. The devastating blaze in 2014 that ripped through acres of national parkland in Chile, gulping down thousands of thousand-year-old trees, is probably a sign of things to come. Global temperatures are rising, forests drying out, consumption and extraction show little sign of decline. Chile's national tree is now officially endangered.

The plight of the ancient forests has prompted legislation: logging was banned in 1976, the Chilean Law of Recuperation of Native Forest and Forestal Promotion passed in 2007. Nevertheless, within four years the araucaria was included in the IUCN's Red List of Threatened Species. Such an unwelcome claim to fame has added momentum to local, national and international conservation initiatives. The Chilean Fundación Mar Adentro, based in the Pehuén forest in Auracanía Andina, encourages better understanding of the region's environmental heritage through art and education, in an effort to influence attitudes to trees whose presence may still be taken for granted. The timber trade is now carefully restricted, while renewed efforts to plant Pehuén seedlings and reseed areas devastated by fires are under way. As araucarias evolved in a highly volcanic region, they are pioneer plants after major conflagrations, with a capacity to spring up again on devastated slopes. Still, the prospects of these arboreal Methuselahs are far from certain.

The effort to save the araucaria is an international as well as national responsibility. The Chilean National Parklands protect what sometimes seems a perpetually shrinking population of native trees but also works with international botanical partners to raise araucaria awareness – and saplings. When the Eden Project was launched in Cornwall, the gardeners had a special nursery of prickly charges in the Chilean Arboretum, courtesy of the Royal Botanic Gardens in Edinburgh – long established as a centre for conifer conservation. Victorian photographs of the Edinburgh Rock Garden show young araucarias, scaly branches outstretched, growing out of round grass mounds. In between are miniature mountains built from basalt pillars pillaged from Staffa and the Giant's Causeway. Ideas about conservation have changed considerably since 1860.

The Royal Botanic Gardens' araucarias are now grown mainly at the Benmore Gardens near Dunoon. The grand monkey puzzles near Benmore House are the legacy of the estate's Victorian owners, who were delighted to discover how well conifers from around the world will grow in the mild, extremely damp climate of Argyll. On the wooded hill above, beyond the Japanese Valley and the Bhutan Glade, you find yourself in the Chilean Rainforest – a plantation of young trees that are growing into an araucaria grove. The botanists at Benmore work with conservation charities such as Rainforest Concern to protect conservation sites in Chile, too. The Reserva Nasampulli, secured in the 1990s, provides a natural wildlife corridor linking depleted patches of ancient araucaria and so demonstrating how forests might be revitalised for the future. Suitable sites in other countries can lend their slopes to the Chilean tree, helping to strengthen the biodiversity and resilience of the Andean forests and offering Europeans a taste of South America without a long-haul flight. If you come across an unexpected cluster of spiky monkey puzzle trees, like those standing guard at the entrance to Crarae Gardens on Loch Fyne, they may look like an attempt to recreate nineteenth-century gardening styles. Their real purpose is international conservation.

Although we can all do our bit to protect threatened species, by turning even a tiny patch of ground into a mini zoo for bees, butterflies and small birds, it may be wise to think twice before leaping in to plant your own araucaria. My fingers are crossed for our rehomed tree, but I sometimes wonder what will happen if it does shoot up and out. Monkey puzzles need a bit more room than a bee house or small, flowering, pollinator plant. The acid-rich, volcanic mountains of the Scottish Highlands have the space, soil, rain and specialists to give the young araucaria a fighting chance. And if Chile's signature trees seem out of place in Argyll, they are only swelling the ranks of exotic botanical migrants in Scotland's hospitable Victorian gardens. The recent history of Highland forestry also shows just how accommodating to non-native conifers the hills have proved. Miles and miles of Sitka spruce are now being felled and replaced with native broadleaves, but for much of the twentieth century, picturesque views of Scotland featured lochs and castles nestling among steep and very dark wooded slopes.

An arboreal sense of place is rather different from that of the average human. One of the many reasons why I like listening to foresters is their habit of talking happily about the movement of species before the continents divided. If we go back far enough, it turns out that the araucaria is a kind of ancient Yorkshireman. A piece of Whitby jet in a Scarborough antique shop is a fossilised remnant of a monkey puzzle tree, which must have been growing over 180 million years ago. What might seem out of place on first encounter is often just a sign of present-day thinking. The monkey puzzle at Stalling Busk turns out to be a native after all.

Sherwood Forest

~

A valon, Camelot, Elfland, Narnia: known to everyone, visited by few. These are the places beyond the everyday, outside history, alive in myths and minds. Parallel worlds with their own being and ways of working, worlds to slip into at your peril, to return from if you can. Old storytellers knew more than most about the ways into otherworlds, which bird to follow, which tree to crouch beneath, which bough to seek, which pale beauty to kiss or be kissed by, which wardrobe door to open. To those with a strong preference for the daylight world of the down to earth, their stories carried health warnings about what to avoid: fairy mounds, woodland pools, green-eyed strangers, unknown barges, precarious bridges. Forests were decidedly hazardous. Sherwood Forest might not be riddled with gingerbread houses and fairy folk, but it grew its own giants and green men. This was the home of legendary outlaws, figures out of place in regular society, but utterly in place in the ancient hunting forest. Here the trees furnished bows for Will Scarlet, long staffs for Little John, venison for Friar Tuck, firewood for roasting game and keeping the cold at bay. The vast area of woods and clearings offered safe havens, the tracks through the forest chances to rob the rich and redistribute their wealth. As everyone knows who has been to the pantomime, seen the films and TV series, played the computer games, or heard the stories, it is the domain of Robin Hood, Maid Marian and the Merry Men. Unlike most fantasy worlds, though, 'Sherwood Forest' has its everyday double.

For those who live in central Nottinghamshire, Sherwood Forest is as much part of the neighbourhood as the local schools and supermarkets. It has, of course, been there much longer than Edwinstowe's gift shops and garages, longer than the fire station and the football ground, the barber's and the bistro, the youth hostel and the care home. Yet all these unremarkable features seem more integral to contemporary life than a phenomenon that has been there for ever. Although many of the businesses have Robin-related names and Sherwood-style gifts, Edwinstowe's international claim to fame now seems oddly tangential to the daily world of getting up and getting on with life. It has fallen out of place simply by being there for such a very long time. And yet, by outliving the present of every age, Sherwood Forest has the air of another world, out of time, out of place, out of sync with the M1, which runs parallel to the western boundary less than ten miles away.

Admittedly, the car park and clearly marked paths smack of twenty-first-century heritage policy. A recovering slag heap visible from the car park is quickly left behind as visitors are organised into the right route: across the road, along the path by the craft complex in the converted coach house, up the slope, down past the Tree Charter pole to the Visitor Centre, through the picnic and play area and on towards the forest. There are open fields to the left and an unpaved path ahead leading visitors onwards through scattered trees. Instead of a dark, fathomless forest, slim trunks with graceful branches spread about, with a few stouter residents and the promise of older trees beyond – birch, oak, holly – and small signs offering advice on what to look out for, from stag beetles and tree pipits to outlaws. Depending on what you have come for, you might be lucky enough to catch a glimpse of a redstart or Will Scarlet. In twenty-first-century Sherwood, the RSPB has joined forces with Robin Hood, but it's too early to say whether the birds or the brigands have a better chance of survival.

As the paths enter the ancient forest, the air begins to change. Through the nettles and the bracken, the denser holly and craggier birches, a sense of timelessness grows. It's too far from the road to hear the passing cars. The stillness is punctuated by the brisk call of a chiffchaff, the hoarse shout of a pheasant or a dog walker, the chatter of a family party. In summer, the green canopy, thickening with leaves and birdsong, blots out the traces of modernity. In winter, the brown leaves layered underfoot, the tangled brambles and wispy twigs set the everyday world at a distance. As light breaks on the shorter days, catching the scarlet haws and holly berries, dim shapes of older trees cocooned within the pale birches begin to emerge.

The limbs of these veterans are pocked and twisted. Their trunks, once tall and straight, bear the scars of persistent campaigns by the wind and weather. Black and blasted boughs stand high as broken masts amidst waves of fresh green or thin twigs. They stand becalmed, as if in waiting, though their dead beams will never again sprout buds. Still the upper branches ramify into thousands of erratic twigs and irregular leaves. Bristling bunches of new life, turning from bud to leaf, blond to green, refreshing again as the Lammas leaves open, before gashing gold and falling. Elderly trees have their own individual style: the age-old annual changes enhanced by the odd stag-head stump or well-worn ring mark of an amputated branch. Former trees without limbs or leaves stand in unapologetic magnificence. Though slightly askew, they are among the most intriguing figures in the forest. Once the corrugated old bark has gone, the trunk lightens and cracks like a volcanic landscape, olive-green with lichen, burnt sienna with rot, lamp black with caves. The forest is full of strange beings and openings into unknown worlds.

Over the years, the survival of Sherwood's ancient oaks has been helped by the way gales pass through their entrails rather than beating against solid sides, though at times the life-saving hollows have proved risky. During the twentieth century, concrete was poured into the gaping gullets of some of the oldest trees by their well-meaning guardians.

The stately congregation of ageing trees steadies visitors for their encounter with the biggest of them all. An arboreal colossus holds court in a huge clearing of its own. A gargantuan girth with branches spread wide, it sidelines every other tree. The full span from twig to ultimate twig must be at least twice the height of the tallest branch, with each limb thicker than a normal trunk. At least four ancient oaks seem to have been bound together by some titanic forester of a forgotten age. And as for the massive trunk, centuries of slow growth stand still within its broad, furrowed, grey chest. Hard to think it was an acorn once. The entire forest takes bearings from here, the heart of the arterial tracks, the destination of all comers. This is the oak of all oaks in Sherwood, the 'Major Oak', grand patriarch of the woods.

The old heavyweight has come to be at risk from its own magnificence. The great outstretched branches need serious support from a discreet Zimmer frame of steel poles and cones. A circular fence keeps visitors at a respectful distance and safe from falling logs. Transfixed by the twists of the high branches, the knots and ridges, creases and cavities, the tiny figures gaze expectantly. The tree once known as the Queen Oak grants an audience to anyone, explanation to none.

The ancient tree now seems somewhat at odds with its surroundings simply by having outlived all its contemporaries. When King John galloped through Sherwood Forest from his palace at Clipstone in pursuit of deer and wild boar, the oak was just a sapling among other saplings. Later, as a mature tree, it might well have been felled for building houses, churches or ships, along with so many of its old companions. Yet here it is, with a grey Gothic-arched cave and crevices, a world in itself impervious to the goings-on around. The trunk was already yawning broadly when the Duke of Newcastle started breeding spaniels and building his great mansion at nearby Clumber

Park in the eighteenth century. I would like to think that its temporary identity as 'The Cockpen Tree' was inspired by its rippling
leaves, recalling the outline of a cockerel's crest, but the nickname
referred to the unlucky fowl bred, fed and penned inside the capacious trunk until ready for cockfighting.

The tree derives its current name not from any innate superior-
ity to its old companions, but rather from a passionate eighteenth-
century dendrophile called Major Hayman Rooke. Enthusiasm for
antiquities, inanimate or natural, drew him to the Duke of
Portland's estate at Welbeck to admire the famous old trees of
Sherwood. He was not disappointed. Strangest of all was the
Greendale Oak, with its huge trunk chopped away to form a
flourishing arch for the Duke's carriage. On either side of the
carriageway was the grand pair of Porters – Little and Large –
standing at heights of 88 and 98 feet. The Duke's Walking Stick
was even taller, its height accentuated by the unusual dearth of
lower branches. And yet this towering tree was still not as distinctive as the magnificent seven-pronged pollard known as the Seven
Sisters, which grew like a giant wooden fork, though it was already
down to six when Rooke encountered it. The Parliament Oak,
where King John held an emergency assembly in 1212, was also
showing its age, the head of the main trunk bare of leaves, branches
like giant fingers reaching for the clouds.

Here was living history – but history in danger of disappearing.
The oaks were a very substantial link to past centuries: some
revealed tangible traces of those who had lived and worked there in
earlier ages – letters cut into the inner wood of some of the great
trees marked out their royal patrons – 'W+M' for William and
Mary, 'IR', James Rex – perhaps even John? The inexorable process
of slow decay meant that the living tablets would one day be gone.
The action of Time's file might be less visible, but in the end it was
just as effective as the woodman's axe. Rooke's desire to record the
living monuments of Sherwood Forest was compelling – and
urgent. There were far more ancient trees than time to draw them.

Sherwood Forest in the 1770s, though sadly diminished from its medieval heyday, retained much of its traditional layout. Rather than continuous thick tree cover, it was broken into woods and grazing areas, large estates and small scattered villages. The best stretch of all, in Rooke's opinion, was a beautiful 1,800-acre wood known as Birklands after the mass of birches growing in and around the forest oaks. Whether he counted or merely estimated the 'ten thousand old oak trees', Rooke's awed description gives us a vivid sense of the forest's character 250 years ago and the prominence even among so many old trees of 'a most curious antient oak'. His own name has fared better with wood preservative than any other remedy he might have taken against oblivion, since his favourite tree went on to borrow his rank and so ensure his place in the annals of Sherwood Forest. Rooke is the Major Oak's very own Major.

So impressed was he by the scale of the great tree that he took three measurements of its girth. The lowest, near the ground, was 34 feet and 4 inches in circumference. At one yard above, it measured 27 feet and 4 inches, and a yard above that, 31 feet and 9 inches. What surprised him most was that the 'wonderfully distorted trunk' had clearly been much larger in the past. He examined the tree inside and out, noting the interior decay and the hollowing effects of its extreme age, which he guessed at about a thousand years. In his portrait of the 'majestic ruin', Rooke caught the distinctive form of the Major Oak, with its squat, stocky, hollowed trunk and broad, bushy crown. His careful drawings and measurements act as an invaluable gauge for the tree's subsequent growth. Edwardian postcards suggest some gain around the waist and sagging at the shoulders since Rooke's visit, but also show how little the great oak changes over decades. It has not altered very much in size or shape since. To see old pictures of a familiar form, with men in whiskers and waistcoats, women in long dresses and large hats, brings home the difference between the lifespan of a healthy oak and a human being. Generations of children have grown up, grown old and gone in the time it takes for an oak to gain a few extra rings or lose a few branches. The ancient oaks of Sherwood Forest are portals into the past and future. Their boughs, whether green, golden or grey, form arches to allow the curious into other lives and worlds.

Rooke's enthusiasm for Sherwood – or perhaps his awareness of the Duke of Portland's pride in his ancient oaks – meant that his *Description and Sketches of some Remarkable Oaks, in the Park at Welbeck* dwelt more on the fortunes than the misfortunes of the forest. Other observers were more forthright – William Gilpin, whose home was in the New Forest, was deeply troubled by the destruction of Britain's ancient woodlands. His 1791 book of *Forest Scenery* was an effort to open contemporary eyes to the picturesque beauty of old trees and to preserve the memory of the old forests that once covered so much of Britain. Since Sherwood Forest was among the most famous, Gilpin was especially dismayed to find it 'a scene of great desolation'.

More than three decades after Gilpin sounded the alarm, Jacob Strutt made his own pilgrimage to the great oaks of Sherwood – only to find that many of those sketched by Hayman Rooke were gone. His exploration was rather less thorough than Rooke's and, in any case, many of those recorded by Rooke in the 1770s had evidently been in a state of extreme age. Still, the noticeable depletion of oak trees over half a century reinforced Gilpin's gloomy judgement. In the intervening years, demand for timber had caused havoc among the old forests of Merry England. War always takes its toll on trees: the Royal Navy needed thousands of mature oaks for each of its battleships. The loss of a single ship might mean the death of hundreds of men and thousands of oak trees. As the Napoleonic conflict wore on, what remained of Sherwood Forest shrank further.

Not all the trees were pressed into the service of the Crown – oaks continued to be needed for tanning, building, barrel making and furniture, while rapidly expanding industries and nearby cities took an unprecedented toll. Storms and tempests, as ever, took their share of trees. As land was enclosed and large estates grew larger, trees were felled to make room for roads and farms as well as for timber and other, less practical, reasons. Byron's family seat at Newstead Abbey is at the heart of Sherwood Forest, but when he inherited it from his eccentric uncle – known locally as the 'wicked' Lord Byron – all the old trees in the estate had been felled because of a family dispute. The young trees had also been cut down and sold off as firewood to bakers in nearby Nottingham. Although Byron planted an oak beside the Abbey when he took possession of the family seat, he was himself indirectly responsible for the destruction of a group of tall trees on the Chaworth family's neighbouring estate. As a teenager, Byron would ride through Sherwood Forest like a knight of old, dreaming of Mary Chaworth. Some years later, when both were unhappily married, he recalled his early love for her in 'The Dream', fondly evoking Annesley:

> the hill
> Was crown'd with a peculiar diadem
> Of trees, in circular array, so fix'd,
> Not by the sport of nature, but of man:
> These two, a maiden and a youth, were there
> Gazing—the one on all that was beneath
> Fair as herself—but the boy gazed on her.

When Mary's husband John Musters read the poem, he was so enraged that he had the entire coronet of trees chopped down. For one reason or another, the forest that once covered most of Nottinghamshire was steadily disappearing.

William Gilpin's dismay over the depletion of Sherwood Forest was deepened by a sense of cultural vandalism. This was the traditional home of 'the illustrious Robin Hood', who was enjoying a major revival at this time. Folk ballads were generally popular, but the old tales of Robin Hood, newly published by Joseph Ritson, spoke with special force in an age when the rights of the common man were hotly debated and expanding industrial towns were heightening awareness of the value of the countryside. The image of an outlaw band sustained by the natural produce of the forest, ready to protect the poor and redistribute excess wealth to the needy, had strong appeal to many, while those less sympathetic to social and political reform warmed to Robin's loyalty to King Richard and defence of English ideals in the face of French villainy. In novels such as *Ivanhoe*, national animosities stirred by the Napoleonic Wars were aired and explored among the thickets of Nottinghamshire's ancient hunting forest. As Robin Hood emerged from old scattered tales and medieval ballads as a substantial character, he needed somewhere to live – and where better than Sherwood Forest?

In the older ballads, Robin roamed around Nottinghamshire and across the North of England, from Barnsdale and Wakefield to Clitheroe and Lancaster. Robin Hood's Bower was near Sheffield, his Bay just south of Whitby. But there is something about a Forest that fits the stories better. The Jacobean poet Michael Drayton evidently thought so. In *Poly-Olbion*, his long, winding poem about England's places and stories, Robin Hood, along with Will Scarlet, George-a-Green, Much the miller's son and 'Tuck the merry friar' are firmly situated in the forest at Mansfield, camouflaged in suits of Lincoln green and living on venison:

> Which they did boil and roast, in many a mighty wood,
> Sharp hunger the fine sauce to their more kingly food.
> Then taking them to rest, his merrymen and he
> Slept many a summer's night under the greenwood tree.

Late-Georgian readers, keen on early modern literature, Robin Hood and the great outdoors, agreed: from henceforth, Robin Hood and Maid Marian were imagined living an idyllic life in Sherwood Forest. The ancient oaks, rooted there rather longer than the legends, had just the right character for accommodating a bold outlaw band. The Shambles Tree, already fitted with hooks for hanging venison carcases, needed a more romantic name and so became Robin Hood's Larder, and, with its massive spread and natural cave yawning wide to hide outlaws, the Major Oak must of course be his headquarters.

For all this mental travelling in Sherwood Forest, the trees continued to disappear. The more the forest decreased, the more visitors arrived in person to see the remnants. Illustrated story-books, green-capped figurines, arrow-shaped horse brasses and door knockers, fat Friar Tuck toby jugs and Robin Hood plates captivated new generations in the Railway Age. As the network expanded, so did visitor numbers – and the fame of individual trees. A colourful poster printed in 1897 to advertise the new Lancashire, Derby and East Coast Railway grouped small portraits of Chatsworth, Bolsover Castle, Clumber Park, Rufford Abbey, Thoresby Hall and Welbeck around the leafy A-list celebrity. The Major Oak commanded centre stage in the Dukeries.

Late-Victorian visitors could catch the train to Edwinstowe and walk under the greenwood tree. It was like stepping into another world, far removed from the smoky cities, railway towns or even modern, increasingly mechanised farms. Tennyson was so taken with the 'hundreds of huge oaks' growing around the well-beaten path through the forest that he embarked on a musical version of Robin Hood – with somewhat mixed success. But if the characters seemed rather wooden, the oaks came alive: 'Gnarl'd—older than the thrones of Europe—look, / What breadth, height, strength— torrents of eddying bark!' For the ageing poet laureate, the old patriarch oaks seemed 'as it were, / Immortal, and we mortal'.

As steam carried thousands from the noisy cities of Victorian England into the green world of Robin Hood, the coal-powered engines contributed to its destruction. The old trees were at risk not only from their admirers, who would clamber up to pose and picnic, or see how many could squeeze inside, or light a fire to create an authentic outlaw atmosphere, but also from the deep coal deposits far below. Once the rich seams of the deeper Nottinghamshire coalfield were discovered, Sherwood Forest's ancient character changed more decisively than ever before. Visitors alighting from steam trains at Edwinstowe were only a mile from the Thoresby mine. By then, the whole area once covered in woods and heathland was filling with smoke, wheels, pitheads and sheds. Shafts descended deep into the ground at Bestwood, Bilsthorpe, Blidworth, Clipstone, Cresswell, Kirkby, Mansfield, Ollerton, Rufford, Warsop and Welbeck. Tourists in search of Lord Byron's old haunts found new mining villages at Newstead and Annesley.

Beneath Sherwood Forest lay a parallel world of coal dust and tunnels, pit ponies and wooden props, where teams of men hacked and heaved in the dark, re-emerging exhausted at nightfall after long hours of labour. At times, the ground shook as a tunnel collapsed or gas exploded deep underground. If the day-trippers to Sherwood Forest were escaping the grime of modern cities, those who lived in the new mining villages were not. The democratic traditions of Robin Hood still inspired them to band together and demand better conditions, and eventually to strike for the survival of their livelihood. The parallel worlds above and below Sherwood Forest were not as separate as they may have seemed.

Two world wars brought further devastation to Sherwood Forest. Intense demand for coal and timber meant the loss of thousands more trees. The forest became a key site for military exercises, training camps, ammunition stores and gun emplacements. Trees that escaped felling were subject to damage from grenades and artillery fire. It is remarkable that any of Major Rooke's 'Remarkable Oaks' survived at all. But there they stood, ring-marked by smoke and fumes of kinds unknown to the inner heartwood, going through the wars as they had so many times before.

For the generation that found themselves alive in 1945, the idea of an old, untouched England was more powerful than ever.

Between the wars, a Britain filled with pretty villages, peaceful fields, slow rivers and flourishing trees had taken mental root; after years of bombardment and anxiety, people sought reassurance that something of the old country survived. Those who had seen Errol Flynn swinging across the screen in his neat green doublet and tights in 1938 were also curious about whether Hollywood's 'Sherwood' was anything like the real Sherwood Forest. With the military gone, leaving some of the ancient trees in place, the old Forest was opening again. By the 1950s, the oaks of Birklands were clocking over 15,000 visitors in a single summer's day.

Fame can have its downside. As would-be Robin Hoods scrambled into the ancient trees, they often broke branches or trod too hard on the ageing bark. The impact of the Major's admirers on the ground around did nothing for his health, as air was forced out by unwitting feet, crushing and compressing the vast underground world of roots, invertebrates, fungus and soil. If the protective fence that now keeps us at several arm's lengths from the old tree feels at odds with dreams of free living in the wild woods, it is acting as security for the Major and future generations of admirers. Even with the safe enclosure and vigilant foresters to guard it, the ancient oak was injured during the lockdown of 2020 when a would-be outlaw climbed over the fence and up the trunk, breaking off a three-foot section.

Although the old trees have suffered over the years from the comings and goings of human beings, they have maintained a magnetic power. As a boy in the 1950s, John Palmer fell under the enchantment of Sherwood Forest. Half a century later, he gained special permission to fulfil his lifelong sense of obligation to the woodland monarch by collecting five hundred acorns from the Major Oak to put in pots, and watch as they turned into oaklings. Since then, he has planted them in a Dorset field, fending off the combined threats of voles, ants, rabbits, droughts, gales and floods. In five centuries or so, the Major's descendants may be as tall and broad as the grand old patriarch and enjoying their second home on the south coast. Oak trees have always been celebrated for their staying power and their mobility – remaining in place longer than most other living things, but also reaching out elsewhere. The naval officers who once sailed away in oak-built ships often took pocketfuls of acorns to plant in distant countries. Sherwood Forest's miniature reincarnation in Dorset adds another parallel world to the Forest's multi-dimensional existence in space and time.

The Major Oak is so well propped and protected that the biggest threats are probably the smallest: the attractively named, but potentially deadly, two-spotted oak buprestid beetle and the oak processionary moth. The beetles are harbingers of acute oak decline, a fatal condition marked by deep, weeping wounds in the bark, and they prey on withered trees suffering from chronic oak die-back. The little brown moths operate through other tactics, marching nose-to-tail in arrow formations, munching their way through thick clusters of foliage to leave even the mightiest oaks stripped bare. The quiet determination of these tiny oak assassins is chilling, but expert arborists are intent on their elimination. Sherwood Forest is now a designated European Special Area of Conservation – internationally recognised for its exceptional importance and rich biodiversity. The old oaks are host to hundreds of animals, insects, spiders, birds and bats, the surrounding woodland to rare ferns, flowers and butterflies. Despite their turbulent life stories, more than nine hundred ancient oaks are still standing (more or less), while the annual eruption of acorns offers a regular, renewable promise of fresh growth.

Serious conservation work has been under way since the 1950s, when Sherwood Forest was declared a UK site of Special Scientific Interest. It has recently come under the care of the RSPB. Work to clear intrusive plants and manage deadwood, with the aim of ensuring light levels conducive to healthy regeneration, is already helping to recover the natural richness of Sherwood Forest. The restoration of ancient clearings, heaths and commons – as much part of the medieval forest as the oaks and birch – will give birds dependent on mixed terrain a fighting chance. The noisier species are often most evident in the woods – jackdaws and jays, wood-peckers and warblers. On a clear day you might just catch the high-pitched tweets of tiny goldcrests in the tall pines or notice the slight movement of a bark-brown tree creeper on an old oak trunk. Tree pipits and woodlarks like open heathland, too. A grey log or lichen-covered stone on the heath offers safety to nightjars until daylight falls away and they fly low across the heath in search of beetles and moths. In the twilight world of Sherwood Forest, the old hunting grounds come alive with dark, flitting shapes repos-sessing their old haunts.

Wickenby

~

The scarlet cups of field poppies stand out against the tangle of bramble bushes, burdock and tall nettles. Bearded barley shimmers away behind a straggle of parched grass. Thin, white-haired thistles hang over the low-lying plantain along the edge of ageing concrete. A flat, cracked, ghost road runs towards a horizon marked by a row of tiny trees, evenly spaced as a worn-out bristle brush. The vanishing point of the rough, parallel lines is hidden by a light, pocked heap of lime and a lower mound of something dark that might be soil or manure. The way is chipped and crossed with irregular ravines: a rough, buff plain pitted with shallow craters, splattered with dried mud and scattered patches of tired tarmac. Brambles feel their way along the veins in the concrete. A single pathfinder, green leaves spread out like a lizard's feet, winds its way across, testing the ground as it creeps towards an unknown target. Russet-red explosions of midsummer sorrel. Heartsease with flowers all lemon yellow, as if their blue caps have come off when jumping up into the air. An isolated clump of white campion, dark-stalked and thin-leaved, transforms a hot, frayed square into a black-and-white still. The old runway at Wickenby is empty now, but high above, a single kestrel holds its wings firm against the current, and eyes the bleached ground for signs of life.

Across the narrow lane, everything's tidier. Close-shaven grass runs along the well-defined lines of a working airfield. It's not very large, but the smooth, charcoal-grey strip is long enough for the few light aircraft at the far end. I remember taking off from here years ago, in a red-and-white-striped four-seater plane. It made me gasp as it rose suddenly and steeply, before wheeling around over the flat fields for fifteen minutes or so. We could see small brick houses, smaller Massey Ferguson tractors and, smallest of all, a herd of Lincoln Reds grazing imperturbably. Everything was a strong red against the green fields and summer trees. I don't remember taking much notice of the white watchtower or the wide curve of the grey hangar – at the time such familiar buildings hardly registered at all. Active RAF bases were a common sight, disused airfields even more so. We used to walk the family dogs along old concrete tracks in the middle of ploughed fields – they provided welcome causeways in the wet winter mud. I was not aware, when grappling with clutch control at the abandoned airfield at Ludford, that I was learning to drive at what was once a site for secret weapons. This was probably just as well, given my seventeen-year-old nerves behind the wheel. My father, who was attempting to teach me, had no worry about the old peri-track turning into a racing circuit – I failed my first test for driving too slowly.

Odd stretches of wartime runway, broken walls and underground shelters were still commonplace in rural areas. Even today, it is not unusual to come across a rusty sheet of corrugated iron or a few old concrete posts with collapsing chain-link fencing protruding from an unkempt hedge. Long, moss-covered, semicircular Nissen huts and squat, grey pillboxes still lie low in many woods and fields and coastal scrublands. They are almost part of the landscape. Almost.

Between 1939 and 1945, the face of Europe changed – suddenly, dramatically, shockingly. In Britain, thousands of acres of farmland were covered in concrete runways and quickly constructed camps.

The tiny airfields that had popped up with the new aviation craze in the thirties were mostly militarised and renamed: Balivanich in the Hebrides took on a new identity as RAF Benbecula, while Coventry Aerodrome turned into RAF Baginton and the airfield at Exeter (rather less imaginatively) RAF Exeter. In the eastern counties, especially, airfields, landing strips and decoy sites were rapidly laid down by teams of Irish workmen. At the outbreak of the Second World War, Yorkshire had around fifteen airstrips; by 1945 there were nearly forty RAF stations there. East Anglia saw similarly rapid expansion, while Lincolnshire offered room for even more. Tennyson would have been astounded to feel his native county juddering with low-flying aircraft. He regarded railways with deep suspicion, preferring in most of his poems to eschew mechanised transport in favour of horses, boats and barges. By 1943, his birthplace in the small village of Somersby was encircled by RAF stations – at Bardney, Coningsby, Manby, Spilsby, Strubby and Woodhall Spa. Had his Northern farmer 'old style', a man preoccupied with land and inheritance, lived for another century, he would have had something to say about the wholesale requisitioning of farmland.

William Hoskins, writing soon after the war, certainly did. In a brief concluding chapter of his 1955 book, *The Making of the English Landscape*, he rounded on the wartime leaders and scientists for their destruction of 'the gentle, unravished English landscape'. The real culprit was the MOD: 'Airfields have flayed it bare wherever there are well drained stretches of land, above all in eastern England. Poor devastated Lincolnshire and Suffolk!' Hoskins could not have predicted that what he saw as the agents of destruction might one day strike people as precious remnants of a vanished past. Since then, the few who flew the propeller planes of the Second World War have become fewer and fewer. Lincolnshire is now known as 'Bomber County', home to one of only two Avro Lancasters still capable of flight, and the International Bomber Command Centre at Bracebridge Heath. Plans are under way to erect a life-sized steel sculpture of a Lancaster bomber above the site where it crashed in 1942, close to the county border with Nottinghamshire. That the RAF presence is still strong so many years after the wartime personnel have gone is gin clear.

The airfields deplored by Hoskins began to disappear as soon as the war ended. Many farmers recovered their fields and ploughed up the triangular runways for grass and grain. Once demobbed, some of the servicemen stationed at isolated RAF bases stayed to become farmers themselves. A young Australian called John Varley, posted to the Lincolnshire Wolds in the early 1940s, married a local girl and farmed the land requisitioned by the Air Ministry at Ludford Magna. He never bothered to finish demolishing the buildings and left the perimeter track in place.

While some wartime airfields rapidly returned to agriculture, leaving little more than the ghost of a memory or a strip of hard-standing for resting combine harvesters and grain silos, others were gradually repurposed. Some, such as the nuclear power plant at RAF Annan or the Atomic Weapons Research Establishment at RAF Aldermaston, remained in government service during the Cold War. At the Royal Naval Air Station at Crail in Fife, the Joint Services School for Linguists offered very discreet opportunities for National Service to bright young conscripts including Alan Bennett, Michael Frayn, Peter Hall and Dennis Potter. Other ex-flying stations have had more peaceful afterlives as schools, golf courses, housing estates or factories. The 800-acre Nissan plant in Sunderland spreads out over the former site RAF Usworth, while the rather more niche production of Lotus cars takes place further south at the old RAF base at Hethel in Norfolk. Sleek Lotus classics stand stationary among hundreds of other old cars in the British Motor Museum at ex-RAF Gaydon, just off the M40. Bomber County Beer, an especially powerful brew, is made in a craft beer brewery at the disused RAF station at Elsham Wolds. The international airports at Belfast, Edinburgh and Glasgow have at times been known as RAF Aldergrove, Turnhouse and Abbotsinch.

Welsh holidaymakers heading for Ibiza or Tenerife may not be aware that Swansea Airport was once RAF Fairwood Common, any more than Scots think of Inverness Airport as RAF Dalcross. I was surprised when flying to Aberdeen for the first time that my father announced I would be 'landing at Dyce at eleven hundred hours'.

Some of the airfields built in the 1940s did continue as operational stations, evolving with advances in aviation. Successive generations of young pilots learned to fly Jet Provosts, Tucanos or Hawks under the Red Dragon Badge of RAF Valley in Anglesey. Britain's oldest RAF station at Northolt is now the only active base in London, but like other older airfields built for the Royal Flying Corps, it has served successively as a civil and military hub. RAF Scampton, famous in turn for the Dambusters Raid, Vulcan bombers and the pyrotechnics of the Red Arrows, was finally closed in 2022. Local residents who almost grew accustomed to the dark shadow of vast triangular wings passing overhead, and the roar of fast jets weaving in and out of formation, with multicoloured, criss-crossing vapour trails, are now looking anxiously to the future of the site. Will it be a Heritage or Asylum centre next?

Nostalgia for the RAF has grown with the contraction of the service. The UK's only fully working Lancaster still rumbles into the sky on special occasions, escorted by the veteran Spitfires and Hurricanes of the Battle of Britain Memorial Flight. Former airfields lend themselves to large aviation museums – there are a lot of them. Whether visiting the Helicopter Museum at Weston-super-Mare, the Lashenden Air Warfare Museum in Kent or the National Museum of Flight in East Lothian (once RAF East Fortune), you step into the past among old aircraft. Robert Sage, Life President of the Yorkshire Aviation Museum until his death in 1994, knew more than most about the site's wartime character as RAF Elvington. He took off from the airfield on many bombing raids, until, one night in 1943, his Halifax was shot down over Belgium and he spent the rest of the war in a POW camp. At the

Imperial War Museum at Duxford, the surviving wartime hangars help to give some sense of what it was like during the Battle of Britain. For those with a cool head and a steady stomach, there is even a chance to take to the air in a Spitfire.

But you might get a better sense of the wartime generation by walking quietly across a small or disused airfield and feeling the lives that were lost. The woods around the old station at Finmere are full of stray debris. In winter, the dried oak leaves build up, but can't quite bury the moss-covered concrete, the doors leading down into the ground. Low brick walls, blotched with damp, mark the sunken guard houses. Through the straight, ribbed trunks of the healthy trees you can make out the forms of wartime buildings. When you get closer they are only tired shells. At dawn or dusk especially, when the air is thick with the residue of intense activity, the sense of emptiness is profound.

Though no longer an RAF station, Wickenby Airfield, like Finmere, has not entirely lost its original character. The fields commandeered from the Bowsers' farm in 1941 are still home to an aerodrome eighty years on – it is just rather different in scale. The old bomber base is now used for light planes, the old watchtower houses a museum commemorating the wartime airfield. What seemed both frighteningly out of place and yet welcome to the local community when it suddenly appeared in the 1940s has come to be the village's best known feature.

When the airfield opened in 1942, Wickenby was home to 12 Squadron. Originally formed for the Royal Flying Corps, 12 Squadron had first seen action flying biplanes at the Somme. Some years later, as an RAF squadron based in France, the crews operated monoplane bombers with the unlikely name of Fairey Battles. After desperate missions over Belgium and the Netherlands, they were forced back to Britain, where new airfields were opening every few days – as many as 125 in 1942 alone. As the war took its toll on the RAF, the bombing campaign demanded more and more men and planes, so 626 Squadron was formed to strengthen the force at Wickenby. The new squadron's motto – 'To Strive and Not to Yield' – took inspiration from Tennyson but, in tune with the times, cut the line to the bare essentials. Tennyson had Ulysses, the ageing veteran of the Trojan War, in mind when composing the stirring lines. The men of 626 Squadron were mostly about twenty-one. Their badge was a trireme with its eye fixed on the breakers ahead, their battlecraft an Avro Lancaster, facing waves of Messerschmitts, flak and ack-ack. The grand motto was swiftly adapted by those aboard: 'To Press on Regardless'.

Young men from all over the world found themselves at British bases. RAF stations included airmen from as far afield as Australia, Canada, the Caribbean, France, New Zealand, Poland, South Africa and Sri Lanka. None could have seemed a less likely destination than Wickenby. In November, when the fog is so thick you can hardly see your own feet, when driving rain turns the surrounding fields to dank mud pools and Siberian winds sweep across from the North Sea, it can seem quite bleak. And all the more so for anyone brought up in a hot, sunny climate. Very few of those stationed at Wickenby during the war are still alive, but some felt moved in later life to share their experiences with friends, family and historians. In the 1990s, Patrick Otter listened to wry recollections of bitter cold weather and spartan billets from some of the long-retired servicemen and -women. Their memories chime with Peter Baxter's account of his months at Wickenby as a Flight Engineer with 12 Squadron. What stuck in his mind, as in many, was the bewildering remoteness of the airfield. He had never heard of RAF Wickenby when he set off for active service at the age of twenty. Wickenby still takes a bit of finding, but during the Second World War, with all the signposts taken down for reasons of national security, it was a real achievement to get there at all.

I wonder what Richard Dimbleby thought when he arrived at Wickenby as a war correspondent to join the crew of a Lancaster on an overnight bombing mission. Although he never overcame his airsickness, he reported on at least twenty raids for the BBC.

The surviving recordings of his reactions to feeling the plane dive, seeing the bombs drop, the fireballs, the burning buildings and the anti-aircraft guns, while doing his best to maintain a calm tone and impartial focus on the facts, convey as vividly as any wartime memoir the full horror of these missions, the scale of the destruction, the courage of the young crews. The chances of returning to base unscathed were slim. Of 125,000 servicemen in Bomber Command during the Second World War, 57,205 died. Thousands more were wounded or shot down and taken prisoner. Those wounded in action were often back in the air within a week. Peter Baxter recalled that after six weeks of bombing raids, the men were allowed to take a week's leave, which 'helped to soothe our jangled nerves', adding that in no time at all, 'we were back at Wickenby and in action again'. He felt lucky to have been allowed leave – the three friends he made on arrival at the base in November 1942 were all killed within the first month.

Baxter found the silver birch woods around the airfield soothing – they softened the bare, unfamiliar landscape. The naturalist Eric Simms, also stationed at Wickenby, may also have sought relief among the trees. Perhaps between raids, he stood in the woods listening to the blackbirds and thrushes, or stared across the open fields observing lapwings in their element. But the birds took flight in the face of the unaccustomed company in the air. If Simms spent any time birdwatching during his months on active service at Wickenby, he made no mention of it in his autobiography. The chapter on life in Bomber Command is the only one to omit any reference to birds or natural history. Instead the months at Wickenby are a sequence of increasingly dramatic recollections of bombing raids, reaching a peak on the night when his plane was accidentally bombed by another Lancaster and had to limp home with a critically wounded air gunner and an unwanted cargo of incendiary bombs. His wartime recollections close with lines composed at Wickenby in January 1944:

Friends can die, as if in the routine of a day,
Some quietly, unobserved, and others in the cataclysm.

To which he added, 'I have been very fortunate, and for me each
day since the war has been a kind of bonus – a gift to be treasured
and not frittered away.' Along with the birds, he left out his own
DFC, awarded for outstanding bravery in the skies.

The RAF had birds of their own – the homing pigeons which
accompanied crews on every mission. When a Lancaster from 12
Squadron crashed into the sea in May 1943, the crew's pigeon flew
home alone to Wickenby, triggering a search for the missing crew.
After five days, Flight Sergeant Scott and his men were miraculously spotted in the North Sea and rescued from their tiny dinghy.
The use of homing pigeons, vulnerable to attack from raptors,
prompted the Government to issue the 'Destruction of Peregrine
Falcons Order' in 1940, by which peregrines and their young had
to be shot and any eggs destroyed. Since then, the diktat has been
deplored by naturalists tracing the catastrophic decline in twentieth-century peregrine populations. But the brutality was of its time.
The wartime cost in all kinds of life is higher than the highest flyer.

The comedian and writer Michael Bentine, best known for
co-creating *The Goon Show*, was posted to Wickenby in 1943. His
initial attempts to join the RAF had been thwarted first by his dual
Peruvian-British nationality and then by a near-fatal overdose of
typhoid vaccine, which left his eyesight irreparably damaged. He
finally joined up after being arrested by military police, who were
under the mistaken impression that he had gone AWOL and
charged him accordingly – with desertion. As he was on stage
arrayed in Shakespearean doublet and hose at the time of the arrest,
they might have paused to wonder about whether he was really
attempting to lie low. It took an intervention from the Peruvian
ambassador to uncover the trail of misunderstanding and allow
Bentine to enlist as an RAF Intelligence Officer. His first posting
to Wickenby made a deep impression. As a non-flying officer, he

saw the young bomber crews night after night, preparing for action, 'dangerous, frightening and, in winter especially, bitterly, morale-sappingly, cold'. One night in particular stayed with him. On 16 December 1943, Bentine was returning to base just before midnight, when he caught sight of a friend in the moonlight. As he waved to 'the tall moustachioed figure', Arthur Walker acknowledged the gesture but carried on towards his own billet. The following morning, Bentine learned that Walker had been killed the night before when his Lancaster crashed in low cloud a few miles from Wickenby. At the moment when Bentine saw him so clearly in the moonlight, Walker was already dead.

Whether the sense of humour that sustained Michael Bentine's post-war career was sharpened by trauma or had always acted as a defence against what he witnessed is hard to tell: there is little humour and a great deal of horror in his memoir, *The Door Marked Summer*. He was prepared to admit that the wackiness of the Goons owed something to the war – 'Comedy catharsis isn't a bad description.' Like the St Trinian's cartoons of Ronald Searle, who only narrowly survived years as a POW forced into hard labour on the notorious Burma Railway, much post-war comedy demonstrated an intense sense of liberation accentuated by very dark jokes.

Although Bentine was haunted by memories of Wickenby, many veterans dwelled on more entertaining anecdotes. Those who chatted to Patrick Otter remembered the local pubs with particular fondness – the White Hart at Lissington, the Red Lion in Market Rasen, the Adam and Eve in Wragby. One night, cycling home without lights after a pub crawl in Market Rasen, they were stopped by a line of local policemen, arms linked, right across the country lane. The Air Force revellers did not think much of the fines meted out in the Magistrates' Court: 'it was all right to navigate across Europe by night without lights, but not, it seemed, from Market Rasen to Wickenby.'

My father, a young air gunner through most of the Second World War (though never stationed at Wickenby), was far more inclined to tell tales of high jinks than of aerial combat. 'Are you there, Moriarty?', which involved vigorous blindfold battles with rolled-up newspapers, was a standard Mess game. It included variations such as balancing on a bottle before launching the first blow or making a chap spin round and round before sending him staggering off to meet an equally befuddled opponent. Airmen with time off from their more serious duties also worked out how to create black footsteps across a high white ceiling. This requires an elaborate pyramid of furniture and a pair of boots covered in coal dust attached to broom handles. 'Shouldn't have joined if you can't take a joke,' was one of my father's lifelong catchphrases, handy for many situations, though easily outdone by his favourite, 'The sun's over the yard arm', at 6.01 p.m. Even on the rare occasion when he did speak of being wounded at altitude, it was with breathtaking matter-of-factness and a huge sense of gratitude for coming out alive. That stoic readiness to get on with whatever needed doing, combined with a capacity for closing the hangar doors and getting on with ebullient socialising once it was done, evidently stood him in good stead. Whether it all seemed different in the small hours is impossible to know, and I wouldn't have dreamed of asking. The wartime photos of young bomber crews with well-trimmed moustaches and cheerful, ready-for-anything expressions remind me of him very much.

It is often the next generation who feel the strongest need to recall the conflict, regardless of their parents' stiff upper lips and deadpan humour. 626 Squadron was disbanded in 1945 and the RAF abandoned the site eleven years later. Three decades on, RAF Wickenby was marked by memorials raised by volunteers determined that those stationed there should never be forgotten. If you walk from the hangar to the aerodrome's main gate, the path runs straight between a memorial avenue of young Swedish white-beam. The slim trees stand proud in perfect symmetry beside the trimmed hedge flanking the straight approach road. In spring their white flowers match the watchtower, by late summer their boughs are hung with blood-red berries. Each young tree commemorates someone who served, as the plaques at the foot of their trunks relate. Some are dedicated to whole crews – Jim Wright, Eric Saunders, Doug Tattersall, Wally Smith, Don Hone, Brian Heath and George Shrimpton, who took off from Wickenby in the summer of 1943 in a bomber affectionately known as Sarah. One young crew never saw action, because they were killed the same June in a training flight over the Wolds – Sergeants Yeo, Aston, Sneesby, Hiddleston, Robinson, Soluk and Rennick. John Critchley had better luck. When his Lancaster crashed in a thunderstorm in July 1945, nearby farm workers heard his emergency whistle and pulled him from the wreckage. While the rest of the crew were killed, John, the trainee rear gunner, lived on into his eighties.

Lists of names may not tell us very much about the men whose lives are now defined by their early deaths. Sergeant Frederick Gooch has his own plaque, revealing only his final role as a rear gunner, killed on 23 September 1944 at the age of twenty-four. Flight Sergeant George Chaffe came from Devon to serve in 12 Squadron at Wickenby, and is buried in northern France, at the cemetery in Magny, along with the rest of the crew. What the plaques do bring home is that these young men never had a chance to make a life for themselves after the war and died without knowing the outcome. Arthur Long, on the other hand, who worked alongside Peter Baxter as a Flight Engineer at Wickenby in 1943, lived long enough to see the airfield turn into a museum and to be remembered as the 'genial Welsh gentleman'. There is a tribute to Mary Vickers, too, who, like many local families, opened her home to members of 12 and 626 Squadrons during the war. She lived until she was ninety-four.

At the gate, the stylized bronze frame of a young man hangs suspended by his left ankle. *The Fall of Icarus*, created by Margarita Wood in 1981, stands for all those who flew too close to the sun. In the classical myth, Icarus plunges into the sea as his wings melt, before the eyes of his distraught father. The tall, pointed letters beneath were carved by Ralph Beyer, whose own childhood was spent moving from Berlin to Potsdam, Crete and Switzerland, before his family finally fled mainland Europe for Britain in the mid-1930s. Ralph was eighteen when the war broke out; his mother, who returned to Germany, was arrested and died in Auschwitz. After the war, Ralph carved the texts for the new cathedral at Coventry, built from the wreckage in the hope of everlasting peace. In a similar spirit of reconciliation, the International Bomber Command Centre opened in 2018 on a breezy stretch of Bracebridge Heath to commemorate the aircrews on all sides lost in action during the war.

I sometimes visit one of the older stations, RAF Hemswell, long since repurposed but oddly atmospheric at certain times of year. It was familiar long before I went there, not least because of my father's fondness for old war films ('The Dam Busters March' would often boom out from the garden shed to the surprise of unsuspecting school friends). Although 617 Squadron was stationed at Scampton, the buildings at RAF Hemswell provided convincing locations for the 1955 film of *The Dam Busters*. Unlike so many of the airfields rushed into service during the Second World War, both Hemswell and Scampton enjoyed the solid, cream brick, evenly spaced H-Block buildings of the 1930s. After the station closed, Hemswell acted as a refuge for the Ugandan Asians fleeing Idi Amin's regime. Today, the buildings house a vast array of antiques.

The original neo-Georgian RAF windows shed light on inter-connected, rectangular caves of wonder. Clustering in corners, towering overhead, laid out behind glass or proudly arrayed, are grape-shaped decanters, sapphire rings, red Dinky trucks, flying ducks, découpage fire screens, green baize tables, papier-mâché trays, fading maps, mahogany chairs, cherrywood cupboards, Persian rugs, china pugs, art nouveau jugs, Wally dogs, jelly moulds, Regency coal scuttles, stone bottles, shuttlecocks, footballs, mirror balls, prints, plates, paintings, pots – just a few of the items that come and go. The Antiques Centre is a haven for the abandoned and displaced – a limbo land of the old, outdated but only temporarily unwanted. Here, the relics of homes lovingly created over decades, culled for downsizing or cleared after death are carefully reassembled in unexpected combinations: an enormous pair of French bellows, transformed into a coffee table; a pine pig, rescued from a butcher's closing-down sale and now polished and standing proud on an old naval chest. There are sometimes pictures of Spitfires and Hurricanes by Alan Holt, a former Battle of Britain fighter pilot who spent his later years revisiting formative experiences in paint.

Along the straight paths outside, well kept and weed free as the original residents would have expected, are rows of elderly cherry trees. In summer, the slim, pointed leaves are perfectly in keeping with the surrounding architecture. Two stout veterans stand guard on either side of the entrance to the Canberra building, forming a sword-like arch with their branches for visitors to pass beneath. Above the grand, green parade around the car park, the solid, art deco water tower still keeps watch. These sturdy trees were planted in the 1930s – just before all things Japanese became tainted by the global hostilities. Not many of the young men who saw them as saplings had the chance to grow old and spread so comfortably. But the Hemswell cherries survived the war – and the unpredictable fortunes of peacetime. They are at their best in the spring, when the thick blossom bursts from their ageing boughs to create low-lying clouds of dawn pink.

The Bridge of Sounds

~

Yorkshire and Lincolnshire share the same name for the low rolling hills that would run into each other were it not for the great river mouth and its flat, whiskery cheeks of surrounding land. The Wolds to north and south are part of the same lime-stone escarpment, remnants of chalk deposited some hundred million years ago and shaped since by wind and water. Similar sweeping lines of chalk emerge elsewhere as the Chilterns or the Marlborough Downs and face the sea in gleaming white at Lulworth Cove and Dover.

The country roads in the Wolds twist and turn between fields marked out by neat hedges and odd clumps of oak and ash. Pale cream churches on the gently rolling hills have stood there for centur-ies, reminding parishioners of lives past and the life to come. The compass-needle spires of Huggate and Ganton have always directed attention to the heavens, while further south, across the Humber, Louth's soaring pinnacle now attracts peregrine falcons as a nesting site. But even a squat and stumpy tower looks tall when level-headed hills are surrounded by flatlands. From the old, abandoned church at Walesby, you can look right across the plain to the graceful silhou-ette of Lincoln Cathedral and the Derbyshire hills beyond.

The trees are somehow bigger, too, than in places crowded with chimneys, warehouses, high-rise blocks, or indeed, mountains.

David Hockney's portraits of the Thixendale trees catch the sheer grandeur of mature broadleaves in the Wolds. They just seem to rise and expand to fill the space. From Garrowby Hill, the highest point of the Yorkshire Wolds, the levels stretch away, criss-crossed with a patchwork of crop-coloured fields. Normanby Top, the Lincolnshire counterpart, falls short by 250 feet, but is still the highest point of a vast county, high enough to look over the nearby woods and fields to the fenland beyond.

Heading south from Garrowby or north from Normanby, the fields flatten away towards the coast. This is estuary land, where the great rivers of the North and East Midlands join forces on their way to the sea. The River Humber fills with the fresh water of the Trent, the Derwent, the Ouse, the Aire and the Don and the surging salt of the North Sea. On either side of the river lie mudflats, reed banks, level sands and long straggling roads. A railway runs along the North Bank, linking the villages to the sizeable city of Hull. Across the water, the southern shore is emptier until it banks round to Immingham and Grimsby. Along both coasts, a motorway loops towards the estuary. There, a pair of narrow towers, startlingly bright, straight, vertical, look as if they must have been dropped from space.

The Humber Bridge has the longest single-span suspension in Europe. When it opened in 1981, it was the biggest suspension bridge in the world, longer than those across the Forth or the Severn, longer even than the Bosphorus Bridge or the Golden Gate. An odd claim to fame for this quiet open coastline, with hardly even an island to break the steady flow of the tides.

Once, this unfenced existence was much busier, with Dutch and Danish ships sailing up the estuary to Goole, passing heavily laden Humber keels on their way down the Trent to Hull. Those crossing the estuary, north or south, would catch a ferry. But for the last forty years, lorries, cars, vans and coaches have been streaming across the water a hundred feet in the air, cradled by great grey cables and swags of steel.

From a distance, the traffic's hardly visible – just tiny moving specks along a horizontal line. Nothing distracts from the soaring pair of concrete ladders set up for Titans to step into the clouds. The northern pair have their feet firmly on the ground, their more southerly twins appear to be floating in the sea. In fact they are standing on the solid Kimmeridge clay that lies deep below the sand and gravel of the seabed. The sodden ground selected for the towering bridge turned out to be even more unstable than anticipated. When the site engineers uncovered an artesian well beneath the water, the building work was suspended rather than the bridge. It began to seem doubtful whether the project would ever be finished.

The construction team, acclimatised to the high winds and snowstorms blowing in from the North Sea, were used to halting the project, as days became weeks, weeks turned into months and the costs rose more surely than the concrete towers. Even when work was under way, things went at a steady pace. David Wilkinson, who was part of the painting team, remembers the daily routine of clocking on at Hessle, taking the lift up the tower, crossing over to Barton on the mesh swag, before setting off again up the great cables to start work, down again for a tea break, then up again for an hour before the lunch break. 'You can see why it took so long to build it.' When you listen to his experience of walking, or even rolling about, on the swaying metal walkway some five hundred feet above the river, it's remarkable that it was built at all.

Nine years is hardly a pulse in the arteries of the Humber, which people have been crossing and recrossing for the last 4,000 years. The idea of a bridge, like so many engineering dreams, goes back to the days of Queen Victoria. For the railway magnates, broad estuaries like the Humber or the Solway were serious, but not insurmountable obstacles. They made plans for tunnels and bridges, though it was not until 1959 that the Humber Bridge Act was finally passed, giving a green light to the gargantuan construction. To help things on their way, the new county of Humberside, formed from sections of North Lincolnshire and the East Riding, inauspiciously came into being on 1 April 1974. This did not have quite the desired effect: the news that they were now living in Humberside made people on both banks realise just how strongly they belonged to their old counties. The bridge designed to bring people together was opened by Queen Elizabeth, at last, in July 1981 under celebratory aerial streams of red, white and blue. Fifteen years later, Humberside dissolved into its old dual identities.

Though so startlingly out of place while being built, the Humber Bridge had arrived to stay. Neither Yorkshire nor Lincolnshire, the great, steel giant is somehow its own place. This Atlas of a bridge holds an entire world – the massing, grey clouds and patches of blue sky surge above the long thin strip of road, while just below, everything's light and opalescent. It's more of a divider than a bridge, slicing across the air as if to cut the turbulent sky from the smooth sea. The winds and tides travel through, yet still it somehow contains time. At the Humber Bridge, norms are oddly inverted, visitors disconcerted. To go across on foot means going up. And up.

You can see a very long way even before you reach the top of the flights of stairs. The view upriver seems as wide as looking out to sea. Spaces of sand and shining channels and banks and broad water go on and on into the far distance. Bushy trees edge the beach on the north shore, then woods, flat fields, low houses, and a distant pair of wind turbines, turning briskly in the steady blast. From high aloft you can stare over to the chimneys of the tile factory near Barton-upon-Humber and trace the westward path to a nature reserve. The long line is blurred by tall reeds, making it impossible to see where the land ends and the sea begins.

In an area where the shores are regularly flooded by high tides, and the sand slopes slowly underwater, boundaries are naturally fluid. Reed Island on the southern shore, surrounded by invisible channels, seeped in seawater, submerged in tall sedges, is too amphibious to reach. Not far from here, George Stubbs secreted himself for almost two years to study the inner workings of horses. I've often wondered where he hung their carcases, which old barn offered the space and silence he needed to draw the layers of flesh, muscle and bone. Such intensity must surely have left its trace on the place; a sudden waft of rotting bodies, mingling with the salty air. But the reeds just sway as the breeze sweeps through, giving nothing away.

The path over the bridge is below the level of the cars: high in the air it still has an odd feeling of beneathness. Above the traffic, the steel wires shoot away so high that it's hard to focus on the impossibly elongated zigzaggery. Up and down, up and down, longer and longer and longer. Craning upwards, you begin to lose balance, which is rather unnerving at such a height, especially with Lycra-covered cyclists speeding by.

The footpath is punctuated by small, round drains. Dried tarmac grilles, presumably designed to prevent small objects or animals cascading down, give these troubling holes the look of clouded eyes. It's hard not to gaze into them, mesmerised and disoriented by the strangeness of the place. These are portholes to the sea below, so far down that you might be staring into the centre of the Earth. Tiny, sandy waves signal that the Neptunists were right all along and the Earth's core is made not of fire, but water.

Before the bridge, river-crossings were different, though neither the hazy rawness nor the salt water's deep swell has changed. Less swift, but no less unsettling than walking over the bridge, foot passengers used to put themselves in the hands of wind-browned ferrymen to brave unpredictable waves. The business of moving between Yorkshire and Lincolnshire demanded more time than a few minutes taken by cars or half an hour on foot. On his way to Hull from Lincoln in the 1720s, Daniel Defoe spent four hours being biffed and buffeted in an open boat along with fifteen horses, a dozen cows and seventeen other seasick passengers. So memorable was the experience that on the way back he opted for a long journey round by land instead. Though an unpleasant surprise for the author of *Robinson Crusoe*, the sea route across the estuary was just part of the daily routine for many. The names of the twin villages, North and South Ferriby, are permanent reminders of ancient trips across the broad river. When Bronze Age boats were unearthed on the Yorkshire side, it became clear that people had been pushing off and mooring there since around 2000 BCE.

Until construction of the bridge was finally under way, paddle steamers operated a regular timetable, picking up and dropping off passengers in Hull and New Holland. The unromantic Humber was the place to see castles moving on the water, because the ferries carried the unlikely names of *Tattershall Castle*, *Lincoln Castle* and *Wingfield Castle*. For the men who worked the steamers, it was a regular routine of people, livestock, cars, carts, vans, tractors from Yorkshire to Lincolnshire, from Lincolnshire to Yorkshire, backwards and forwards, day in, day out. The steady rhythms of the paddle boat worked with the currents and the tides. From January to December, everything flowed. The ferries breasted the brown waves bravely to carry their cargos to the quay.

At the heart of the old paddle steamers were pounding pistons and blazing furnaces. As a small child, the strange smell of coal, mingling with oil and smoke, the shining cylinders and the deafening noise made me feel that the whole boat was about to explode. The men in charge, with dark, greasy hands and smears of coal dust on their foreheads, were surprisingly cheery and chatty in the circumstances. As the last working fleet of paddle steamers in Britain, the Humber ferries were remnants of an older era. No matter that planes now moved faster than sound and human beings had walked on the moon, the ferries chugged on regardless. But the rising bridge finally rendered them redundant.

When the *Wingfield Castle* retired from duty on the Humber, she was destined for Swansea. The harbour turned out to be too constricted, so instead she steamed north to Hartlepool and became a Maritime Museum. The *Tattershall Castle* headed south to find a new berth as a quirky pub on the Thames, opposite the London Eye and a short walk from the Houses of Parliament. It's now quite hard to imagine her as a working ferry paddling across the Humber in all weathers. The *Lincoln Castle*'s retirement plan meant remaining much closer to her old workplace. She too was turned into a pub and moored on the foreshore at Hessle, before moving downriver to the Grimsby docks. In 2010, she was sent off for scrap.

Crossing the river is quieter now. Even on foot, the noise of the overhead vans and cars and HGVs and tractors is whisked away into the air. Walking across in January, when there are not many people about, the blast cocoons you from the road, while the ice-cold air blots out most of the coast. But still the echoes are eddying below and old voices streak the biting wind. As the wind squeals and the wires shudder, it's easier to hear with the mind. Though the bleak bank is empty and the view barred by steel, it's surprising what's there. The tides carry shoals of stories, the sands can be stirred by unexpected storms. A bridge doesn't always take you where you expect to go.

Whether it's a cohort of Roman soldiers marching straight across at low tide or Bronze Age boatmen in sewn-plank craft may depend on who is listening or what gets caught in the mental nets. For centuries, ropes were twisted and tarred on the banks of the Humber. But the long line of time is untwisted and shaken and frayed and remade in places where everything is oddly suspended. In between the wires, beneath the gulls' shrieks or the calls of passing geese, are churning paddles and a steam engine's clank and the deep blare of a hooter in ghostly percussion. Picks at the chalk quarry and the grinding wheels of the whiting mill carry across the water to the clattering Barton brickworks. CalMac ferries were made here, too, leaving their clanks and hammers pounding in the air. Softer now, the rattle of sails being hoisted, reefed or rent. Heavy cargos of French wine and linen, Dutch cheese and Russian hemp move upriver, past boatloads of lead and grain, Nottingham lace, Midlands metalwork, woollens and Staffordshire pots. The skipper's orders and the sailors' shouts play over the mutterings of ferry passengers. Somewhere on the wind, you might catch the strong, clear voice of William Wilberforce, passing piles of tobacco and sugar bales on his way from Hull.

This is a crossing place for poets. On the Humber's cold banks, Andrew Marvell felt the unbridgeable gap between his desire and his coy lady. He had good reason to distrust the treacherous tides, which swept away his father during a rough estuary crossing. Philip Larkin knew the coastal shelves and black-sailed ships of the Humber, too. But the ferries offered him comfort and company. When Douglas Dunn arrived from Scotland to take up a post at Hull, they would take the ferry back and forth, enjoying the longer opening hours on board. Their words, too, are echoing on the winds, cooler and clearer as the years go by.

The river carries voices with a higher pitch. There is Jane Brown, fortified by the word of God on her way to Hull's Female Penitentiary. Her passionate preaching reaches through the years and miles to the solid Methodist chapels on the flatlands beside the Humber, where strains of Wesleyan hymns rise heavenwards. Mary Wollstonecraft went to school in Beverley, returning to the East Riding a few years later with a baby girl, to wait fretfully at Hull for the right wind to carry them away to Scandinavia. The plaintive sound of little Fanny Imlay may just be detectable in the tern's cry. Or perhaps it's the sound of schoolchildren caught on a sandbank as the tide rushes in. The wind carries the coughings of a small engine and then the steadier sound of propellers. It might be a little plane competing with the steam ferries, flying a handful of passengers from the airfield at Hull or Kirmington in the 1930s. But I like to think that it is Amy Johnson returning home after her solo flight to Australia. Her message to young people – to abandon 'Safety First' and see the world – is blown away by a sudden, fresh gust and the scream of a gull, swooping.

High above the waters of the brown Humber, I like most of all to catch the laughter of Dorothea Thickett, lighting up the winter air. Even in her eighties, bedridden and shaken after a heart attack, my Great-Aunt Dorothea was delightful company. I can only imagine what she must have been like when she was twenty. When the survivors came home from the Western Front, the Thickett sisters were waiting and ready to help them forget. Dorothea was the first of the three girls to get to the theatre in Hull, which meant travelling to Barton to take the ferry across the river and back again after the show. But whether it was the journey, or the play or the company, no sooner was Dorothea back at home than she wanted to see the show again. And again. By Saturday afternoon, her elder sisters and their favourite friends were setting off, too, to catch the last performance.

They hardly felt the cold, wrapped in light shawls and anticipation. Once aboard the ferry, they watched the moon rise over the great black estuary, like the spotlight that would soon be arcing above the stage. Moonlight and champagne, chiffon dresses and a steam engine, with a vast expanse of water to wash away memories and submerge the mud. Life was starting again. It was almost like seeing the sea for the first time. Except that everything was thrown into relief by the darkness behind. Look forward, face the buffeting wind and the strong tides, trust the ferryman who knows the way so well. The crossing does not take long. You are soon on the other side, ready to be dazzled.

But then the ferry juddered and stopped. One moment it was charging onwards, the next moment, everything went black. No one moved as the silence descended, no gasps, no cries, no questions, no rage. The great dark pause was like eternity, opening to engulf them after all. Everyone knew about the estuary tides and sandbanks. No wonder, then, that as the ferry thudded and rocked, no one spoke.

It was Margery Thickett's friend, Peter, who lit the first match with an elegant flourish. All that had happened was that the ferry had run onto a sandbank – no Titanic disaster, nothing to fear. In a matter of minutes she would be afloat again and they would all be in Hull by seven. Plenty of time to relight the lamps and have another glass of wine. The captain confirmed what everyone knew: they had run aground and would just have to wait until the tide lifted the ship again. And so they waited. But the only thing that moved were the hands of wrist and pocket watches and they were moving slowly – but still more quickly than anyone wished. At seven o'clock, the ferry remained stuck fast. All they could do to keep other thoughts at bay was imagine the audience thronging the warm bar in happy expectation. As hopes sank with the sea water, anxieties were bubbling up and eddying in the dark. Stranded in the middle of a black, trackless channel, the silence thickened with unstoppable thoughts. No chance now of floating free.

Dorothea did not know very much about tidal currents, but she was quite an expert in diverting attention.

'I can tell you what happens in the first act,' she announced brightly, at exactly 7.30 p.m., the moment when the theatre curtain would be rising.

So they sat down and made a space for Dorothea to tell them a bit about the play. She introduced the characters, described their costumes and gave a very vivid account of the set. They could almost imagine they were in the stalls, as she ran through the lighting and the cast. Then she began to hum the overture, before breaking into the opening number. After seeing the play so often, Dorothea knew the songs by heart – and always enjoyed an audience. Before the end of the act, they were all joining in and no one felt quite so desperate for the ferry to move. This was just as well, because it stayed where it was, stuck fast as the sands emerged into a narrow island, dimly outlined against the black waves.

After a brief interval of beer and boiled sweets, which Mr Wilson brought out of his bag, Dorothea let it be known that she could continue, if requested. A round of applause sent her straight onto a little stage they put together from tables and benches. Before she went on with the plot, she reminded them of the melody and everyone started to sing. On went the story, on went Dorothea, on went the singing into the coldest hours of the night.

As dawn broke over the wide expanse of water, the deck began to move at last and the ferry started to float free of the sand. With the first gleams of light, a host of white wings swooped suddenly out of the birdless silence, cutting through the long night. One of the flock alighted for a moment on the railings of the ferry, with something dangling from its bill. Sometimes Dorothea remembered it as a gull, sometimes a tern. Either way, it always took the final bow.

Acknowledgements

Earlier versions of 'A Crossing with Red Pillars' and 'Otters and Cockles' first appeared in *Archipelago* 9 (2014) and 12 (2019); some material from 'Sherwood Forest' was published in 'The Story of Major Oak, one of Britain's most awe-inspiring trees', *Financial Times* (28 October 2016). For making possible and accompanying my trip to Staffa in the footsteps of Keats, I would like to thank Turan Ali of Bona Broadcasting and BBC Radio 3. Bernard O'Donoghue's 'Geese Conversations', first published in *Archipelago* and then in *Farmers Cross*, is quoted here by kind permission of the poet and Faber and Faber.

This book is indebted to many years of travels and conversations, as well as to related reading. It is not possible, then, to thank by name everyone who has contributed, whether directly or indirectly. Particular thanks are due to Peter Davidson, Andrew McNeillie and Bernard O'Donoghue, who kindly read draft sections, and for other help of various kinds to Turan Ali, Ben Brice, Steph Gassor, Helen Greenstreet, Jason Griffiths, Peter Harper, Alexandra Harris, Simon Kövesi, Hermione Lee, Ann Lindsay, John Purser, Nick Roe, Martin Rogers and Jeremy Stafford. My greatest debts are, as ever, to my family: my parents, grandparents, Dominic and Rachael, and to Malcolm, who travelled with me on many a wild goose trip and still maintained unwavering support for this book.

Springs and Sources

Allen, Nicholas, Nick Groom, and Jos Smith, eds., *Coastal Works: Cultures of the Atlantic Edge* (Oxford: Oxford University Press, 2017)

Archipelago, ed. Andrew MacNeillie (Thame: Clutag Press, 2007—)

Auden, W. H., *Collected Poems*, ed. Edward Mendelson (New York: Random House, 1976)

Baker, J. A., *The Peregrine, The Hill of Summer and Diaries: The Complete Works*, ed. John Fanshawe (London: William Collins, 2017)

Barnes, Julian, *Pulse* (London: Jonathan Cape, 2011)

Barringer, Tim, et al., *David Hockney: A Bigger Picture* (London: Royal Academy, 2011)

Bateman, Meg, and John Purser, *Window to the West: Culture and Environment in the Scottish Gàidhealtachd* (Sleat: Cló Ostaig, 2020)

Baxter, Peter, *I Flew with Nine Wing Commanders: The Story of my Career in the Royal Air Force* (University of Lincoln, 1985), https://ibccdigitalarchive.lincoln.ac.uk/omeka/files/original/1524/30282/BBaxterPDBaxterPDv1.1.pdf

Benfield, Tim, *Memories of Edgcott in the 20th Century* (Edgcott Millennium Committee, 2000)

Bennell, Alan P., *Logan Botanic Garden* (Edinburgh: Royal Botanic Garden, 2003)

Bentine, Michael, *The Door Marked Summer* (St Albans: Granada, 1981)

Berridge, Vanessa, and Sally Beauman, 'Island Retreat', *The Lady* (12–18 February 2002), http://www.alanhoward.org.uk/island.htm

Bevan, David W., ed., *Scarborough: A Guide and Souvenir presented to the Delegates of the Conference of the National Union of Teachers, 1924* (Hull and London: A. Brown and Sons, 1924)

Bewick, Thomas, *A History of British Birds*, 2 vols (Newcastle: Sol Hodgson and Edward Walker, 1797–1804)

————, *The Fables of Aesop, and Others* (Newcastle: E. Walker, 1818)

Binns, Jack, 'Mr and Mrs Farrer', *Transactions of Scarborough Archaeological and Historical Society* 26 (1988)

————, *The History of Scarborough North Yorkshire* (Pickering: Blackthorn, 2001)

Blackhall-Miles, Robbie, 'Monkey Puzzles: An Iconic Tree Under Threat', *Guardian*, 7 May 2015

Black's Guide to England and Wales (Edinburgh: Adam and Charles Black, 1864)

Brett, David, *A Book Around the Irish Sea: History without Nations* (Dublin: Wordwell, 2009)

Brodie, Ian O., 'The "Rock of Names"', Wordsworth Grasmere (21 May 2019), https://wordsworth.org.uk/blog/2019/05/21/the-rock-of-names/

Brooke, Rupert, *The Collected Poems*, ed. George Edward Woodberry (New York: Dodd, Mead and Co., 1931)

Brown, Geoff, *Herdwicks: Herdwick Sheep and the English Lake District* (Kirkby Stephen: Hayloft, 2009)

Buckinghamshire Gardens Trust, *Dorton Spa*, site dossier 2019 https://bucksgardenstrust.org.uk/wp-content/uploads/2020/08/Dorton-Spa-BGT-R-R-site-dossier-29-Oct-19.pdf

Bullamore, Colin P., *Scarborough and Whitby Watercolourists* (Whitby: Horne, 1976)

Burchell, Helen, 'A Handy Bandy Guide . . .' (BBC Cambridgeshire, 2014), https://www.bbc.co.uk/cambridgeshire/content/articles/2006/02/15/bandy_sport_feature.shtml

Burns, Robert, *The Poems and Songs of Robert Burns*, ed. James Kinsley, 3 vols (Oxford: Clarendon Press, 1968)

————, *The Letters of Robert Burns*, ed. G. Ross Roy, second edition, 2 vols (Oxford: Clarendon Press, 1985)

Byford, James S., *Moorland Heritage* (New Mills: Kinder Press, 1981)

Byram, Carmela Semeraro, ed., *Hidden Voices: Memories of the First Generation Italians in Bedford* (Bedford: Community Arts, 1999)

Byron, George Gordon, Lord, *The Complete Poetical Works*, ed. Jerome J. McGann, vol. 4 (Oxford: Clarendon Press, 1986)

Calderwood, Roy, *Times Subject to Tides: The Story of Barra Airport* (Erskine: Kea, 1999)

Camden, William, *Britannia* (London: 1587–1607); trans. Philemon Holland (London: 1637)

Campbell, John Lorne, ed., *The Book of Barra: Being Accounts of the Island of Barra in the Outer Hebrides* (Edinburgh and London: Routledge, 1936)

Campbell-Culver, Maggie, *The Origin of Plants: The People and Plants that Have Shaped Britain's Garden History since the Year 1000* (London: Headline, 2001)

Carter, Ian, and Gerry Whitlow, *Red Kites in the Chilterns*, second edition (Chinnor: Chilterns Conservation Board, 2005)

Chrystal, Paul, *Old Hessle: with Anlaby, North Ferriby, West Ella and Willerby* (Mauchline: Stenlake, 2019)

Clare, John, *The Natural History Prose Writings of John Clare*, ed. Margaret Grainger (Oxford: Clarendon Press, 1983)

———, *The Later Poems of John Clare, 1837–1864*, ed. Eric Robinson and David Powell, 2 vols (Oxford: Clarendon Press, 1984)

———, *The Letters of John Clare*, ed. Mark Storey (Oxford: Clarendon Press, 1986)

———, *The Early Poems of John Clare: 1804–1822*, ed. Eric Robinson and David Powell, 2 vols (Oxford: Clarendon Press, 1989)

———, *Poems of the Middle Period, 1822–1837*, ed. Eric Robinson, David Powell, and Paul Dawson, 5 vols (Oxford: Clarendon Press, 1996–2003)

———, *By Himself*, ed. Eric Robinson and David Powell (Manchester: Carcanet, 1996)

Clifford, Sue, and Angela King, *England in Particular: A Celebration of the Commonplace, the Local, the Vernacular and the Distinctive* (London: Hodder & Stoughton, 2006)

Clough, Peter, *Inverewe* (Edinburgh: National Trust for Scotland, 1994)

Cocker, Mark, and Richard Mabey, *Birds Britannica* (London: Chatto & Windus, 2005)

Cook, Robert, *Bucks Bricks: A History of Bletchley and Calvert Brickworks and the London Brick Company* (Frome: Baron Birch, 1997)

Coward, Noël, *Autobiography* (London: Methuen, 1986)

de Cuéllar, Francisco, *A Letter Written 4 October 1589 by Captain Francesco de Cuellar*, trans. Henry Dwight Sedgwick Jr (London: Elkin Mathews, 1896)

————, *Captain Cuellar's Adventures in Connacht and Ulster*, trans. Robert Crawford (University College, Cork, 2011), https://www.ucc.ie/research/celt/published/T108200.html

Cunliffe, Barry, *Roman Bath Discovered* (London: Routledge, 1971)

Cunningham, Alan, *Traditional Tales*, ed. Tim Killick (Glasgow: Association for Scottish Literary Studies, 2012)

Dean, Edmund, *Spadacrene Anglica. Or, the English Spa Fountain* (1626), ed. James Rutherford (Bristol and London: John Wright and Sons; Simkin, Marshall, Hamilton, Kent and Co., 1922)

Deeks, Roger, and Jason Griffiths, eds., *Reading the Forest: A Forest of Dean Anthology* (Gloucestershire: Douglas Maclean, 2022)

Defoe, Daniel, *A Tour Through the Whole Island of Great Britain*, ed. Pat Rogers (Harmondsworth: Penguin, 1971)

Drayton, Michael, *Poly-Olbion* (1612/22), in *The Works of the British Poets: Volume Third, containing Drayton, Carew, and Suckling*, ed. Robert Anderson (London: John and Arthur Arch, 1795)

Elwes, Henry John, and Augustine Henry, *The Trees of Great Britain and Ireland*, 8 vols, privately printed (Edinburgh, 1906–13)

English Forests and Forest Trees, Historical, Legendary, and Descriptive (London: Ingram, Cooke and Co., 1853)

Evelyn, John, *Sylva, or A Discourse of Forest-Trees and the Propagation of Timber* (London, 1664)

————, *Silva: or A Discourse of Forest-Trees and the Propagation of Timber*, 'with Notes by A. Hunter' (London, 1776)

————, *The Diary of John Evelyn*, ed. E. S. De Beer (London: Everyman, 2006)

Ferguson, Richard S., *A History of Westmorland* (London, 1894)

Fiennes, Celia, *The Illustrated Journeys of Celia Fiennes, 1685–c.1712*, ed. Christopher Morris (Cheltenham: Sutton, 1995)

Franklin, Benjamin, *The Autobiography and Other Writings* (London: Everyman, 2015)

Frost, Lorna, *Railway Posters* (London: Shire, 2013)

Garnett, Mark, *From Anger to Apathy: The Story of Politics, Society and Popular Culture in Britain since 1975* (London: Jonathan Cape, 2007)

Gedye, David, *Araucaria: The Monkey Puzzle* (Bluntisham: Orakaria Press, 2019)

Gilpin, William, *Remarks on Forest Scenery; and other Woodland Views*, second edition, 2 vols (London: R. Blamire, 1794)

Gray, Adrian, *Sherwood Forest and the Dukeries* (Chichester: Phillimore, 2008)

Green, Peter, Mike Hodgson, and Bill Taylor, *Wings over Lincolnshire* (Leicester: Midland Publishing, 1994)

Groome, F. H., *Ordnance Gazetteer of Scotland: A Survey of Scottish Topography*, ed. Francis H. Groome (Edinburgh: Thomas C. Jack, 1884–5)

'Guides to the Lakes' (updated version, 2022), https://www.lakesguides. co.uk/html/lakemenu.htm

'Haaf Netting' (3 March 1965), BBC Archive, https://www.bbc.co.uk/ archive/haaf-netting/zrtvhbk

Hallam, Vic, *Silent Valley: The Story of the Lost Derbyshire Villages of Derwent and Ashopton*, revised edition (Sheffield: Sheaf, 1989)

———, *Silent Valley at War: Life in the Derwent Valley, 1939–1945* (Sheffield: Sheaf, 1990)

———, *Silent Valley Revisited* (Sheffield: Sheaf, 2002)

Hardy, Thomas, *The Return of the Native* (London: Macmillan, 1913)

Hayter, Alethea, *The Wreck of the 'Abergavenny': One of Britain's Greatest Maritime Disasters and its Links to Literary Genius* (London: Macmillan, 2002)

Historic England, https://historicengland.org.uk/

Hoare, Philip, *Noël Coward: A Biography* (London: Sinclair-Stevenson, 1995)

Hodgson, William, *The Shepherd's Guide* (Ulverston, 1849)

Hogg, James, *The Shepherd's Calendar*, ed. Douglas Mack (Edinburgh: Edinburgh University Press, 1995)

Holt, J. C., *Robin Hood*, revised edition (London: Thames and Hudson, 1989)

Hoskins, W. G., *The Making of the English Landscape* (1955; Toller Fratrum: Little Toller, 2013)

Hoyle, Norman, and Kenneth Sankey, *Thirlmere Water: A Hundred Miles, a Hundred Years* (Tottington: Centwrite, 1994)

Hutchinson, Robert, *The Spanish Armada* (London: Weidenfeld & Nicolson, 2013)

Illingworth, Cayley, *A Topographical Account of the Parish of Scampton: In the County of Lincoln and of the Roman Antiquities Lately Discovered There* (London: 1810)

Jacobs, Peter, *Bomber Command Airfields of Lincolnshire* (Barnsley: Pen and Sword, 2016)

Jenkins, David, and Mark Visocchi, *Mendelssohn in Scotland* (London: Chappell, 1978).

Keats, John, *Letters of John Keats*, ed. Hyder E. Rollins, 2 vols (Cambridge. Mass.: Harvard University Press, 1958)

———, *The Poems of John Keats*, ed. Jack Stillinger (Cambridge, Mass.: Harvard University Press, 1978)

King, Melanie, *A Secret History of English Spas* (Oxford: Bodleian Library Publishing, 2021)

Kingdon Ward, F., *Plant Hunting on the Edge of the World* (London: Victor Gollancz, 1930)

Kingshill, Sophie, and Jennifer Westwood, *The Fabled Coast: Legends and Traditions from around the Shores of Britain and Ireland* (London: Cornerstone, 2012)

Kipling, Rudyard, *The Complete Verse*, ed. James Fenwick (London: Kyle Cathie, 1996)

Kirkup, James, *The Submerged Village, and Other Poems* (London: Oxford University Press, 1951)

Knight, Stephen, *Robin Hood: A Complete Study of the English Outlaw* (Oxford: Blackwell, 1994)

Knight, William, *Through the Wordsworth Country*, third edition (London: Swan Sonnenschein, 1898)

Kövesi, Simon, '"pieces of naked water . . . make me melancholy": John Clare plashing in the pudges', paper delivered at 'Wordsworth, Water, Writing', Online Conference (10 September 2020)

Larkin, Philip, *Collected Poems*, ed. Anthony Thwaite (London: Faber, 1988)

Lawson, Basil, *Thirlmere: Across the Bridges to the Chapel, 1849–1852: From the Diary of Reverend Basil R. Lawson, Curate of Wythburn*, ed. Margaret Armstrong (Keswick: Peel Wyke, 1989)

Lea, Hermann, *Thomas Hardy's Wessex* (London: Macmillan, 1913)

Lear, Edward, *A Book of Nonsense* (1846; London: Everyman's Library, 1992)

Leask, Nigel, 'Fingalian Topographies: Ossian and the Highland Tour, 1760–1805', *Journal of Eighteenth-Century Studies* 39 (June 2016), 183–196

———, 'Fingal's Cave', European Romanticisms in Association (13 August 2018), https://www.euromanticism.org/fingals-cave/

———, *Stepping Westward: Writing the Highland Tour, c. 1720–1830* (Oxford: Oxford University Press, 2020)

Lindsay, Ann, *Seeds of Blood and Beauty: Scottish Plants and Collectors* (Edinburgh: Birlinn, 2005)

Lingard, Ann, *The Fresh and the Salt: The Story of the Solway* (Edinburgh: Birlinn, 2020)

Lockhart, James MacDonald, *Raptor: A Journey Through Birds* (London: Fourth Estate, 2016)

Lodge, David, *Changing Places* (Harmondsworth: Penguin, 1985)

Loth, Calder, 'Flemish Bond: A Hallmark of Traditional Architecture', Institute of Classical Architecture and Art (30 November 2011), https://www.classicist.org/articles/flemish-bond-a-hallmark-of-traditional-architecture/

Mabey, Richard, *Flora Britannica: The Definitive New Guide to Wild Flowers, Plants and Trees* (London: Sinclair-Stevenson, 1996)

MacCarthy, Fiona, *Byron: Life and Legend* (London: John Murray, 2002)

MacDiarmid, Hugh, *The Islands of Scotland* (London: Batsford, 1939)

Mackenzie, Compton, *Whisky Galore* (London: Chatto & Windus, 1947)

———, *My Life and Times*, 10 vols (London: Chatto & Windus, 1963–71)

MacNeice, Louis, *I Crossed the Minch* (London and New York: Longmans, Green and Co., 1938)

Macpherson, James, *The Poems of Ossian and Related Works*, ed. Howard Gaskill (Edinburgh: Edinburgh University Press, 1996)

Macpherson, John, *Tales from Barra: Told by the Coddy*, foreword by Compton Mackenzie, introduction by John Lorne Campbell (Edinburgh: Birlinn, 1992)

Mann, Geoffrey B., *Passage of Humber* (North Ferriby: Lockington, 1983)

Marsden, Philip, *The Summer Isles: A Voyage of the Imagination* (London: Granta, 2019)

Martin, Martin, *A Description of the Western Islands of Scotland*, second edition (London, 1716)

Marvell, Andrew, *The Poems of Andrew Marvell*, ed. Nigel Smith (London: Routledge, 2003)

Middleton, Paul, *England's Lost Lake: The Story of Whittlesea Mere* (Peterborough: FastPrint, 2018)

Mills, A. D., *A Dictionary of British Place Names*, rev. ed. (Oxford: Oxford University Press, 2011)

Milton, John, *Paradise Lost*, ed. Alastair Fowler (London: Longman, 1981)

Morris, Richard, *Yorkshire: A Lyrical History of England's Greatest County* (London: Weidenfeld & Nicolson, 2018)

Musty, John, 'Brick Kilns and Brick and Tile Suppliers to Hampton Court Palace', *Archaeological Journal* 147 (1990), 411–19

National Monuments Service (Ireland), 'Wreck Viewer', https://www.archaeology.ie/underwater-archaeology/wreck-viewer

Newbolt, Henry, *Poems: New and Old* (London: John Murray, 1913)

Niall, Ian, *The Way of a Countryman* (1965; Ludlow: Merlin Unwin, 2012)

Nixon, Philip, and Hugh Dias, *Exploring Solway Firth History* (Derby: Breedon, 2007)

O'Donoghue, Bernard, *Farmers Cross* (London: Faber, 2011)

Otter, Patrick, *Lincolnshire Airfields in the Second World War* (1996; Newbury: Countryside Books, 2009)

Paterson, Leonie, *How the Garden Grew: A Photographic History of Horticulture at RBGE* (Edinburgh: Royal Botanic Garden, 2013)

Pearce, Cathryn, *Cornish Wrecking 1700–1860: Reality and Popular Myth* (Woodbridge: Boydell, 2010)

Pennant, Thomas, *A Tour in Scotland, and Voyage to the Hebrides; MDCCLXII*, second edition, 2 vols (London, 1776); with an Appendix by Joseph Banks

Penoyre, John and Jane, *Houses in the Landscape: A Regional Study of Vernacular Building Styles in England and Wales* (London: Faber, 1978)

Pevsner, Nikolaus, *The Buildings of England: Leicestershire and Rutland*, rev. ed. Elizabeth Williamson (London: Penguin, 1984)

Pryor, Francis, *The Fens: Discovering England's Ancient Depths* (London: Head of Zeus, 2019)

Rackham, Oliver, *Trees and Woodland in the British Landscape*, revised edition (London: J. M. Dent, 1990)

———, *The Ash Tree* (Toller Fratrum: Little Toller, 2014)

Ramshaw, David, *The Carlisle Ship Canal 1821–1853*, revised edition (Carlisle: P3 Publications, 2013)

Rawnsley, Hardwicke Drummond, *Literary Associations of the Lake District: Westmoreland, Windermere and the Haunts of Wordsworth* (Glasgow: James MacLehose, 1894)

———, 'A Crack about Herdwick Sheep', in Rawnsley, *By Fell and Dale at the English Lakes* (Glasgow: James MacLehose, 1911), pp. 47–72

Rawnsley, Willingham Franklin, *Highways and Byways in Lincolnshire* (London: Macmillan, 1914)

Reilly, Jill, 'Interview with Annie Prangnell on 14 August 1990', https://www.iwhistory.org.uk/brickmaking/prangnell/Annie-Prangnell-interview-Reilly.pdf

Rice, Matthew, *Village Buildings of Britain* (London: Little, Brown, 1991)

Riding, Christine, and Richard Johns, *Turner and the Sea* (London: Thames and Hudson, 2013)

Ritson, Joseph, *Robin Hood: A Collection of All the Ancient Poems, Songs, and Ballads, Now Extant, Relative to that Celebrated English Outlaw*, 2 vols (London, 1794)

Rooke, Hayman, *Descriptions and Sketches of Some Remarkable Oaks, in the Park at Welbeck, in the County of Nottingham, a Seat of His Grace the Duke of Portland* (London, 1790)

Rotherham, Ian, *Sherwood Forest and the Dukeries: A Companion to the Land of Robin Hood* (Stroud: Amberley, 2013)

Royal Botanic Garden Edinburgh, https://www.rbge.org.uk/

Royal Botanic Garden Edinburgh (Logan), https://www.rbge.org.uk/visit/logan-botanic-garden/

Royal Society for the Protection of Birds, 'Wildlife Guides' and 'Reserves', https://www.rspb.org.uk

Scott, Stewart, *Airfield Focus: Scampton* (Peterborough: GMS Enterprises, 1994)

Searle, Muriel, *Spas and Watering Places* (Tunbridge Wells: Midas, 1977)

Shakespeare, William, *The Complete Works of Shakespeare*, ed. David Bevington, fourth edition (Harlow and New York: Longman, 1997)

Shepherd, Nan, *Wild Geese: A Collection of Nan Shepherd's Writing*, ed. Charlotte Peacock (Great Shelford: Galileo, 2018)

Sheridan, R. B., *The Works of Sheridan* (London: Oxford University Press, 1930)

Shulman, Nicola, *A Rage for Rock Gardening: The Story of Reginald Farrer, Gardener, Writer and Plant Collector* (London: Short Books Ltd, 2002)

Simms, Eric, *Birds of the Air* (London: Hutchinson, 1976)

Smit, Tim, *The Lost Gardens of Heligan* (London: Gollancz, 1997)

Smollett, Tobias, *The Expedition of Humphry Clinker*, ed. Angus Ross (Harmondsworth: Penguin, 1967)

Spanning the Humber: Souvenir Opening 1981 Humber Bridge (Kingston upon Hull: Cherryprint, 1981)

Steam-Boat Companion, and Stranger's Guide to the Western Islands and Highlands of Scotland, The, second edition (Glasgow: Lumsden and Sons, 1825)

Stewart, Katharine, *A Garden in the Hills* (Edinburgh: Mercat, 2001)

Stewart, Rory, *The Marches: Border Walks with My Father* (London: Jonathan Cape, 2016)

'Stewartby Historic Brickworks Chimneys Demolished', BBC News (26 September 2021), https://www.bbc.co.uk/news/uk-england-beds-bucks-herts-58665319

Strutt, Jacob George, *Sylva Britannica; or, Portraits of Forest Trees, Distinguished for their Antiquity, Magnitude, or Beauty* (London, [1830])

Swaysland, W., *Familiar Wild Birds* (London, Paris, New York, Melbourne: Cassell, 1903)

Taylor, Derek J., *Through England from a Side-Saddle: The Great Journeys of Celia Fiennes* (Cheltenham: The History Press, 2021)

Taylor, John, *All the workes of Iohn Taylor the water-poet Beeing sixty and three in number. Collected into one volume by the author: with sundry new additions corrected, reuised, and newly imprinted* (London, 1630)

Tennyson, Alfred, Lord, *The Poems of Tennyson*, ed. Christopher Ricks, second edition, 3 vols (Harlow: Longman, 1987)

Thorold, Henry, and Jack Yates, *Lincolnshire: A Shell Guide* (London: Faber, 1965)

Traill Dennison, Walter, *The Orcadian Sketch-Book: Being Traits of Old Orkney Life, written partly in the Orkney Dialect* (Kirkwall: William Peace, 1880)

———, *Orkney Folklore and Sea Legends*, ed. Tom Muir (Kirkwall: Orkney Press, 1995)

Turner, E. S., *Taking the Cure* (London: Michael Joseph, 1967)

Turner, J. M. W., '*Staffa* sketchbook 1831' ('Sketchbooks, Drawings and Watercolours'), https://www.tate.org.uk/art/research-publications/jmw-turner/staffa-sketchbook-r1135105#entry-main:fn_1_3_6

Turner, Roger, *Capability Brown and the Eighteenth-Century English Landscape*, second edition (Chichester: Phillimore, 1999)

Tyler, Ian, *Thirlmere Mines and the Drowning of the Valley* (Keswick: Blue Rock, 2005)

Viney, Michael, 'Solving the Puzzle of the Monkey Puzzle Tree', *Irish Times*, 7 August 1999

Voices from the Forest, https://www.voicesfromtheforest.co.uk/

Wadsworth, Michael P., *Heroes of Bomber Command: Yorkshire* (Newbury: Countryside Books, 2007)

Walford, Edward, *Old and New London: Volume V* (London: Cassell, Petter and Galpin, 1878)

Watkins, Charles, *Trees, Woods and Forests: A Social and Cultural History* (London: Reaktion, 2014)

Westwood, Jennifer, and Jacqueline Simpson, *The Lore of the Land: A Guide to England's Legends, from Spring-Heeled Jack to the Witches of Warboys* (London: Penguin, 2005)

Whyte, William, *Redbrick: A Social and Architectural History of Britain's Civic Universities* (Oxford: Oxford University Press, 2016)

Wittie, Robert, *Scarborough Spaw* (York, 1660, 1667)

Wordsworth, William, *The Poetical Works of William Wordsworth*, ed. E. De Selincourt and H. Darbishire, 5 vols (Oxford: Clarendon Press, 1940–9)

——, *Benjamin the Waggoner*, ed. Paul F. Betz (Ithaca: Cornell University Press, 1981)

——, *'Poems, in Two Volumes' and Other Poems, 1800–1807*, ed. Jared Curtis (Ithaca: Cornell University Press, 1982)

Index

Index